For Newt
1987–2000

About the Author

Dave Johnson writes about technology from Seattle, Washington. He writes a weekly electronic newsletter on digital photography for *PC World* magazine and is the author of three dozen books that include *Robot Invasion: 7 Cool and Easy Robot Projects, How to Do Everything with MP3 and Digital Music*, and *How to Do Everything with Your Palm Handheld* (the latter two with Rick Broida). His short story for early readers, *The Wild Cookie*, has been transformed into an interactive storybook on CD-ROM. In his spare time, Dave is a drummer, scuba instructor, and wildlife photographer.

Dave started writing professionally in 1990, before anyone had a chance to talk him out of it. Prior to that, he had a somewhat unfocused career that included flying satellites, driving an ice cream truck, loading bombs onto B-52s in a remote region of Michigan, stocking shelves in a Jersey City grocery store, teaching rocket science, photographing rock bands, and writing about interstellar penguins. He's still not playing in a psychedelic band, but at least he's found steady work.

About the Technical Editor

Jennifer Kettell has written and contributed to more than a dozen books, including *Microsoft Office 2003: The Complete Reference*. She has designed Web sites for a wide range of professional, commercial, and nonprofit entities. In her spare time, Jenn dabbles at writing fiction, travels, and tries to grab the camera fast enough to photograph her homeschooled children at work before their chemistry experiments explode. Jenn lives in Arizona with her husband, children, assorted pets, and lots of dust bunnies.

How to Do *Everything* with Your

Digital Camera
Fourth Edition

Dave Johnson

McGraw-Hill/Osborne

New York   Chicago   San Francisco   Lisbon
London   Madrid   Mexico City   Milan   New Delhi
San Juan   Seoul   Singapore   Sydney   Toronto

The *McGraw·Hill* Companies

McGraw-Hill/Osborne
2100 Powell Street, 10th Floor
Emeryville, California 94608
U.S.A.

To arrange bulk purchase discounts for sales promotions, premiums, or fund-raisers, please
contact **McGraw-Hill**/Osborne at the above address. For information on translations or
book distributors outside the U.S.A.

How to Do Everything with Your Digital Camera, Fourth Edition

234567890 DOC DOC 0198765

ISBN 0-07-226163-3

Acquisitions Editor	Megg Morin
Project Editor	Samik Roy Chowdhury (Sam)
Acquisitions	
Coordinator	Agatha Kim
Technical Editor	Jennifer Kettell
Copy Editor	Emily Rader
Proofreader	Chris Andreasen
Indexer	Broccoli Information Management
Composition	International Typesetting and Composition
Illustration	International Typesetting and Composition
Series Design	Michelle Galicia and Peter F. Hancik
Cover Series Design	Dodie Shoemaker
Color Insert Design	Lyssa Wald

This book was composed with Adobe® InDesign®/MAC.

Contents at a Glance

Contents

Acknowledgments

Thanks to all the great folks at Osborne who are always fun to work with—especially folks like Megg Morin and Agatha Kim. I'd also be remiss not to thank Kristin Hersh, Bob Mould, Jack White, and Peter Himmelman because their music, as usual, was the soundtrack that played through 16 chapters of writing, editing, and photography. Finally, let me thank all the selfless models who posed for me as I shot picture after picture for this book, which include Kris, Evan, and Marin.

Thanks also go out to Geoff Coalter at Canon USA, to Michael Bourne at Mullen PR and Olympus Imaging America, and to Nancy Lichtman and Sony Electronics Inc for their help with the images on the cover of this book.

Introduction

Welcome to *How to Do Everything with Your Digital Camera*. This is not your typical book on digital photography—I wrote this book with the intention of answering all the questions I had about digital cameras and photography techniques when I was starting out, and then slipping this back in time through a wormhole. I never found the wormhole, but I did write the book for today's fledgling digital photographers.

I've been a photographer for over 20 years, and in that time I've read a lot of books and magazines about the art and science of photography. It seems that this is a good time for a book that explains everything you could possibly need to know about digital photography in the space of a few hundred pages.

A tall order, I know.

Nonetheless, I know what it feels like to have a new digital camera and search fruitlessly for the answers to seemingly obvious questions. I've read too many books that make passing references to "control your depth of field with the aperture" without explaining what either the aperture or depth of field actually is. Or mention that you need a lot of pixels to print an 8×10-inch picture without ever telling you how many pixels you actually need.

So when I wrote this book I mapped out all of the things I wondered about when digital cameras were new back in 1996, and when I was starting out as a film photographer in the 80s. I went right to the beginning and decided to cover photography techniques like lighting, composition, and close-ups. Hopefully you'll find that the book walks you through the key steps of using a digital camera—from working with memory cards to file formats, to editing images on a PC, to printing, and finally, to sharing your images.

The world of digital photography is changing fast. It's finally crawling out of its infancy, but it has a way to go before digital is as easy to use as a 35-mm point and shoot camera. But this is a great time to purchase and use a digital camera, and I hope that some of my enthusiasm for the digital medium comes through. I love the freedom and flexibility that a digital camera gives me; armed with my Nikon D100 or Sony Cyber-shot DSC-L1, I can take pictures without worrying about buying film or using it before it expires. I can instantly preview my work and download just the images

I want to keep. I particularly like the fact that I can print 8×10- or 13×19-inch enlargements exactly the way I want without trying to convey imprecise instructions to some tech in a photo shop. I've even used a digital camera underwater when scuba diving, and that, too, is a whole new and exciting world of photography that is made dramatically easier by digital cameras.

I wrote this book so that you could sit down and read it through like a novel if you'd like to—but I realize few people will actually do that. If you're looking for specific information, I've organized the book so topics should be easy to find. Part I kicks things off with the basics of using your camera. I begin by explaining how to shop for a digital camera and how to operate the most common controls on digital cameras. From there, I delve into stuff you need to know no matter what kind of camera you have—stuff like composition, lighting, close-ups, and how to take advantage of the special features on your camera.

Part II of the book is all about getting the images from the camera into your PC. I talk about how to use file formats such as JPG and TIF, and how to care for the memory cards that come with your camera.

I'm guessing that most of you will be keenly interested in Part III—at least that's one of the most exciting parts for me. This is where you can learn how to edit digital images as if your PC were a sort of digital darkroom. Sure, there are simple techniques in here like how to crop and resize images, but I also write about cool special effects—adding text, changing images so they look like they were painted, and even creating Hollywood-style "bluescreen" effects.

While the techniques I describe in this book are all done with Corel's Paint Shop Pro, you don't have to be a Paint Shop Pro user to get the most out of it. Instead, you can easily find the same tools in your favorite program, whether that's Adobe Photoshop Elements or Ulead Photo Impact, and follow along with that program.

Finally, the book ends with Part IV, a few chapters that explain how to print and share your images. I tell you exactly what you need to know to get great results—like optimizing your printer, using the right paper, and calculating how large you can print your image based on how many pixels it has. And then you can learn how to share your images—on the computer screen, in email, on the Web (even without any programming), and in devices like Palms and digital picture frames.

To help you along, you can find special elements to help you get the most out of the book:

■ **How-To**   These special boxes explain, in a nutshell, how to accomplish key tasks throughout the book. You can read the How-To box for a summary of what the chapter at large is explaining.

■ **Notes**   These provide extra information that is handy for trivia contests but isn't essential to understanding the current topic.

■ **Tips**   These tell you how to do something a better, faster, or smarter way.

■ **Sidebars**   These talk about related topics that are pretty darned interesting, but you can skip them if you prefer.

■ Within the text, you'll also find words in special formatting. New terms are in italics, while specific phrases that you will see on the screen or need to type yourself appear in bold.

Want to email me? You can send questions and comments to me at: cameraquestions@bydavejohnson.com.

My Web site is located at bydavejohnson.com, and you're welcome to visit there and check out other books or my photography anytime you like. I also write a free, weekly email newsletter for *PC World* magazine called *Digital Focus*. You can subscribe to *Digital Focus* by visiting pcworld.com and clicking on the newsletters link. Each week I offer digital photo and editing tips, answer reader questions, and award prizes to reader-submitted photos. Join—it's a blast!

Thanks, and enjoy reading the book!

Part I Your Camera

Chapter 1

Welcome to the Future

How to…

- ■ Navigate around your digital camera

- ■ Distinguish between point-and-shoot and professional camera features

- ■ Pick a camera resolution based on print size

- ■ Conserve battery power

- ■ Tell the difference between a digital and optical zoom

- ■ Shop for a new digital camera

- ■ Choose gear and accessories for a digicam

This chapter is called "Welcome to the Future," and I mean it. I'm convinced that digital photography is, for most people and in most situations, the best way to take pictures. And the technology just keeps getting better all the time.

With a digital camera, it's possible to take photos and review them instantly—while they're still stored in the camera—to see if they turned out the way you wanted. From there, you can transfer them to a computer and easily crop them to size, adjust color and brightness, even perform special effects on them if you want to, and then print the final result to exactly the size you like for a frame in your living room. Then you can take the same picture and e-mail it, post it to a web site, display it on a TV, or show it to friends from your handheld organizer. The beauty of digital imaging is its immediacy and versatility—just try to do those things with an old 35mm or Advanced Photo System (APS) camera.

So if you've recently bought a digital camera, congratulations—you've made the right choice. In this chapter, we'll take a quick look at your camera and at digital cameras in general. And if you're still shopping for your camera, flip to the box "Choose a Digital Camera," where I tell you what to look for when you head off to make your purchase.

A History Lesson

When I was a kid, my dad bought a darkroom kit so he could develop his own photographs. I clearly remember that box, and how it sat, untouched, on top of a hall closet. For years. Why did my dad never get around to setting up his darkroom? In a nutshell, it was just too much trouble.

Darkrooms require, well, darkness. You have to have a room that you can dedicate to the task and trust that people won't come barging in while you're developing film (or hang their wet bathing suits in there when you're not watching).

And then there are the chemicals. Film processing is all about using nasty, toxic chemicals that, if you were running a business, would get the attention of OSHA. When I worked in the space launch business, I'm sure that some of the rocket fuels we used weren't as frightening as the chemicals that home darkroomers routinely expose themselves to. Who wants to muck around with that stuff?

Oh, yeah—and it isn't all that easy, either. Black-and-white processing isn't really brain surgery, but working with color film is tough. It's not a hobby you can master in a few weeks, to be sure. And the whole point of having your own darkroom is so you can get better results than the corner store delivers, right?

No wonder my dad never got too far with his darkroom kit.

These days, digital photography gives you the same flexibility as those old chemical darkrooms—the ability to brighten or darken an image, crop it down to generate a better composition, and print enlargements in a variety of sizes—but without the chemicals, without the steep learning curve, and without dedicating a part of your house to nothing but photography. How did we get here?

A Slow Evolution

These days, some digital cameras can compete with the best 35mm Single-Lens Reflex (SLR) cameras in terms of resolution and image quality. Obviously, it hasn't always been this way.

When you consider the first digital cameras that debuted in the early 1990s, it's a miracle that anyone used them at all. The first models you could buy for under a grand included the Logitech Fotoman, Kodak DC40, Apple QuickTake 100, and the Casio QV-10. They were strictly for gear-headed early adopters who bought them just to try out the nascent field of digital photography. They certainly weren't particularly useful, since they offered poor image quality, limited resolution, and substandard optics. Early digital cameras generated low-resolution images with a mere 376×240 pixels and, soon thereafter, 640×480 pixels—barely enough to fill a computer screen when set to the lowest Windows resolution. That was if you could figure out how to get the images out of the camera and into your PC.

Those early digital cameras typically had plastic lenses, and the light sensor that captured the image was a component called a Complementary Metal Oxide Semiconductor (CMOS) chip. CMOS chips were popular because they were cheap and required very little power, but they created horribly fuzzy pictures. Charge-Coupled Devices (CCDs) cost a small fortune in comparison, so CMOS chips found their way into many of the first cameras. See Figure 1-1 for an example of the difference between an image taken with a CMOS chip (on the left) and a CCD (on the right).

FIGURE 1-1 Older cameras with CMOS sensors (left) typically offered lower image quality than those with CCDs (right).

NOTE *CMOS is making a comeback—the technology has improved dramatically, some new cameras with CMOS chips work as well as CCDs, and they cost less to boot. Since some of the best professional cameras on the market now include CMOS sensors, don't ignore a new model just because it has a CMOS sensor.*

In the early days, Video Graphics Array (VGA) resolution (640×480 pixels) established itself as the first real standard size for digital images. Digicams came equipped with sensors capable of capturing 640×480-pixel images, which was ideal for display on a computer screen, posting on web pages, or e-mail, but you couldn't really print such a picture. On a typical inkjet printer, you'd get a photograph that measured just 3 inches across.

Then came *megapixel*. "Mega" means million, and the term simply refers to the maximum number of pixels the camera can capture. A megapixel camera can create an image with a million pixels—for example, 1000×1000, 860×1200, or any other pixel dimension that multiplies out to about a million dots of information. The first megapixel cameras raised the bar for everyone. Like owning last year's laptop with a slow processor, no one wanted to own a VGA camera. That started the race we're still in the midst of today.

Today, most digital cameras capture anywhere from 2 to 5 megapixels, with many 6- and 8-megapixel cameras tempting photographers as well. And it doesn't end there. Some high-end cameras capture even more pixels—we're starting to

FIGURE 1-2 More megapixels means more resolution, which is handy for changing the composition of your picture through cropping, as well as for making good-quality prints.

see pro-level cameras with 12 million and more. Why the fuss over pixels? Well, as I alluded to earlier, the more pixels you have, the sharper your image is, and consequently the larger it can be printed. If you'd like to print a digital photo at 8×10 or larger, for instance, a VGA or 1-megapixel camera simply won't cut it—each pixel would be the size of a postage stamp. Take a look at Figure 1-2. On the left is a detail from a picture taken at 640×480 pixels. On the right is the same detail, but it's cropped from a 3.3-megapixel image. As you can see, the smaller image has fewer pixels to work with, and that's why it looks so grainy. Obviously, you need lots of pixels to print pictures at a large size, and that's why each year we see ever larger-resolution digital cameras hitting store shelves.

The Future of Digital Cameras

These days, the trend for cameras is both bigger and smaller.

Bigger pictures—most folks never make prints larger than about 8×10 inches, and that means a 3- or 4-megapixel camera is generally good enough for them. But for those folks who definitely want larger pictures—such as 11×17 or 13×19 (well within the ability of some consumer-priced wide-format inkjet printers)—you need more pixels to keep those huge images sharp. So camera manufacturers are responding with cameras that snap 6-, 8-, and even 12-megapixel pictures. These cameras aren't usually very affordable—they clock in between $500 and $1,500—but they're an option for anyone who wants the ultimate in digital photography today.

And cameras are getting smaller. So small, in fact, that many phone companies are selling mobile phones with built-in cameras. This is kinda cool, since you can always take a picture if you have your phone handy. But camera phones have some serious limitations. Like the early days of digital cameras, camera phones still take really lousy pictures with low resolution, bad contrast, and washed-out colors. This isn't limited to just the cheapest camera phones—pretty much all camera phones sold in the United States are like that today. Of course, they'll get better. In Japan, camera phones have as much resolution as some of the best digital cameras and take really good pictures. But that day has yet to dawn here in the United States.

There's one other trend in digital photography: an effort to satisfy traditional film photographers. Right now, the most common kind of digicam is the point-and-shoot model, like the Nikon CoolPix 5400 in Figure 1-3. They look like 35mm point-and-shoot models and automate most of the features needed to take pictures.

But SLR digital cameras (referred to as Digital SLRs, or just D-SLRs) are getting more popular all the time. These cameras, like the Canon Digital Rebel and the Nikon D100 (in Figure 1-4), don't cost a lot more than top-of-the-line point-and-shoot cameras did just a few years ago, but they feature interchangeable lenses, powerful flash units, and a wealth of manual controls. In a nutshell, they work and behave just like the best SLRs from the film world. Photographers who love their old 35mm SLRs finally have a digital alternative.

If you have a trusty old SLR and want a digital camera that's just like it, this is a good time to be getting into digital. Only a few years ago, the price of these

FIGURE 1-3   Point-and-shoot digicams promise great results without a lot of effort or expense.

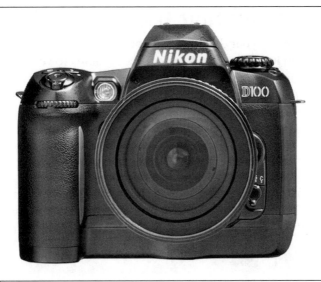

FIGURE 1-4   SLR-style digital cameras offer lot of resolution, plus plenty of advanced photographic control.

pro-oriented cameras was $5,000 and beyond. Right now, you can find the Canon Digital Rebel for under a thousand dollars!

So prepare for more dramatic price drops in the future. In fact, this table shows how digital camera prices, on average, have plummeted in the past few years:

	Under 1 Megapixel	1–2 Megapixels	2–3 Megapixels	3–4 Megapixels	4–5 Megapixels	5–6 Megapixels
1999	$839	$663				
2000	$716	$461	$885			
2001	$141	$377	$532	$815	$1,733	
2002	$85	$264	$345	$556	$805	$1,982
2003	$71	$193	$310	$477	$725	$1,066
2004	Built into phones	$150	$230	$375	$650	$750
2005	Built into phones	$50	$175	$225	$550	$700

Basics for Choosing Your Own Digital Camera

If you haven't yet made your digital camera purchase—or if you are planning to upgrade—you're in luck. The field has never been more crowded with excellent choices, and technology advances keep making these cameras better each year.

Even though the camera field is evolving all the time, the basics really don't change. The next few sections cover the most important elements to consider when shopping for a camera.

Resolution

First and foremost, figure out how much resolution you need. This should be the very first decision you make, since it determines what cameras you will be evaluating. Use this handy little guide to decide what megapixel range you need:

Megapixels	Print Size
1 megapixel	3×5-inch prints
2 megapixels	4×6-inch prints
3 megapixels	8×10-inch prints and 4×6-inch prints from a crop of the original image
6 or more megapixels	13×19-inch prints and 8×10-inch prints from a crop of the original image

Remember that even if you choose a camera with lots of resolution, such as a 6-megapixel camera, you can set it to capture lower-resolution images—even a mere 640×480 pixels—making your camera quite versatile. Why would you do that? Well, suppose you are on vacation and your camera's memory card is almost full—but you are taking pictures that you know you'll only use to make 4×6-inch prints. In that case, might want to shoot at a lower resolution so you can hold more pictures than you would normally be able to do at full resolution.

Optics

It is a camera, after all—not a computer. Don't forget that the optics are important. Your camera's optics should be made of glass, not plastic, and multiple "elements" (a lens made of several glass components instead of a single hunk of glass) help keep everything in sharp focus through the camera's entire zoom range.

Also consider what kind of pictures you want to take. Having a camera that has a fairly wide angle lens is good for landscapes, indoor shots, and general-purpose photography. If you want to take portraits or wildlife shots, a longer reach is important. But take a look at the specs for a digital camera—what the heck is a 9.3mm lens? Is that wide angle? Telephoto? Who knows? That's why most digital cameras also advertise their focal length in "35mm equivalents"—in other words, if this digital camera were a 35mm camera, its 9.3mm lens would give you the same picture as a 50mm camera, for instance. Many photographers know that 20–35mm is considered wide angle, while 50–90mm is thought to be "normal"—great for portraits, for instance. Anything over 100mm is thought to be "telephoto," good for pulling in distant scenes. 200mm or more is considered a powerful telephoto.

Be sure to check the "35mm equivalent" numbers for an indication of the camera's real value.

Choosing a Zoom

A zoom lens lets you change the focal length of the camera. In simple terms, it lets you choose how much the camera magnifies the image, and zoom lenses let you zoom in and out of a scene for the perfect composition. In general, the greater the zoom, the better. You'll commonly see 2x, 3x, and perhaps even 5x zooms on digital cameras. With some simple finger pressure, you can use your camera to go from a normal or wide-angle view to telephoto. The effect of a 4x zoom is apparent in Figure 1-5, taken with a 3-megapixel digital camera at both ends of its zoom range.

FIGURE 1-5   Zoom lenses are popular because of their flexibility when composing pictures.

Beware, though, of a camera's *digital zoom*. While optical zooms move the lenses around to actually magnify the image, a digital zoom simply grabs a block of pixels in the middle of the scene and processes them to make the image look bigger. Since the result is grainy and blurry, I suggest that you ignore digital zoom ratings when evaluating a camera and just look at the optical zoom ratings.

Memory

The more memory your camera holds, the more pictures you can take. It sounds simple, but don't forget that cameras come with all different kinds of memory solutions. In general, it really doesn't matter whether your camera uses Compact Flash, SmartMedia, Memory Stick, Secure Digital, or xD memory—the only things to consider are cost and capacity:

- **Capacity** If you only want to carry a single memory card on a long trip and store a huge number of images, a CompactFlash digital camera is your best choice. You can get CompactFlash cards in capacities well beyond 1GB. (Imagine a thousand images on one card!) Other memory formats top out around 512MB, and the nearly extinct SmartMedia card holds just 128MB. (Not many new cameras have SmartMedia slots anymore, but you may own a camera that uses this format.) Of course, you can also buy several memory cards and carry spares, which can be cheaper than buying one really huge card (regardless of what kind of memory card your camera uses). Personally, I own several 256MB memory cards and bring them along as spares when I use my camera—it's a lot cheaper than buying a single 1GB card.

- **Cost** The various memory card formats play a lot of leapfrog when it comes to price, so you might want to shop around for memory cards before you commit to a specific camera. Of course, the newest memory card formats (we're looking at you, xD) cost a bit more than the more established memory cards, like CompactFlash. See Chapter 9 for details.

Flash

Almost all digital cameras come with a built-in flash. The real issue is how well the flash works. Check to see what the maximum range of the flash is and if it works when the camera is in macro, or close focus, mode. Otherwise, you might be unable to use the flash when taking macro photos. You might also want a flash with special features like these:

- **Red eye reduction**   This mode preflashes the subject to try to minimize reflected light from the pupil known as *red eye*.

- **Force/fill**   Force or fill flash is used to reduce shadows outdoors or in otherwise adequate lighting when the flash might not fire.

- **Rear curtain flash**   This mode fires at the end of a long exposure. It comes in handy at night so that light trails precede the main subject, illuminated by the flash.

Some cameras also come with sync ports or hot shoes that allow you to connect more powerful, external flash units.

Special Effects

Since digital cameras are part computer, they can be programmed to do some neat tricks that were inconceivable with traditional film cameras. Few of these effects are necessary; in fact, I'd choose a camera based on solid features like the zoom, lens quality, and overall handling before looking too hard at whether the camera included a video mode or sepia tint. Nonetheless, these are some of the effects you may see:

- **Movie mode**   Some cameras can capture short, low-resolution video clips as well as still images. Don't confuse this with real, high-quality digital video, though—the results are strictly for web pages.

- **Tint modes**   With special settings, you can take black-and-white or sepia-tinted stills. Remember, though, that you can achieve the same effect in an image editor on the PC after the picture is taken, so you aren't losing anything if your camera lacks this feature. In fact, it's usually better to start with a full-color image; that way you can do whatever you like to it later and always have the high-quality original to fall back on.

Transferring Pictures

Getting images out of your camera is just as important as taking the pictures to begin with.

Of course, most digital cameras use a USB cable to transfer images to the computer. USB is a common, standard cable that connects most external gadgets to computers. But some cameras include even more convenient solutions, such as docking stations as shown in the first illustration next page that "sync" the pictures as soon as you place the camera on the desk.

If you like to view your freshly shot images on a television or want to record them, slide-show style, directly to a VCR, then you should definitely consider a camera with a video-out port. Using an ordinary RCA-style composite video cable, you can connect the camera to a TV, VCR, or some other video display unit.

Other cameras include adapters that accept the removable media card and connect to the computer directly. The advantage with these devices is that you can transfer images without draining the camera batteries, and transfers are often easier to do, since you drag-and-drop images from a folder on your desktop. Even if your camera doesn't include one of these gadgets, you can add one later.

Memory card readers, such as the one in the following illustration, let you pop the memory card from your camera into your PC and copy the pictures as if they were stored on a floppy disk. Any computer or office supply store should have a wide array of removable memory card readers to choose from, and they all tend to cost under $30 or so.

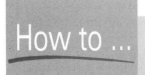

Choose a Digital Camera

When you're shopping for a digital camera, make a checklist of features and capabilities you want based on these criteria:

- **Resolution**   Decide how large your finished images need to be, and look for cameras that can take pictures in the appropriate "megapixel" range. If you usually want to make 4×6-inch prints, get a 2-megapixel camera. Three megapixels is great for 8×10s.

- **Zoom**   The bigger the zoom, the more you can enlarge the image. But pay attention to the lowest number of the zoom range, which indicates the wide-angle rating, and the biggest number, which is the telephoto setting. Ignore the digital zoom rating, which is more of a marketing gimmick than a useful photo feature.

- **Memory**   How large is the memory card that comes with your camera? Does the camera also have special internal memory so you can take a few pictures even if you forget the memory card at home?

- **Flash**   Consider the flash range and special features such as red eye reduction. For serious flash photography, look for cameras that accept external flash units.

- **Batteries**   Does the camera take standard AA batteries or special lithium ion batteries? Does it come with a wall adapter or a battery charger?

- **Picture transfers**   One last issue to consider is how the camera transfers images to the PC—this is a convenience issue. Does it use a standard USB cable? A docking cradle? Does the camera come with a removable memory card reader?

Gear You'll Need

Every hobby has its accessories. Here's a short shopping list of things you might consider buying as you become a more avid photographer:

- **A camera**   It goes without saying that you will want a digital camera, but don't rush into the purchase. You can even use a film camera to begin with, and scan the images into the PC for editing and printing. If you've read the previous sections of this chapter and decided what features are important to you, you can shop like a pro.

■ **An adequate PC**   Crunching data to process digital images takes a bit more horsepower than you might be used to when working with Word or Excel. These days, a good "digital camera rig" includes at least a 1.5 GHz processor and no less than 256MB of Random Access Memory (RAM). If you want to work with really big images—like 6-megapixel pictures—then consider 512MB or even 1GB of RAM. You might be surprised to learn that more memory is generally more useful than a faster processor.

■ **Batteries**   Digital cameras are power hogs. If your camera uses AA-style batteries, I highly recommend buying two sets of rechargeable batteries, since they'll pay for themselves before you can say "alkaline." If your camera didn't come with an AC adapter, I suggest that you buy one from the camera vendor's accessories store so you can power the camera when you're transferring images to the PC or displaying images on a TV. No matter what kind of battery your camera takes, have at least one spare that can be fully charged all the time.

NOTE   *It's worth pointing out that rechargeable batteries last a lot longer these days than they used to just a few years ago. If you tried rechargeables back before the turn of the century and were unimpressed, give them another shot—they're a lot better these days.*

■ **Memory**   Buy the biggest memory card you can afford, or a combination of two cards each with reasonable capacity. The measly 16MB memory card that came with your camera won't last a day when you're on vacation, so having a 256MB, 512MB, or even a gigabyte card is almost essential. A spare card, if it's in the budget, can keep you going when you fill up your main card far away from your PC. (And if you're on a budget, remember that two 512MB cards are usually cheaper than a single 1GB card.)

■ **Image-editing software**   Your camera probably came with some rudimentary image editor, but it may not be up to the task. Try a few out, and buy the image editor that you like the best. I like Paint Shop Pro (www.jasc.com), Adobe Photoshop Elements (www.adobe.com), and Digital Image Suite (www.microsoft.com). See Chapter 11 for more info on image-editing software.

■ **Tripod** If you want to extend your photography into the world of close-ups or long-range telephoto images, a tripod is a necessity. It needn't be large or heavy, since most digital cameras are significantly lighter than their film camera counterparts.

■ **Camera bag** Choose a bag that lets you arrange your camera and accessories in a way that they're protected from theft and damage, but easy to use when the time comes to shoot a picture. Look for bags that don't really look like they're holding camera gear—that might make them less of a target by thieves.

Features, Gadgets, and Goodies

No two digital cameras are the same. Each camera maker is known to some greater or lesser extent for implement-specific kinds of features—such as interchangeable lenses, bodies that swivel around the lens, or movie recording features. If you cut through all those goodies, though, you'll find that most cameras share many of the same fundamentals. Let's start at the top and cover your camera's fundamentals.

The Optics

At the heart of every camera, no matter how it stores its images, is an optical system, as you can see in Figure 1-6.

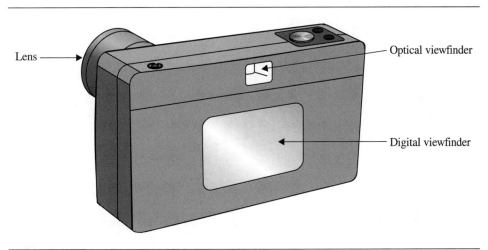

Lens

Optical viewfinder

Digital viewfinder

FIGURE 1-6 Almost all digital cameras rely on an optical system that includes both an optical viewfinder and a digital viewfinder, or LCD display.

Most digital cameras have two distinct viewfinders—an optical one and a digital one. In most cases, the optical viewfinder is composed of a glass or plastic lens that shows you your subject directly—it's just a plain window that lets you see through the camera to the other side. The digital viewfinder is a large Liquid Crystal Display (LCD) that reproduces what the camera's image sensor is actually seeing.

Which one should you use? Whichever one you like. You'll get better results, though, if you understand the difference between the two. With a majority of cameras, you do not actually see exactly what the camera sees when you look through the optical viewfinder.

Here's why: When taking pictures from a distance, the optical viewfinder and lens see essentially the same thing. Close up to your subject, though, they clearly see two different things (as you can see from Figure 1-7).

The digital viewfinder, on the other hand, shows you exactly what the camera sees, and thus is the most accurate gauge of your potential photograph. You won't want to use your digital viewfinder all the time, though. For starters, it uses a lot of power, and you can get more mileage out of your camera's batteries by using the optical viewfinder instead. In addition, the LCD display can be very difficult to see in certain lighting conditions, such as outside in mid-afternoon.

TIP   *Some cameras allow you to turn off the LCD display to conserve power. Leave the display off most of the time to get more battery life.*

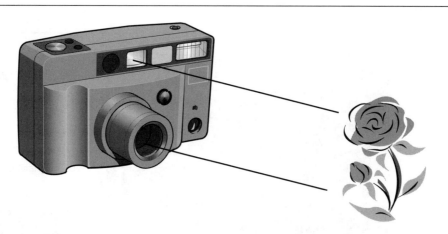

FIGURE 1-7   The optical viewfinder and the camera's lens don't always see exactly the same thing, especially when close up to the subject.

1

Power Systems

Your digital camera, of course, takes batteries. Some digital cameras rely on a standard set of AA batteries or their rechargeable equivalents.

An increasingly common practice is for manufacturers to design cameras around special lithium ion battery packs. The advantage is that these batteries are much smaller than a foursome of AAs, so the camera itself can be much smaller. You can see the size difference between the battery compartments of a Canon PowerShot A75 (left), which uses AA batteries, and a Sony CyberShot L1 (right), which features a tiny lithium ion battery:

On the downside, with lithium ion batteries you can't just pop in ubiquitous AA batteries when the cells run dry, which means you need to keep one or more spares on hand.

Here's a little advice to help you get the most mileage from your batteries:

- Insert batteries according to the diagram on the camera body—make sure you align the battery's positive and negative ends correctly.

- Don't leave batteries in the camera for an extended period of time. Some kinds of batteries may leak when fully discharged, and if that happens, your camera can be ruined.

- Don't mix and match fresh and used batteries, or batteries of different kinds (such as alkaline and rechargeables).

■ If your camera takes NiMH batteries, it's a good idea to run them all the way down before recharging them. If you have lithium ion batteries, though, do just the opposite: charge them more frequently, before they have a chance to fully discharge.

■ When you can, run your camera using AC power (power via a wall outlet) to conserve your batteries for when you really need them.

Some digital cameras come with their own AC adapters, while for others AC adapters are an optional accessory. Check the camera body for an AC adapter connector. If you can connect the camera to a wall outlet, especially during image transfers to the PC, you can significantly extend the length of your battery's life.

Taking Care of Batteries

Digital cameras are battery hogs, plain and simple. You shouldn't expect the batteries in a digital camera to last very long since they are responsible for running a number of key functions within the camera:

■ The imaging system, including the exposure controls and the zoom lens motor

■ The LCD display

■ The flash

■ Picture storage

That's a lot to expect from a set of batteries. You might typically expect to get between 100 and 200 shots from a set of batteries, depending on how aggressively you use features such as the zoom and LCD display.

Rechargeable Versus Alkaline   If your camera uses typical AA-style batteries, you should avoid alkaline batteries. Instead, invest in one or two sets of NiMH rechargeable batteries. Yes, they're initially more expensive. But they quickly pay for themselves, since you can use rechargeables several hundred times before they stop holding a useful charge. Do the math: Let's say that you use your camera every weekend for a year and you have to replace the batteries about once a month. Here's how the cost stacks up over the course of a year:

AA Alkaline (Such as Energizer "Titanium" High-Performance Batteries)	NiMH Rechargeables (Charger and One Set of Batteries)
12 × $8 = $96	$20

Batteries Don't Last Forever

Rechargeable batteries lose a teeny tiny little bit of their life every time you charge them. You can extend the life of these batteries by only recharging them when they're actually run down; "topping them off" is like a regular recharge in that it heats the chemicals in the battery casing, which slowly reduces the battery's life.

The more you use your camera, the more obvious the cost savings become. Once you've bought your first set of rechargeable batteries, additional sets are less expensive (usually under $10) because you don't have to buy another charger. So you can see how useful rechargeables actually are.

TIP

In general, I avoid compact digital cameras that use proprietary lithium ion batteries. Yes, I know that they're all the rage these days, but I like the security of knowing, in a pinch, that I can simply pop in a pair of AA batteries and keep shooting. If I have a camera with a fancy lithium ion brick and no spare, I'm out of commission until the battery charges.

Get the Most Out of Your Batteries   With so many demands on your camera batteries, it's not all that surprising that they don't last very long. But there are certainly things you can do to extend the life of your batteries, making them last longer between charges or replacements. Just follow some of these commonsense tips:

■ **Use the optical viewfinder.** If your camera lets you, turn off the LCD display and look through the optical finder instead. The LCD screen is one of the biggest energy hogs on your camera, and you can significantly extend the value of your batteries by not using it.

■ **Don't review your pictures.** Likewise, avoid gawking at your pictures on the camera's LCD display. Of course, feel free to review them briefly. But save the slow, careful replays for your computer screen.

■ **Disable the flash when you don't need it.** Sure, there are excellent reasons to use it, even outdoors, but if you are shooting subjects that are 40 feet away and the flash can't possibly help, turn it off. Your batteries will thank you.

■ **Leave the camera on.** If you're taking a lot of pictures in a brief time, don't turn the camera off after each and every picture. You might think that you're conserving battery life, but in fact you're burning energy every time the camera has to power on. That's especially true if your camera has to retract the zoom lens every time it powers down and extend the lens when you turn it on again.

■ **Use AC power when it's available.** When you're transferring images to the PC, don't rely on battery power. You should have an AC adapter to power the camera when you're working at your desk near electrical power. If your camera didn't come with an AC adapter, it's probably wise to invest in one for exactly this reason. The AC adapter might also come in handy if you're shooting a lot of pictures inside a house from a somewhat stationary position. You can save battery life for when you really need it by tethering yourself to an AC outlet.

If your batteries die in the middle of a shoot and you don't have any spares, here's a trick you can try that might give you a few extra shots: turn the camera off, wait a minute, and then turn it back on. Often you can sneak in a few more pictures before the batteries are completely exhausted.

Memory Storage

Memory cards store your digital images for you. The more memory your camera has, the more images it can store. Most cameras include a memory card with some memory capacity (such as 32MB, 256MB, or 1GB) that, when inserted in the camera, stores images. When it's full, you can remove this card and insert another card for additional storage. Of course, most manufacturers include a pretty small card in the box with the camera, expecting that you will buy one or more additional memory cards for your camera.

You can use the connection cable that came with your camera to transfer images to the PC, or use a memory card reader to directly insert a memory card (see Figure 1-8) to insert the memory into your PC as if it were a floppy disk.

There are five major kinds of memory cards in use today:

■ SmartMedia

■ CompactFlash

■ Memory Stick (and its big brother, Memory Stick Pro)

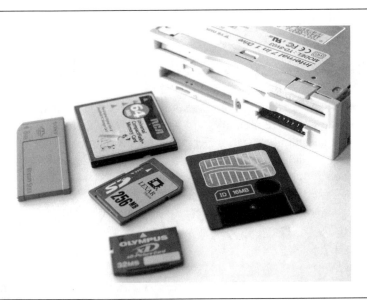

FIGURE 1-8   There are five main kinds of memory cards in use today, and your digital camera probably accommodates at least one of them. Readers, such as the 6-in-1 device shown here, can read your memory card like a floppy disk, eliminating the need for cables.

- Secure Digital (commonly abbreviated SD, along with its little brother, MMC)
- xD

How many images can you fit on a memory card? It has nothing to do with the type *of memory card—all that matters is the resolution of the images and the memory card's total capacity, measured in megabytes or gigabytes.*

Camera Controls

Perhaps the most subjective of digital camera features, the controls are also among the most important because they account for how you interact with your camera. The controls should be comfortable, logical, and convenient. Of course, I can't really tell you which camera has the best controls; you need to experiment with a few cameras to see which you like the best. Try handling cameras in the store whenever you can. Make sure you can reach all of the important buttons and try to pick a camera that isn't littered with so many buttons that you'll never remember how they all work.

How Many Pictures Memory Cards Can Hold

How many images can you fit on a memory card? You can use this handy chart to decide what size memory card—or how many memory cards—to take on your next family vacation. This chart is just approximate, because the exact number of pictures you can fit on a memory card depends on how much "compression" your camera applies to each picture:

	16MB	32MB	64MB	128MB	256MB
2-megapixel	17	35	71	142	284
3-megapixel	13	26	53	106	213
4-megapixel	8	16	32	64	128
5-megapixel	6	12	25	51	102
6-megapixel	7	14	27	53	107

Digital cameras typically feature two distinct control systems: on-body buttons and dials, and onscreen menus. Figure 1-9 shows some body controls, such as a diopter dial (for adjusting the eyepiece to your personal eyesight), a shutter release button, and zoom controls. The onscreen menu (see Figure 1-10) is commonly used to adjust less frequently used controls, such as resolution settings, exposure compensation, and special effects filters. That's not always the case, though, as you can see in Figure 1-11. This camera uses a button—the one with the star—to change the resolution without resorting to a menu system.

And don't forget that the best camera in the world is the one you actually have with you. That means that small is usually better than big—even if a somewhat bulky camera seems to have a great assortment of features, a smaller, sleeker model that actually fits in a purse or pocket might be a better bet.

You need to take the time to review your camera manual to find out how to operate all of your camera controls. Without knowing how your camera works, you can't really learn to take great pictures.

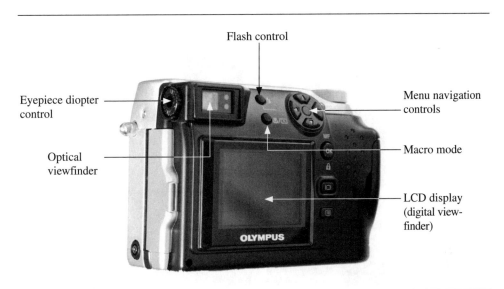

Flash control

Eyepiece diopter control

Optical viewfinder

Menu navigation controls

Macro mode

LCD display (digital view-finder)

Most of these controls are common to all digital cameras.

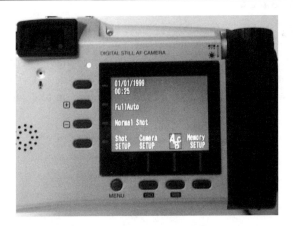

Digital cameras use a series of menus in the LCD display to operate the more advanced or less frequently used features.

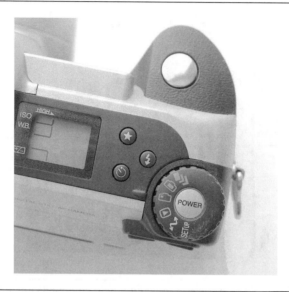

FIGURE 1-11   The star symbol is sometimes used to indicate resolution.

The Upgrade Race

Do you need to get a new camera next year just because the megapixel bar has been raised—or some other cool new features have surfaced?

No, you don't. Just like your desktop computer, a digital camera isn't obsolete just because a new model came out with more bells and whistles. It's only obsolete when it no longer does what you want it to do. Find a camera you like and stick with it.

Chapter 2

Understanding Exposure

How to…

- Tell the difference between analog and digital camera operation
- Distinguish between slide and negative photography
- Select ISO settings for digital and film cameras
- Match aperture and shutter speed settings for correct exposure
- Use the Sunny 16 Rule
- Modify the Sunny 16 Rule based on ISO and lighting conditions
- Adjust exposure manually
- Tweak exposure with your camera's EV settings
- Choose metering modes for better pictures
- Use exposure lock to optimize exposure
- Tell when to ignore the camera and make your own exposure decisions

Some people think that photography is akin to magic. They turn on the camera, snap a picture, and a day or two later they've got a mystical re-creation of the scene they saw in the viewfinder. With a digital camera, or *digicam* for short, it's even more magical—the pictures are available instantly! How does it work? Who knows?

The problem with the Abe Simpson approach to photography (which I've so named based on an episode of *The Simpsons,* in which someone took a picture of old Abe and he shouted feebly, "You stole my soul!") is that you can never really improve if you don't know what your camera does or why, or how you can influence the camera yourself to improve your shots. This chapter, consequently, walks you through the exposure process. Here you'll learn what constitutes a proper exposure and how to get one yourself—even on cameras that are mostly automatic.

How Cameras Take Pictures

The best place to start is often right at the beginning—how on earth does a camera take a picture, anyway?

Did you know?

What Happens at the Moment of Exposure

Depending on the kind of camera, the events that take place at the moment of exposure can be quite complicated. In a modern 35mm SLR, for instance, microprocessor-controlled sensors determine the exact amount of light needed to expose a picture at the moment you press the shutter release. The lens automatically adjusts the size of its opening to admit the correct amount of light, and the mirror mechanism that usually lets you look through the viewfinder flips up and out of the way, allowing light to reach the film. Finally, the aperture opens, and the shutter slides open for the programmed amount of time. Point-and-shoot cameras, in contrast, don't use mirror mechanisms to let you see through the lens before the shot, so there are fewer moving parts at the moment of exposure—but the trade-off is that you don't see the picture you're about to take as accurately with a point-and-shoot.

All cameras, regardless of type, work more or less the same way—as depicted in the following illustration. They open their shutter for a brief time, allowing light to enter. That light then interacts with a sensitive photo-receptor (such as film or a computer chip), and an image is recorded. Let's start by looking at a traditional 35mm camera to give us a little perspective.

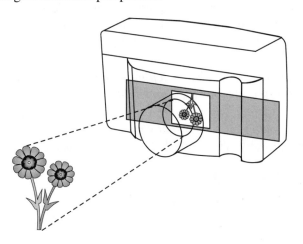

Inside a 35mm Camera

Traditional cameras rely on good old-fashioned film. But what is film, really? It's just a strip of plastic that has been coated with a light-sensitive chemical. The chemical soup on the film is loaded with grains of silver halide. When exposed to light, the silver halide reacts, and that is the essence of photography. The longer the film is exposed to light, the more the silver is affected.

There are two kinds of film in common use today: negative film and slide film. They work a little differently, but the end result is similar. When you use color negative film, also referred to as reversal film, the film itself becomes a "negative" image of the scene you photographed. After processing—which includes letting the film sit in a chemical bath that coaxes the grains of silver to visually materialize on the film—the negative is used to create positive prints of the scene. It's a two-step process, and one that is highly subjective. When creating prints from negatives, photo-finishers often tweak the picture to improve its appearance. Of course, what the corner shop considers an "improvement" may not be what you were trying to achieve, and that explains why your pictures never seem to benefit from filters, exposure changes, or any of the other corrections you try to make when taking pictures.

But I digress. The other kind of film, simple slide (or reversal) film, uses a color positive development process: after fixing the slide film in its chemical bath, the film becomes slides that can be held up to the light to display images. Because of their far simpler development process, slides can't be tweaked by the processor. What you and your camera do determines how they turn out—and in that way, slide photography is much more like digital photography in a sense.

No matter what kind of film you have, it eventually needs to be exposed to light. When you take a picture, you obviously press the shutter release. The shutter release instructs the camera to open the shutter blades for a brief period of time and then close them again. If all goes well, that is just long enough to properly expose the film.

If you want to shoot with 35mm film, scan the results, and then edit and print the results on your PC, you might want to work with slide film. Slides are more exacting—they require you to nail the exposure fairly precisely, but they'll better represent what you actually photographed than will the local photo shop's vision of what you photographed.

The ABCs of Film Speed

As you no doubt know from shopping for film, not all canisters of 35mm film are alike. Film is differentiated principally by its speed, or ISO number.

2

What ISO Means

ISO stands for International Organization for Standardization, and that's the group that helped establish how the film numbering scheme works. Film around the world uses ISO numbers, so you can buy it anywhere and it'll all work the same. In the United States, photographers used to call this system ASA, which stood for the American Standards Association. That term was essentially abandoned about 20 years ago, so if you want to be considered a gristled old geezer, you can refer to ISO numbers as "ASA numbers."

A film's ISO number refers to how sensitive it is to light. The lower the number is, the less sensitive it is—requiring long exposures or very bright scenes.

A fairly typical ISO number for ordinary daylight photography is ISO 100. Increasing the ISO to 200 doubles the sensitivity of the film, meaning it would only take an exposure half as long to capture the same picture; dropping back to an ISO of 50 halves the sensitivity of the film, requiring an exposure twice as long as an ISO of 100.

The ISO number has a tangible effect on the mechanics of photography. To see why, look at Figure 2-1. This diagram shows a typical camera body as a picture is taken. The lens is equipped with a diaphragm—called an *aperture*—that has

FIGURE 2-1   Every camera—no matter what it uses for film—controls the exposure with some sort of aperture and shutter settings.

a certain diameter and consequently is designed to allow a specific amount of light through to the film. With ISO 100 film in specific lighting conditions (say, at midday), the shutter might need to open for a 250th of a second (1/250) to adequately expose the picture.

But what happens if we instead try to take the same picture with ISO 200 film? The film is exactly twice as sensitive to light as the previous roll of film. And that means, all other things being equal, that we only need to leave the shutter open for half as long (a 500th of a second, or 1/500) to take the same picture.

That's not all. Suppose you're trying to take a picture in late afternoon, when there isn't as much light available? You might need to leave the shutter open for 1/30 in that situation to gather enough light with ISO 100 film. That shutter speed is a bit on the slow side, though. Not only might you jiggle the camera as you're taking the picture (it's hard to hold a camera steady for 1/30), but your subject might move as well, causing a blurry picture. You can probably guess what the solution is—stepping up to ISO 200 film will enable you to grab that picture at a much more reasonable 1/60, and ISO 400 would halve the shutter speed yet again, to a crisp 1/125.

The F/stop Ballet

So far so good—but there's one other aspect to consider, and that's the fact that camera lenses can change the diameter of their aperture, thus letting in more or less light as needed.

The size of a camera's aperture at any given moment is called the *f/stop,* also sometimes referred to as the *f/number* of the lens. F/stops are represented by numbers that start with "f/"—such as f/2, f/5.6, and f/11. The larger the number, the smaller the opening, so an f/22 is very, very small (not much light gets through to the film), while a lens set to f/1.2 is a huge opening that floods the film with light. Changing the camera setting by a "whole" f/stop, such as from f/5.6 to f/8 or f/11 to f/16, doubles or halves the available light, depending on which way you're going. If you adjust a lens from f/8 to f/11, for instance, you've reduced the light by half.

We'll talk about f/stops in more detail in Chapter 3 (it's really important, yet really simple), but for the moment take a look at Figure 2-2. This diagram shows the relationship between the f/stop and the shutter speed. As you reduce the shutter speed, you need to increase the diameter of the aperture in order to have enough light to take a properly exposed picture.

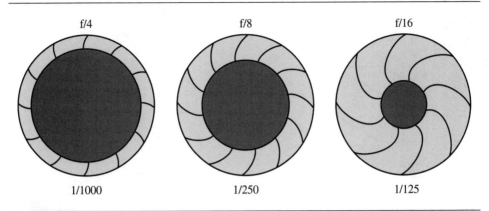

f/4   f/8   f/16

1/1000   1/250   1/125

FIGURE 2-2   Each of these combinations results in the same amount of light reaching the film.

Of course, there's a relationship between aperture, shutter speed, and your film's ISO rating. Look at Figure 2-3. At any given film speed, you can take a picture with a specific aperture/shutter combination. If you double the film speed without changing the lighting conditions, though, you have to adjust the aperture and the shutter speed so that you still get a properly exposed picture.

So let's apply all this newfound knowledge. Suppose you want to take a picture of lions frolicking at the zoo near dusk. The aperture is wide open at f/2—it won't open any farther. Nonetheless, your camera needs to use the relatively slow shutter speed of 1/15 of a second to take the shot. You know the image would be a blurry mess at that sluggish shutter speed, so what is there to do? Take a look at your film speed. It's ISO 100. Well, you might be in luck. If you're willing to pop the film out of your camera and put in film that's two f/stops (often, just called "stops") faster, you can keep the aperture at f/2 and change the shutter speed to 1/60. That's probably good enough to get the shot. Just do it quickly—it isn't getting any brighter out, and if you dally, you might find you need to increase the speed by three stops by the time you get the film loaded and ready to go.

How Digicams Are Different, but Kinda the Same

All that talk about f/stops, shutter speed, and ISO settings may seem irrelevant to your digital camera, but it's not—all cameras use these concepts, even though they're sometimes disguised fairly well. The main difference between a digital camera and a film camera, of course, is the fact that digicams don't use film.

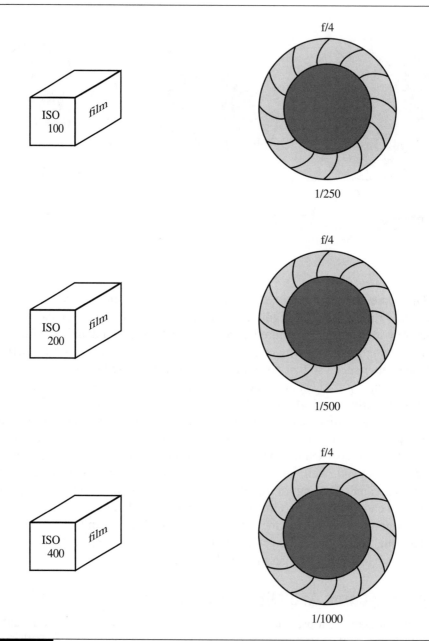

FIGURE 2-3   Film speed, known as the ISO number, also affects shutter speed and aperture.

About F/stops

You probably don't need to know this, but it might come in handy during a trivia game some day. Mathematically, f/stops are the ratio of the focal length of the lens divided by the diameter of the opening of the diaphragm. Thus, when you divide the focal length of the lens by a very small opening, you get a large number, while dividing the focal length by a comparatively large diameter gives you a smaller number.

That means you never load anything that has a specific ISO value into the camera. So how does the camera actually work?

It is quite simple. When light enters the camera at the moment of exposure, it doesn't hit light-sensitive silver halides that are fixed in a chemical broth. Instead, the light hits a computer chip that acts as a sensor and is usually called a CCD (though some cameras use a CMOS sensor instead, both of which I talked about in Chapter 1). The sensor is light sensitive, and each of its many pixels register changes in light just like the film's many grains of silver react individually to light (see Figure 2-4, where you can imagine the grid representing the pixel-filled sensor, with the image being generated by each pixel receiving a different amount of light). In other words, the silver grains in film and the pixels in a CCD or CMOS sensor are essentially the same thing. They contribute to your picture in the same way, and both are the smallest components that make up your picture.

The sensor makes a picture by noting the variation in light rays that travel through the camera lens. The CCD or CMOS sensor passes this information on to the camera's microprocessor in the form of varying electrical charges. The image is then transformed into digital bits and stored on a memory card.

Your camera's image sensor functions like the film in a 35mm camera, except that it differs in one important way—you can't swap the CCD out of your camera and insert one with more light sensitivity for low-light photography. The sensor is a permanent part of the camera. Camera makers understand that you might need to change the camera's light sensitivity on occasion, though, and that's why many cameras can have their ISO rating "adjusted" on-the-fly, whenever you want. In essence, what this does is allow you to "turn up" or "turn down" your camera's sensitivity to light by adjusting the gain of the circuit reading the sensor voltage.

190	200	210	210	200
180	160	100	120	190
160	150	100	153	160
170	160	90	110	110
130	125	90	120	110
125	100	88	120	110
88	100	90	92	88

FIGURE 2-4   A digital camera creates pictures by interpreting a dense grid of light-sensitive pixels instead of chemically reactive grains of silver.

Use ISO for Exposure Control

You can use the ISO control built into your digital camera to vary its sensitivity to light and thus mimic the effect of using different grades of 35mm film. This can come in handy in a number of situations, such as when you're shooting in particularly high- or low-light situations. Remember a few key facts about your digital camera's ISO settings, though:

■ It's not a real ISO adjustment, in the sense that your camera doesn't have real film. All camera makers have somewhat different ways of implementing this feature, but they all use ISO numbers since that's comparable to 35mm film, which most people are at least a little familiar with.

■ Some folks think that by setting their cameras to the highest sensitivity, they'll be prepared for anything and won't have to muck with the camera menu when they're on the go, trying to take pictures. In reality, boosting your camera's sensitivity to light also increases the amount of digital noise you're capturing. More ISO means more fringing, artifacts, and digital detritus, as in the image shown in the following illustration. Sometimes that's unavoidable, but stick with the lowest ISO value you can get away with most of the time. To do that, set your camera's ISO control to its lowest setting or to Auto, which usually accomplishes the same thing.

Change the ISO Setting

If you find yourself in a situation in which the lighting isn't quite right for your picture, it's time to bump up the camera's ISO value. Remember that most, but not all, cameras come with ISO adjustments, so review your user manual to see if this applies to your particular model. Figure 2-5 shows a typical ISO adjustment; you'll probably find it in the onscreen menu system, displayed in the LCD screen at the back of your camera.

FIGURE 2-5   A typical ISO adjustment on a digital camera

Here are some situations in which you might need to increase the ISO:

■ You're shooting in a low-light situation, such as early evening or indoors. Natural-light photos have a certain appeal, and by increasing the light sensitivity of your camera you may be able shoot a picture without using the flash at all. Using natural light can eliminate harsh shadows and produce more natural colors.

■ Your subject is too far away for the flash to have any effect. During the day you might be outdoors and want to take a picture of something, but there's not quite enough light—such as in winter or during very overcast conditions. Your camera wants to use a flash, but your subject is just too far away. As you'll see in Chapter 4, the flash on your digital camera has a very limited range, so to properly expose your picture you need to use "faster film"—that is, increase the camera's ISO setting.

■ You're shooting at night. Most digital cameras have limited ability to take pictures at night or in near total darkness. As a result, if you want to capture anything at all with a night shot, you may need to increase the camera's light sensitivity to the maximum.

TIP   *If night photography interests you, investigate what I refer to as "performance" digital cameras—cameras that include manually adjustable shutter speeds and apertures. Cameras such as the Nikon CoolPix 7900, the Olympus C-8080, and the Canon PowerShot G6 are the sorts of models that are better equipped to deal with very low light such as you'll encounter at night. Using more full-featured cameras lets you perform long exposures for light trails, glowing illuminated signage, and other special effects.*

Perfect Shots with Aperture and Shutter

Let's return to the idea of aperture and shutter speed again for a moment. As you saw earlier in this chapter, they're essential ingredients to creating good pictures. Of course, with most digital cameras, you rarely have to worry about setting shutter speed and aperture size at all for typical photography.

How Cameras Choose Aperture and Shutter Speed

Here's what usually happens: when you apply pressure to the camera's shutter release, the camera's microcomputer samples the scene in front of the lens and determines how much light is needed to adequately expose the scene. With most digicams, the camera selects a shutter speed and aperture combination that is sufficient to get the job done. But, you might be wondering, how does it choose? After all, there are a lot of shutter speed/aperture pairs that will work. To take the same properly exposed picture at ISO 100, any of these combinations should produce exactly the same result:

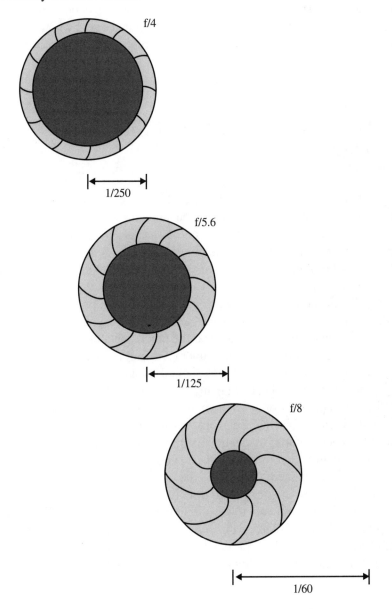

Usually, the camera uses the following logic:

The photographer wants to take a picture using the fastest available shutter speed to minimize camera shake and motion blur from objects moving inside the picture.

Though there are some exceptions, most cameras tend to choose the combination that allows for the highest available shutter speed, limited only by how small they can make the aperture given the current lighting conditions and ISO setting.

The Truth About Shutters

Though I talk quite a lot about shutter speed in this book, the reality is that not all digital cameras have a real mechanical shutter in the sense that 35mm cameras have shutters. 35mm cameras usually have a physical barrier that blocks light from entering the chamber where the film is stored. This mechanism—the shutter blade—moves lightning fast, able to deliver shutter speeds as fast as 1/8000 of a second. That's fast.

Many digital cameras, in comparison, don't have real, physical shutters. You can verify this yourself with a simple experiment: When you press the shutter release on a 35mm camera, you can hear the quick, metallic click of the shutter blade opening and closing. A digital camera may not make any noise at all. Or it might make an obviously fake "click" sound through the camera's speaker. When I got my first digital camera many years ago, I actually had to look at the LCD display on the back of the camera to see if the picture was captured or if, for some mysterious reason, the camera was still waiting to grab the shot.

So if there's no shutter blade, how is the picture actually taken? Often, the CCD is simply turned on long enough to expose the picture. Since the CCD is an electronic component that acts as the camera's film, it can be controlled electronically for whatever exposure time is needed. In addition, the camera's aperture may close completely to keep light from reaching the CCD—prolonged exposure to sunlight can damage this sensitive part of the camera, but the aperture needn't spring open and closed as quickly as the shutter blade in a 35mm camera, so the sound it makes isn't as dramatic. You'll hardly notice it at all.

This isn't always what you want your camera to do, though, and in fact you might sometimes want to choose a slower shutter speed, overexpose the image, underexpose it, or perhaps base the exposure on a completely different part of the picture. That's why you might want to investigate your camera and look for controls that let you tweak the shutter speed and aperture.

Adjust Exposure Manually

The most basic manual exposure control you can exert over your camera involves setting both the aperture and shutter speed. Some digital cameras allow you to set these controls as if you had a fully automatic 35mm SLR. There are two kinds of cameras you may run into with this capability:

- **Point-and-shoot** Most point-and-shoot digicams that include manual settings for aperture and shutter speed require you to use the LCD display to make onscreen menu changes. The camera shown in the following illustration, for instance, uses a pair of buttons on the right side of the LCD display to adjust shutter speed, and another set of buttons on the bottom of the screen to change the aperture settings. It isn't hard to do, but you need to remember first to set the camera to its Manual Exposure mode and then remember which buttons do what for fine-tuning the exposure.

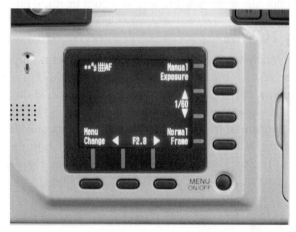

- **D-SLR** A few digital cameras—digital SLRs, for the most part—use traditional SLR controls for making manual adjustments to exposure. Specifically, you can turn the aperture ring on the lens to change the f/stop or use a control on the camera to accomplish the same thing, as shown in the following illustration. Shutter speed is likewise affected with a dial on the camera body, and you can look through the viewfinder to keep tabs on the setting.

To set exposure manually, you must choose a shutter speed and aperture combination that will properly expose your scene at a given ISO. This is a great exercise for new photographers who are serious about learning photography theory.

Use the Sunny 16 Rule

At an ISO of 100, which many digital cameras use for general-purpose photography, you might want to rely on the traditional "Sunny 16 Rule" for a starting point. The Sunny 16 Rule is very old—it dates back to the earliest days of analog photography—and it suggests that when shooting outdoors in bright sunlight you should choose an aperture of f/16 and a shutter speed that's equivalent to your film speed. Since few cameras offer the ability to choose 1/100, most photographers who rely on this rule use 1/125 when shooting with ISO 100 film. Here is a chart that identifies other acceptable combinations. (All of these add up to the same overall exposure.)

Shutter Speed	Aperture
1/1000	f/5.6
1/500	f/8
1/250	f/11
1/125	f/16
1/60	f/22

Keep in mind that these recommendations are just a starting point. Here are some tips that can help you zero in on your ideal exposure:

- ■ Your camera will often recommend an ideal exposure, which you can accept or reject. If the camera considers your setting out of bounds, it may flash a warning in your viewfinder.

- ■ Adjust your exposure based on the ISO setting. If your camera is set to an equivalent of ISO 200, for instance, the Sunny 16 Rule would call for a shutter speed of 1/250 and an aperture of f/16.

- ■ Make adjustments for brighter or darker scenes. If you're shooting in a dark room, for instance, the Sunny 16 Rule doesn't really apply—but it's a good starting point. Open the aperture or lengthen the shutter speed to account for reduced light; close the aperture or shorten the shutter speed to account for increased light.

Use Shutter or Aperture Priority Adjustments

Instead of relying on an all-automatic or all-manual exposure system, you can compromise and use your camera's shutter or aperture bias, if it has one. The idea with these controls is that you select either an aperture or a shutter speed, and the camera automatically selects the other half of the exposure for you.

Aperture and shutter priority modes are discussed in more detail later in this chapter in the section "Using Your Camera's Various Exposure Modes." These settings are usually used to find the right balance between freezing (or blurring) motion in a picture and focusing attention on the subject by sharpening (or blurring) the background of an image.

Tricky Lighting Situations

Not all lighting situations are easy to shoot; that's why photography is both an art and a science. Specifically, it's fairly easy for real-life scenes to trick your camera's exposure sensor and consequently under- or overexpose a picture. You can fix that tendency to some degree on the PC afterward (and we'll talk about how to do that in Chapter 12), but it's much better to expose the picture correctly to begin with. That's because an over- or underexposed image is missing information about colors, texture, and detail that can never be restored; only at the moment of exposure can you ensure that all the information will be in your image.

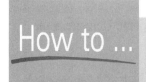 **Improve Your Camera's Dynamic Range**

While digital cameras are just about the equal of film cameras in most respects these days, one area in which they lag behind is dynamic range. Simply put, a digital camera doesn't have the same ability as a film camera to capture the broad range of light and dark elements in a picture.

Most of the time, that's not a problem. But in particularly challenging photographic situations, you'll find that your digital photos lack detail in extremely dark or bright parts of a scene. A common situation is taking pictures in snow—in your final pics, you may find that the snow is a uniform white, with no subtle color variations. Or in scenes with both shadow and sunlight, the sunlit parts will look very, very bright even if it isn't all that bright in real life. In photographic terms, these areas are said to be "blown out." Likewise, digital cameras are far more likely to "blow out" a photo when overexposed than a film camera would, so you need to be careful not to overexpose your photographs.

There are a few techniques for dealing with dynamic range issues. You can bracket your photos (something I talk about later in this chapter) or capture multiple versions of the same image and then combine them afterward on the PC. This is a cool technique that gives you the ability to display a dynamic range that's even beyond the range of what film cameras can do. It only works for static scenes, but here's what you do:

1. Set the camera on a tripod so you can capture two pictures with identical composition.

2. Take one picture with the camera set to expose for the darkest parts of the image. Don't worry if the brighter parts blow out.

3. Take another picture with the camera set to expose for the brightest parts of the scene. The dark regions will be badly underexposed, but that's okay.

4. Use an image-editing program to combine the two photos using layers, bringing the best-exposed parts of both images to the top for a uniformly well-exposed photo. There's even an image-editing program that has made this a key selling point: Ulead PhotoImpact has a feature that automatically combines multiple photos of the same scene into a single, properly exposed image.

There are several solutions to these kinds of problems, and you can experiment to see which works best for you in various situations. Here are some ways you can correct your exposures when you see a problem in the viewfinder:

- **Use exposure compensation.** Use the Exposure Value (EV) control on your camera to intentionally under- or overexpose your pictures beyond what the camera's exposure sensor recommends.

- **Switch metering modes.** Use a different kind of exposure meter to account for high-contrast images.

- **Use exposure lock.** Lock your exposure on a different part of the image, and then recompose the picture and shoot.

To see how to use each of these exposure techniques, keep reading.

Use Exposure Compensation

Most digital cameras come equipped with an exposure compensation control, usually referred to as the Exposure Value (EV) adjustment. The EV control allows you to lock in and use the camera's recommended automatic exposure setting but then adjust that value up or down based on factors that you're aware of but that the camera may not be smart enough to see. Each Exposure Value corresponds to changing the exposure by one stop, such as going from 1/60 to 1/30 (a change of +1 EV since it doubles the exposure) or 1/15 to 1/30 (a change of −1 EV since it reduces the exposure by half).

Take Figure 2-6, for example. In the original picture (on the left), the dark stuffed penguin has confused the camera, making it think the scene was properly exposed when, in fact, it is horribly overexposed. The background and the other animal are nearly invisible as a result. When the camera is set to underexpose the scene by one EV (one stop), however, the scene is much better exposed. The image was salvaged, as you can see on the right side of Figure 2-6.

To use the EV control on your camera, do this:

1. Size up the scene you want to shoot. Decide if it calls for over- or underexposure.

2. If you need to add light to a scene to properly expose it, add exposure by setting the EV control to +1. If instead you need to underexpose the scene, set the EV control to −1. Of course, since you can see the results right away

FIGURE 2-6   The EV control lets you use your own judgment about exposure values instead of relying exclusively on the camera's meter.

in the camera's digital viewfinder, feel free to add or remove EVs until the picture looks about right. Here's a typical digicam display set to EV +2:

3. Take the picture and review it in the LCD display. If you don't like the result, adjust the EV and shoot it again. Of course, keep in mind that the small LCD display on your camera isn't ideal for judging the quality of your pictures. It doesn't show enough detail in the picture or give you a great idea of how well exposed it is. For a thorough analysis of your photos, you'll have to wait until you see them on the computer screen.

Most cameras allow you to adjust exposure by up to three EVs, either positive (overexposed) or negative (underexposed), and some models also allow you to set the EV in increments of one half or one third of an EV at a time for finer control over your scene.

You have a digital camera at your disposal, so frame your picture and take the shot. If you don't like the results, you can take it again with different settings!

Switch Metering Modes

As I mentioned earlier, it's really the camera's exposure sensor—known as an *exposure meter*—that does the majority of the work when figuring out how to shoot your picture. It decides how much light is needed to adequately expose your picture. So it should come as no surprise to learn that cameras distinguish themselves by the kind of meter they use. Some meters are better than others at metering a scene and applying the right exposure.

Center-Weighted Meters

In the old days, most cameras came with a simple center-weighted light meter. This meter measures the light throughout the image but applies more weight, or importance, to the central part of the scene in the viewfinder. The assumption—usually a good one—is that you are most interested in the stuff in the middle of the picture, so the camera tries to get that part of the scene exposed properly. You can see an illustration of a center-weighted light meter in Figure 2-7. A number of digital cameras still rely on this kind of meter for ordinary picture taking.

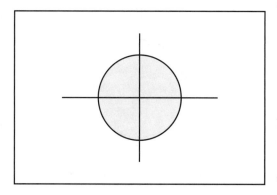

FIGURE 2-7   Many digital cameras use a center-weighted meter like this one.

Matrix Meters

Better than center-weighted metering for routine photo situations, "matrix" or "multisegment" metering is shown in Figure 2-8. A camera that uses matrix metering is usually better at exposing tricky scenes by balancing the lighting needs of several discrete regions within a picture. Instead of concentrating primarily on the middle, matrix meters gauge the light in many parts of the scene at once. If your camera has a matrix meter mode, you should use it most of the time, since it generally delivers outstanding results under a broad range of conditions.

Spot Meters

The last major kind of light meter is called a spot. The spot meter is never the only kind of meter in a camera; instead, it's an option that you can switch to if the center-weighted or matrix meter fails you. As you can see in Figure 2-9, the spot meter measures light exclusively in the center 1 percent of the screen, ignoring the rest of the frame completely. That can come in handy on occasion, but a meter that only measures the light in the central 1 percent of the frame will typically take very poor pictures—either highly under- or overexposed, depending on the situation.

So when should you use the spot meter? Any time you are trying to photograph a scene in which a small subject must be exposed properly for the picture to work

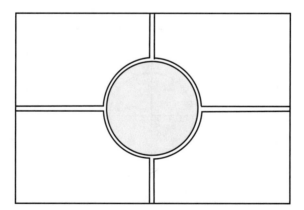

FIGURE 2-8   Cameras with a matrix meter are usually more accurate because they accumulate exposure information from several distinct regions of the frame (like the five regions shown here) and then use a sophisticated algorithm to decide the final exposure for the picture.

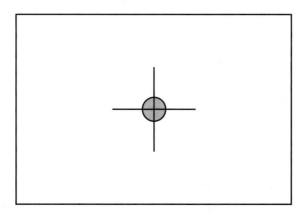

FIGURE 2-9   The spot meter is a great tool for reading the proper exposure in one precise point of the image.

and its lighting is different enough from the rest of the scene that you're worried it won't come out right otherwise. Imagine, for instance, that you are trying to photograph someone who is standing in front of a brightly lit window. If you let the camera decide the exposure, the bright light from the window will radically underexpose the subject. So switch on the spot meter and expose the picture based on the subject. Yes, the window light will be overexposed, but that's okay—the important part of the picture is the person.

Varying the metering mode—especially the spot meter—is best used in conjunction with the third technique, exposure lock.

Use Exposure Lock

Not all cameras offer exposure lock, but those that do are a godsend. Exposure lock is usually achieved by applying slight pressure to the shutter release—not enough to activate the shutter and take the picture, but enough that you feel the button move and the camera itself respond. Here's what happens when you take a picture:

1. Apply slight pressure to the shutter release button.

2. As you feel it depress slightly, the camera's autofocus lens locks the current subject into sharp focus.

3. At the same time, the camera's exposure meter measures the light and locks in an exposure.

4. Apply more pressure to the shutter release to press it in all the way. The camera then takes the picture and saves it to memory.

 *Some cameras use a separate button to lock the exposure. Refer to your camera's manual to see if it has exposure lock, and how to use it.*

The magic of exposure lock is that as long as you continue applying light pressure to the shutter release, the camera will use that "locked-in" exposure information regardless of where you later point the camera. You can lock in exposure information for the sky and then point the camera at your feet and snap the shutter release all the way. You'll take a picture of your feet using the sky's exposure data. You probably wouldn't want to do that since the result will be totally underexposed, but it gives you an idea of the potential.

Some digital cameras have a separate focus lock and exposure lock control; you should check your camera's manual for details. In such cameras, the exposure lock control is a separate button somewhere on the camera (usually where your thumb would fall on the right side of the camera body), often labeled AEL (short for auto-exposure lock). To use it, point the camera where you want to lock exposure settings and press firmly down on the AEL button. Continue to hold the button down while you recompose the photo, and then take the picture by pressing the shutter release.

Exposure lock is a great tool for telling the camera that you'd like to take a picture with the exposure data from one specific part of the scene. Imagine, for instance, a photo of a boy at the beach, taken near sunset. The image can be dramatic, but only if exposed properly. We'd like to capture the overall dark tones inherent in a sunset scene, with exciting splashes of color to light up the subject in a subtle way. Just pointing the camera at the scene might result in the camera averaging the bright and dark bits of the picture, generating an image that might as well have been captured at midday. That would be quite ordinary and not at all what we want.

Instead of taking the average picture, here's what you should do, step by step:

1. Frame the scene in your viewfinder so you know what you want to photograph.

2. Before actually taking the picture, point the camera up into the sky. Include the brightest part of the sky that doesn't also include the sun—that might be overkill. Sounds like guesswork? It is, a little. This is art, not science. You can take the picture, see if you like the result, and reshoot as necessary.

2

3. Press the shutter release partway to lock in the exposure information. You should sense that the camera has also locked the focus at the same time.

4. Recompose your picture. When you're happy with the scene in the viewfinder, press the shutter release all the way to take the picture.

Obviously, you could also choose the spot meter (if your camera has one) and lock the exposure with that instead of the default center-weighted or matrix meter that you used in steps 2 and 3. It's up to you. Take a look at Figure 2-10. This is a real challenge for most cameras, since the subject is a wolf sunning itself in an isolated patch of light. A center-weighted camera would probably average the light in the darker surrounding areas and determine that it needed to select a fairly wide-open aperture to add light to the scene. But that would wash out the poor little wolf. Instead, the best solution is to select the spot meter, frame the wolf carefully, and press the shutter release partially to lock in exposure on the bright subject. Then reframe the picture and shoot.

As you become more confident with your ability to visualize compositions and exposures, you can try different things to get the desired effect.

When to Take Control

As I mentioned at the outset, you may often be perfectly satisfied with the results you can get from the automatic exposure controls in your camera. But there will be

FIGURE 2-10   This wolf is lit very differently than the rest of the scene, so a spot meter is the easiest way to accurately expose the wolf's fur.

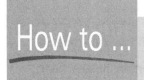

How to ... Use Bracketing for Success

A common photographic technique, and one that you might occasionally want to try, is called bracketing. *Bracketing* your photos is simply the process of taking several pictures, each with a slightly different exposure, so at least one of them will look the way you want. When you're done, review all the bracketed pictures on your PC and discard the ones you don't like.

Suppose you're trying to take a silhouette, for instance (something I'll talk about in more detail in Chapter 4). You need to make sure the subject is sufficiently underexposed that it appears totally dark, with no detail. How can you do that? There are two common methods for bracketing:

- **Use your camera's auto-bracketing feature.** Many digital cameras have something called *auto-bracketing*—turn it on, and it'll take three pictures in quick succession when you press the shutter release. One will be the "proper" exposure, but it'll also capture slightly over- and underexposed images for insurance. Here's an example of three pictures taken at the same time with the auto-bracketing feature enabled:

2

■ **Use exposure compensation.** Take one picture normally, and then take additional photos after changing the EV dial to under- and overexpose. You should start with exposure variations of a half-stop or full-stop (1/2 or 1 on the display), since more than a full stop of exposure compensation can be dramatic.

times when you can do better on your own. Keep your eyes peeled for situations such as those described next.

Very Bright Sunlight

Very bright sunlight can overwhelm your camera, especially if the scene is filled with brightly colored clothing, reflective surfaces, or other tricky subjects. You can reduce the exposure for better exposure. Underexpose the scene by EV –1 for starters, and see if that helps.

Backlit Subjects

If you are taking a picture of someone or something and the sun is behind the subject, you're usually in trouble—the bright background will cause the camera to underexpose the scene. That means the subject itself will look like it's in shadow. You'll get this if you follow the old (and very wrong) rule to put the sun behind the person you're photographing. The best way to shoot an outdoor portrait is to put the sun over your shoulder. Nonetheless, if you find the sun behind your subject, overexpose the scene, such as with an EV +1. Of course, this may overexpose the background, but that's probably okay—your priority is properly exposing the subject in the foreground.

TIP

Try wearing white clothing—it'll essentially turn your entire body into a giant reflector, sometimes allowing you to put the subject between yourself and the sun.

Low Light

In low light, such as at night, indoors, or under thick cloud cover, you can often get better results by overexposing the scene slightly, such as with an EV +1. Vary the EV level depending on how dark the scene actually is.

Consider Exposure When Taking a Picture

Most of the time, you can just compose your shot and press the shutter release. But don't forget to adjust the exposure when necessary. Use this decision process:

- Do I need to adjust the depth of field—that is, make the background more or less sharp compared to the foreground? If yes, then adjust the aperture or shutter or use the aperture priority mode, discussed in the following section.

- Do I need to change the shutter speed to depict motion in the picture? If yes, then again try to adjust the aperture or shutter, or instead use the shutter priority mode, discussed in the following section.

- Is the scene significantly brighter or darker than the camera is designed for? If it is, under- or overexpose the scene.

- Is the subject backlit, such as with the sun behind? If so, overexpose the scene.

- Is the subject especially bright, such as on fresh, bright snow? Try underexposing.

- Do I want to expose the scene based on the lighting in a specific part of the scene? If so, use a spot meter or just lock in the exposure for that part of the picture and recompose the scene.

Use Your Camera's Various Exposure Modes

Almost every digital camera on the market makes it easy to take quick-and-dirty snapshots using an automatic exposure mode. Automatic exposure is great much of the time, but I hope that you will sometimes want to get a little more creative and adjust the exposure of your photographs.

Not all cameras offer the same exposure controls, but here's a rundown of the most common ones, and when you would want to use them:

- **Automatic**   In this mode, both shutter speed and aperture settings are selected by the camera to match the current lighting. Some digital camera automatic modes try to select the fastest shutter speed possible in order to minimize camera shake when you take a picture, while most choose something in the middle, a compromise between speed and depth of field. There's generally nothing you can do to change the settings the camera chooses when set to fully automatic, except for adjusting the exposure compensation (EV) dial to over- or underexpose the scene.

- **Program**   The program mode (usually indicated by the letter *P* on your camera's dial or LCD display) is similar to an automatic mode. Although the camera selects both the aperture and shutter, you can generally modify the camera's selection by turning a dial or pressing a button. The effect: you can increase or decrease the shutter speed, and the camera will adjust the aperture to match. This is a good compromise between fully automatic operation and manual selection. Use this mode if you don't want to worry about devising your own exposure values, but still want some say over the shutter speed or aperture.

TIP   *The program exposure mode is often the best all-around setting for your camera. In this mode, the camera chooses a good exposure setting, but you can turn a dial to tweak the shutter speed. The camera will instantly compensate by changing the aperture setting, keeping the overall exposure the same.*

- **Scene**   Many digital cameras come with a handful of scene modes with names like Night, Portrait, Sand & Snow, Sports, and Landscape. Select the scene name that best represents the kind of picture you're trying to take, and the camera will automatically set the depth of field, exposure, and other factors to give you a good picture. Sports mode sets the shutter speed very high, for instance, while Sand & Snow compensates for the very bright background, which would otherwise underexpose your photo. When used appropriately, these scene modes work great and let you properly expose a wide variety of settings with little effort. Cameras with just a few scene selections may place the icons on the body (such as on a control dial, see illustration), while cameras with many scene selections tend to place them on the onscreen menu.

- **Shutter priority** This setting is usually indicated by the letter *S* on your camera's mode dial or LCD display. Using this mode, you can dial in whatever shutter speed you like, and the camera accommodates by setting the appropriate aperture to match. This mode is ideal for locking in a speed fast enough to freeze action scenes, or slow enough to intentionally blur motion.

- **Aperture priority** This setting is usually indicated by the letter *A* on your mode dial or LCD display. Using this mode, you can dial in the aperture setting you like, and the camera accommodates by setting the appropriate shutter speed. Use this mode if you are trying to achieve a particular depth of field and you don't care about the shutter speed.

- **Manual** The manual mode (typically indicated by the letter *M*) is like an old-style noncomputerized camera. In manual mode, you select the aperture and shutter speed on your own, sometimes with the help of the camera's recommendation. This mode is best used for long exposures or other special situations when the camera's meter is not reliable.

Choose Exposure Modes and Lenses in Special Situations

Now that you know what your camera's various exposure modes are for, you can think about using them when you encounter unique photographic situations. Every situation is a little bit different, but here are a few general guidelines that can get you started.

Portrait Photography

Taking pictures of people can be fun but intimidating. It's hard to get a natural pose from people when they know they are being photographed. The best way to capture good portraits is to work with your subjects so they are a little more at ease. If you're trying to capture spontaneous, candid moments, then back off and try to blend in with the background. If you're trying to capture a fairly formal-looking portrait, you have a little more work cut out for you. It's up to you as the photographer to put your subjects at ease. Talk to your subjects and get them to respond. If you can get them to loosen up, they'll exhibit more natural responses and look better on film. Take pictures periodically as you pose your subjects to get them used to the shutter going off, even if it isn't a picture you intend to keep.

Digital cameras have a cool advantage for portraiture that SLRs don't: the LCD display lets you put your subject more at ease. Try framing your picture using the LCD display, keeping the camera some distance away from your face. That leaves you free to interact with your subject without having an intimidating camera obscuring your head.

The best way to capture portraits is typically with the medium telephoto lens: in the 35mm world, that would be about 100mm. For a typical digital camera, that's near the maximum magnification for your zoom lens. You can see such a portrait in the image on the left in Figure 2-11. The version on the right—which has a fish-eye appearance—is what happens when you take a portrait too close, with the lens set to its wider position. It's also a good idea to work in aperture priority mode if possible. Aperture priority will allow you to change the depth of field quickly and easily as you frame your images. Specifically, good portraits have very shallow depth of field. You want to draw attention to the subject of your picture and leave the background an indistinct blur.

| FIGURE 2-11 | Portraits tend to work best with a moderate telephoto magnification and low f/numbers. |

> TIP
>
> *You can't see the effect of aperture on depth of field in the optical viewfinder, but the LCD display can show you the depth of field. Press the shutter release halfway down. That locks in the focus and triggers the aperture to close to the proper position for the impending picture. It's now—with the shutter halfway depressed—that you can see the depth of field in your picture. Even so, depth of field can be a hard thing to see— especially on an LCD display in bright daylight.*

Action Photography

Action photography is often considered the most exciting kind of photography, but it's also the most demanding for both your technique and your equipment. As in all kinds of photography, you can no doubt take some great pictures with anything from a wide-angle lens all the way up to the photographic equivalent of the Hubble telescope. And wide-angle lenses do, in fact, have a role in action photography. But the essence of many action shots is a highly magnified immediacy—something you can only get with a telephoto lens.

2

The shutter priority setting on your digital camera was born for action photography. To freeze action, you'll need to use a fairly fast shutter speed. Luckily, this higher shutter speed works to your advantage by opening up the aperture and diminishing the depth of field; this focuses the viewer's attention specifically on your subject. On the downside, of course, focusing is more critical since the depth of field is more shallow.

Nature and Landscapes

Unlike action photography and portraiture, which rely on telephoto lenses to compress the action into an intimate experience, landscapes typically work best with wide-angle lenses, which allow you to include huge, expansive swaths of land, air, and sea in a single frame. Zoom out for best results most of the time, and adjust the camera's exposure in aperture priority mode (if possible) to get deep or shallow depth of field, depending on what works best for the picture in question.

Chapter 3

Composition Essentials

How to...

- Use the rules of composition to take compelling photos
- Take less cluttered snapshots by emphasizing a focal point
- Take interesting photos with the Rule of Thirds
- Avoid cropping out important pixels by filling the frame
- Use lines, symmetry, and patterns for artistic images
- Break the rules for more engaging photos
- Understand the relationships among aperture, focal length, subject distance, and depth of field
- Employ depth of field for pictures that emphasize the subject
- Zoom a lens to achieve the right field of view

What does it take to take a good picture? Certainly, it requires more than a mastery of your camera's various controls. If that were all you needed, anyone who knew how to read a camera manual could be Ansel Adams. No, taking good pictures demands a little creativity and a touch of artistry. Perhaps more importantly, though, it takes a solid understanding of the rules of photographic composition and some knowledge—which you can acquire as you get better at photography—of when it's okay to break those rules.

Composition is all about how you arrange the subjects in a picture and how you translate what is in your mind's eye—or even right in front of you—into a photograph. After all, the camera sees things very differently than you do, and in order to take great photographs you have to understand that and learn how to see the world the way your camera sees it.

Taking a picture with a digital camera is really no different than taking a picture with a 35mm camera. That's why in this chapter I will be talking about the rules of composition: what they are, how to use them, and how to break them. If you are already an accomplished photographer and you're reading this book to make the transition to digital photography, you may not need most of what I offer in this chapter. But if you're not an expert, I encourage you to study this chapter. It is only through an understanding of composition that your images will go from snapshots—the ones that bring comments like "What a nice picture of a cat!"—to potential works of art that you'll be proud to frame in your dining room.

Why Composition Is Important

Have you ever been on vacation, pulled out your camera upon seeing a picturesque view, but later been somewhat underwhelmed with the final results? If so, you just learned the first rule of photography: reality, as seen by your camera, is quite different from what you see with your own eyes. If you frame all of your pictures without taking that into account, you will always be disappointed.

There are a few reasons why what your camera sees is different from what you see. First of all, your eyes aren't little optical machines that function in a vacuum. Instead, all that you see is supplemented, enhanced, and interpreted by your brain. In a sense, when you see a majestic landscape while hiking through the backwoods of Kauai, some of the splendor of the scene is actually being added by your mind. Lift the camera to that same view, and you get a totally objective representation of the scene, without any intelligent enhancements. That's because the camera is actually a little optical machine. And it does not have a brain.

And then there's the fact that a camera has a much more limited range of focus, exposure, and composition than you do. When you look at a scene like the Hawaiian landscape I just mentioned, you might think you're seeing a fairly static scene with your eyes. But that's not really the case. In fact, as your eyes dart around, you are constantly recomposing the scene, since you can dynamically change the visual "frame" in which you are viewing the scene. To make matters worse, the apertures of your eyes, called the pupils, change size constantly in response to changing lighting conditions and where you're looking. The result? You don't realize it, but your eyes, working in conjunction with your brain, are creating a visual feast that is difficult, if not impossible, to reproduce on paper.

In comparison, it's amazing that we can get good pictures at all with a camera. Film—and by film I mean both 35mm and digital—has a much narrower exposure range than your eyes because the aperture freezes a single instant in time with a fixed set of lighting conditions. And unlike the magical pictures in the *Harry Potter* series of books, real photographs cannot change their composition or framing on-the-fly. What you see in the viewfinder is, unfortunately, what you are stuck with forever.

What We See

Look around. What do you see? If you look carefully, you'll notice that your field of vision is a rectangle with rounded corners—almost a wide ellipse. In other words, we see the world panoramically. While there are techniques for creating panoramic photographs (which I'll cover in Chapter 12), most of the time this is not the kind of shot we take.

FIGURE 3-1 Turning the camera by 90 degrees to change the composition of a picture can completely change the effect a photograph has on its viewer.

Nope—our job as photographers is to take the panorama that we see with our own eyes and translate it into an attractive photograph using the laws of photographic composition. As you can see in Figure 3-1, there's often more than one way to frame a picture; it's really your job to decide which works best for the kind of photograph you are trying to achieve. In this situation, I had an extremely rare opportunity to photograph endangered monk seals, so I shot many different compositions.

Rules of Composition

For a few pages now I have been alluding to the rules of composition. I hope that you're curious what they might be. In truth, the rules of composition are no more rigid than rules of etiquette or rules of web page design. Certainly, those rules can be important, but they're simply guidelines to help us get the job done. If you violate any of these rules, nothing awful happens (unless you're still living at home when you break the rules of etiquette). And that's why we'll be able to break these rules later on. To begin with, however, we need to learn the rules and apply them.

3

Isolate the Focal Point

I know what you're wondering: what is the focal point? The *focal point* is the main subject of your picture, such as a building or perhaps a person. In other words, the focal point is the main point of interest that the viewer's eye is drawn to when looking at your picture.

You should always strive to consider what the focal point of your picture actually is and then plan your photos accordingly. In my experience, the single biggest problem with photographs taken by new photographers is that they fail to consider what their subject actually is. When you don't know what you're taking a picture of, it's hard to emphasize that element in the final composition. That leads to muddy, confused arrangements in which there is nothing specific for the viewer to look at. Take a look at Figure 3-2, for instance. In this image, there is no real focal point, and thus there is nothing for the viewer to concentrate on. The photographer should have decided what the subject was and then rearranged the image to emphasize that. Indeed, all I would ask of this picture is, "why did the photographer take it?"

When your subject is simply too expansive to be considered a focal point in and of itself, try to contrive a focal point that adds some relief for your viewer. You might try such an approach when you are photographing a mountainous landscape, for instance.

FIGURE 3-2   Without a focal point, your eyes wander the picture aimlessly, looking for something of interest.

In fact, landscapes really benefit from this approach. A tractor, a mountain cabin, or a gaggle of hikers near the horizon allows the viewer's eyes to rest on something familiar, even though the real subject fills up most of the frame. Technically, this is called a secondary focal point. You can see how I used this technique in Figure 3-3 to give the viewer a visual resting spot when looking at the backdrop of mountains. Remember: photography is subjective, and I did not intend for the cabin to be the photo's subject. Instead, the mountains were the subject, but by themselves they would make a terrible photograph.

TIP   *As a general rule, you only want a single focal point in your photograph. More than one main subject is distracting, and viewers won't really know where to look. If I show you a photograph in which several objects have equal visual weight, you probably wouldn't like it, even though you may not be sure why. It is certainly possible to include multiple focal points in an image, but you should do it with care, and only after you have mastered the basics.*

FIGURE 3-3   Secondary focal points add interest to landscapes (and many other sorts of pictures).

Use the Rule of Thirds

Many snapshot photographers don't really think much about the organization of what they see through the viewfinder, so the *Rule of Thirds* helps restore some balance to their photographs. And though this is the second rule I'm going to talk about, in many ways I think the Rule of Thirds is the single most important rule of photography that you can learn and apply.

Here's what you should do: in your mind, draw two horizontal and two vertical lines through your viewfinder so that you have divided it into thirds. In other words, your image should be broken into nine zones with four interior corners where the lines intersect. (See Figure 3-4 for an example of this technique.) It is these corners that constitute the "sweet spots" in your picture. If you place something—typically the focal point—in any of these intersections, you'll typically end up with an interesting composition.

This really, really is the golden rule of photography. Thumb through a magazine. Open a photography book. Watch a movie. No matter where you look, you will find that professional photographers follow the Rule of Thirds about 75 percent of the time. And while the Rule of Thirds is very easy to follow, you may find it somewhat counterintuitive. Many people try to put the focal point of their picture dead smack

FIGURE 3-4   Every picture has four "sweet spots" to which the eye is naturally drawn.

FIGURE 3-5   As a general rule, avoid putting your focal point in the dead center of the photograph.

in the middle of the frame. And trust me—there are few things in life more boring than looking at a picture in which the subject is always right in the middle. Compare the two images in Figure 3-5. I think you'll agree that the one on the right, in which the subject is not in the center, is the better photograph.

> **TIP**   *If you position the subject off-center, the camera may have trouble locking the exposure. This is a perfect opportunity to use the exposure lock/focus lock button on your digital camera, as I mentioned in Chapter 2. Point the camera at the subject and press the shutter release halfway down to lock the exposure on your subject; then reposition the camera to compose the picture just the way you like.*

Fill the Frame

Don't forget to get the most mileage you can out of the frame in which you're working. What the heck does that mean? Essentially, all I am saying is that you should minimize the amount of dead space in a photograph. Once you decide what

3

the focal point of your image is (remember the golden rule of photography!), there's no reason to relegate it to a small portion of the picture. Get close. Zoom in. Walk over to it. Whatever you need to do, do it in order to keep your focal point from being a small part of the overall image. Take a look at Figure 3-6, for instance. When I visited London and took pictures of the Changing of the Guard, I found that the common wide-angle shots of the event resulted in rather unimpressive photographs. I decided that the real star of the show was the guard's face, so I zoomed in for a very tight shot. Certainly, all of your photographs don't need to be this close. Getting a tight shot of your subject is not always a natural or intuitive thing to do; so you should go out of your way to try this technique whenever you think of it.

The "fill the frame" rule certainly applies in the world of 35mm photography, but it is absolutely essential in digital photography. That's because in 35mm photography, it's not difficult to crop and enlarge an image and still retain a reasonable amount of image quality, as long as you don't overly enlarge the final image. In digital photography, however, we're dealing with pixels, not grains of silver halide. And it seems like there are rarely enough pixels to go around.

FIGURE 3-6   This shot is uncomfortably close—thanks to a long zoom lens—and that's why it is so captivating.

If you are using a 3-megapixel digital camera, for instance, the best you can hope to do is print your photograph at 8×10 or perhaps, if you're lucky, at 11×17 inches before the pixels start to become obvious. (See Chapter 15 for details on printing.) That's probably enough resolution for most practical applications, but consider what happens if you need to crop your image because the subject was just too small the way the photograph was originally taken. If you crop out half of the pixels in the photo, you'll have a really hard time getting a good-looking 8×10-inch photograph with the resulting crop. If your digital camera captures smaller images—for example, 2-megapixel—then you can imagine how critical it is to compose the picture properly the first time. There really aren't any pixels to spare.

Move the Horizon

This rule is closely related to the Rule of Thirds. If you follow the Rule of Thirds to the letter, you probably won't make this mistake anyway, but it is important enough to mention explicitly.

No doubt you have seen photographs in which the photographer chose to place the horizon right in the middle of the photograph. Actually, the photographer probably did not make a conscious decision to do this—if he or she had, then the horizon probably would have ended up somewhere else.

Running the horizon right through the middle of a photograph is akin to putting the subject smack dab in the middle. It's boring because it violates the Rule of Thirds. Instead, try putting the horizon along a Rule of Thirds line. As you can well imagine, that actually gives you two choices for where to put the horizon in any given picture. You can put the horizon in the top third or the bottom third of your composition. How do you decide which? It's easy: if you want to emphasize the distant landscape and sky, put the horizon on the bottom third line. If you are taking a seascape where you want to emphasize the foreground, such as in Figure 3-7, the horizon belongs in the upper third of the picture. Of course, these are guidelines. Digital film is cheap—it's basically free. Experiment.

Use Lines, Symmetry, and Patterns

Photographs are two-dimensional representations of three-dimensional scenes. The question, then, is how best to lead viewers through a picture so they get a sense of the real depth that the image is trying to depict.

The answer to that question is simpler than you might think. When you compose an image in the viewfinder, look for natural or artificial lines that might lead the viewer's eyes through the photo. These lines can create a sense of depth and

| FIGURE 3-7 | The horizon usually works best well above or below the center of the picture. |

perspective that is often lost in the two-dimensional photograph. Lines can be formed in almost any situation: you might see a row of trees, the shape of a skyscraper from the ground, or the route of the backyard fence. Personally, I enjoy using the natural flow of a stream or road to lead the eye from one end of the picture to the other. Figure 3-8 is one example of this technique.

While lines like these can fit in with any kind of lens or composition, you may find that this works best when seen through wide-angle lenses. That's because telephoto lenses compress your scene and make it harder to see long, sweeping lines.

Another trick of the trade is to look for repetition and patterns, and incorporate those into your image. Patterns, such as those you see in nature or on manmade objects, can create interesting effects. Like lines, they can add a sense of depth to your images. Try combining these patterns with a sense of symmetry. When you employ symmetry, you are balancing both sides of the photograph. That can also help lead the eye through your image.

FIGURE 3-8   A long, straight road is a powerful tool for creating a sense of implied motion in a photograph.

Use the Foreground to Balance the Background

If you're trying to photograph a distant subject—a landscape or cityscape, for example—a common trick is to place something of interest in the foreground to provide a sense of balance. When done well, the viewer's eyes are drawn

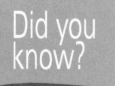

Keep the Horizon Straight

This may seem obvious, but how many times have you seen a photo in which the horizon was a little cockeyed? Vertically oriented pictures can get by with a slightly off-kilter horizon, but if you take a horizontally oriented image and the horizon is not straight, it affects the feel of the photograph. Try to be as careful as possible while photographing an expansive horizon. But if you goof, remember that it's a digital photo. You can always correct for an angled horizon on the computer (see Chapter 11). Any time you rotate or otherwise perform a "correction" on a photograph on your PC, though, you degrade the image ever so slightly. That's something to keep in mind if you want to preserve very high quality.

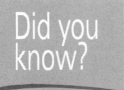

3

Every Picture Tells a Story

Throughout this chapter, and in fact throughout the book, you'll notice references to "leading the viewer through a picture." What do I mean by that? Well, when you've done your job as a photographer, you've created an image with depth, motion, and some sort of story. When you look at a good photograph or painting, your eyes naturally start in one place and move to another. That's in sharp contrast to a typical snapshot that has no particular story to tell, in which the focal point is haphazardly placed and the image is cluttered enough that there's no obvious path for the eye to take. Good artists can use techniques such as lines, symmetry, patterns, and multiple focal points to lead the viewer in a specific way through an image. If you can create an image like that, consider it a success.

immediately to the foreground object, and then they'll wander to the background. This is a very effective technique for adding a sense of depth and perspective to a photograph, as well as giving the foreground a sense of scale. Figure 3-9, for instance, demonstrates this technique.

FIGURE 3-9   The barge in the foreground is the anchor that gives the New York skyline a sense of perspective.

Know When to Break the Rules

Now that I've spent the last few pages telling you what the rules of composition actually are, we can talk a little about how to ignore them.

Don't get me wrong—I love the rules of composition, and I think you should follow them. After you become comfortable with concepts like the Rule of Thirds and filling the frame with the focal point, however, you'll find that you can take even better pictures by bending or breaking those same rules. This is an area of photography that is best experimented with and learned on your own, but here are a few pointers to help you get started:

■ **Change your perspective.** Technically, changing your perspective doesn't break any rules of composition, but it's something few people think about, and it can have a profound impact on the quality of your photos. Simply put, experiment with different ways to view the same scene. Try taking your picture by holding the camera horizontally, and then see how you might frame the picture by turning the camera vertically. Take a look at the picture in Figure 3-10. I originally took this picture as you see it on the left. Afterward, I found that I liked the picture better when I cropped it for a horizontal orientation. As it turns out, most people prefer the original framing, but that's okay: experiment and don't be afraid to try something even if no one else thinks it's a good idea. Get low to the ground or stand up on a chair or table to get a higher perspective on the same scene. You have a lot of options: try them.

■ **Ignore symmetry.** Sure, symmetry is great. But just as often as symmetry works well in a photograph, I have found you can get an even better image if you intentionally skew the photo to strip out the symmetry. When the viewer expects symmetry and doesn't get it, you have introduced tension and drama into an image. And that's not bad, especially if all you've done is photograph some road, train track, or river.

■ **Surprise the viewer.** If you've seen one landscape or sunset, you've seen them all. That's not really true, but it can sometimes seem that way.

3

FIGURE 3-10   Experiment with taking your pictures from many different angles, orientations, and perspectives. After all, you're not paying for the film anymore!

Go for the unusual by framing your picture in a totally unexpected way. One of my favorite tricks is shooting landscapes through the side view mirror of a car—you can see it in Figure 3-11.

■ **Use several focal points.** While most pictures rely on just one or two focal points, sometimes you need even more, especially when you're shooting a picture such as a family portrait. If you're taking a picture with several people in it, you can often overcome a cluttered look by arranging the subjects into a geometric pattern. If the subjects' heads form a triangle shape, for instance, you have introduced order into the photo despite the fact that there are a lot of people in it.

FIGURE 3-11 Successful pictures are often a matter of surprising the viewer.

Use Depth of Field

The last important frontier that you need to understand for proper composition is called *depth of field*. Depth of field refers to the region of proper focus that is available to you in any photographic image. When you focus your camera, you don't get a paper-thin region of proper focus in an image; instead, there's some distance in front of and behind your subject that will also be in focus. This entire region of sharp focus is called the depth of field, or sometimes the depth of focus.

What determines depth of field? There are actually three factors that contribute to the depth of field available to you for any picture you plan to take. Let's look at these factors one at a time and then combine them:

■ **Aperture** The aperture of your lens is the first major factor that influences depth of field. We talked about aperture in Chapter 2—it's the size of the lens opening that determines how much light reaches your camera's imaging sensor. Aperture is measured in f/stops, where lower f/numbers represent bigger openings and higher f/numbers represent smaller openings. In addition, the smaller the aperture's actual opening (or, in other words, the higher the f/number), the greater the depth of field will be. As you can see here, the aperture of your lens directly influences how deep the depth of field is in any given picture:

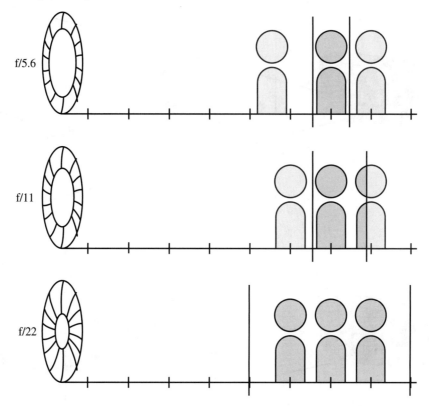

■ **Focal length**   As I'll discuss in the upcoming section "Getting the Most Out of Your Zoom Lens," focal length is just a measure of your lens's ability to magnify a scene. And while most people pay attention to a lens's magnification, depth of field plays an important role here as well. In simple terms, the more you magnify your subject, the less depth of field you have available. When shooting with a normal or wide-angle lens, you have a lot of depth of field. If you zoom in to a telephoto magnification, your depth of field drops dramatically. Likewise, macro photography (also known as close-up photography) has very little depth of field as well, since you are greatly magnifying a small object. See Chapter 5 for details on macro photography. This illustration graphically demonstrates the effect of focal length on depth of field:

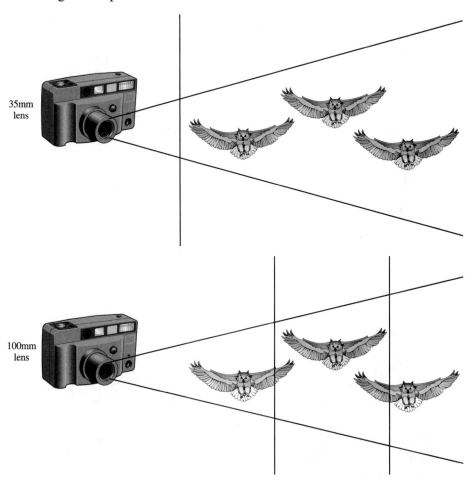

- **Subject distance** Last but not least, your distance from the subject determines how much depth of field you can get in your scene. If you photograph a subject that is far away, the depth of field will be much greater than it is for a subject that is close to the camera. In practical terms, that means the region of sharp focus for a macro shot—where the subject is only a few inches from the camera—is extremely narrow, and you need to focus very, very precisely. If you're photographing something very far away—like a distant horizon—a vast region in front of and behind the image will be in sharp focus. Here is what this looks like graphically:

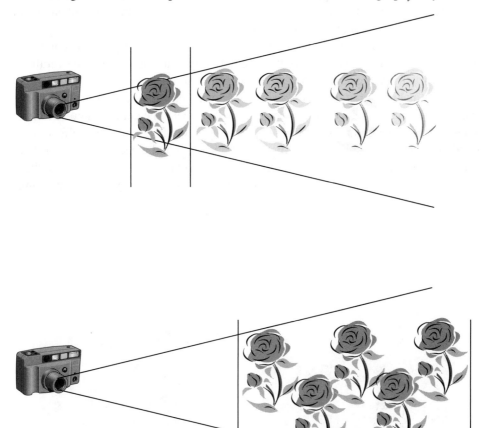

Apply Depth of Field to Your Pictures

As you can imagine, these three factors—aperture, focal length, and subject distance—work together in any shooting situation.

Specifically, suppose you try to take a picture with an aperture of f/5.6. At a given distance from your subject, and at a given focal length, that f/stop will yield a certain depth of field. But what happens if you change the other two factors? If you get closer to the subject, such as if you walk toward it, or if you increase the focal length by zooming in, the depth of field decreases.

So what is the point of all this? Why do you care about depth of field at all? The answer is that depth of field is an extremely important element in the overall composition of your photographs. Using depth of field, you can isolate your subject by making sure it is the only sharply focused person or object in the frame. Alternatively, you can increase the depth of field to make the entire image—from foreground to background—as sharp as possible. Figure 3-12 shows the effect of depth of field on a simple portrait; on the left, the child in the background is in sharp focus thanks to a deep depth of field. On the right, nothing has changed except the f/stop. By decreasing the f/number (and thus increasing the size of the lens opening),

FIGURE 3-12 Varying the aperture changes the depth of field.

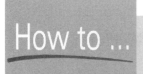 **Maximize Depth of Field**

There are three ways to maximize the depth of field in your image:

■ Use a lens with a short focal length, such as the normal or wide-angle setting on your camera's zoom.

■ Focus on a distant subject. If you're trying to get both a nearby tree and a more distant house in focus simultaneously, for instance, focusing on the house, rather than the tree, is more likely to deliver both subjects in focus.

■ Use the smallest aperture you can, such as f/11or f/16. This is often the easiest element of your picture to control and the reason that many digital cameras have an aperture priority mode for dialing in an aperture setting for your photos.

Not surprisingly, you can minimize the depth of field in a picture by doing exactly the opposite of these things.

the background child is now blurry and indistinct. I think either of these two pictures would make a great album cover for some psychedelic band. But I digress.

Get the Most Out of Your Zoom Lens

As I mentioned in Chapter 1, your digital camera probably comes with a zoom lens that allows you to vary the focal length from a wide-angle or normal perspective all the way through some moderate telephoto length.

As you probably recall, focal length is just a measure of the magnification the lens provides. A larger focal length produces greater magnification; hence long focal length lenses are great for capturing fast action or enlarging objects that are moderately far away. You can see the effect of a zoom lens on magnification in Figure 3-13.

FIGURE 3-13   These three views, all taken from the same position, show the effect of a zoom lens on the magnification of the subject.

Take a Zoomed Picture

Not all special effects need to be done inside a computer. The *zoomed* picture, like the one in the following illustration, is a good example of a special effect that you can do "in the lens" of your camera without doing any processing on the computer whatsoever. Unfortunately, there are very few digital cameras that will let you achieve this effect. To take a zoomed picture, you need a digital camera that allows you to change the zoom setting during the exposure; generally, only professional SLR-style digital cameras are capable of this feat.

If you do have a camera like the Olympus e20n or the Nikon D100, however, here's how to do it. Start by choosing a scene that you want to zoom through. You'll get the best results with a brightly colored subject and a simple background that won't be too busy. Mount your camera on a tripod to minimize camera shake. If you have very steady hands, you might want to try holding the camera yourself.

Set your shutter speed for about 1/4 of a second. You'll need that much time to slide the zoom lens during exposure. Then, just as you press the shutter release, start zooming with a firm, steady, and consistent motion. Just as in golf, be sure you follow through the zoom motion even after the shutter releases.

That way, you won't stop moving the zoom in the middle of the exposure. You may need to practice this a few times to get the shot right; remember, electronic film is free.

A key fact to remember, however, is that the focal length of the given lens also affects the camera's angle of view. Because a telephoto lens magnifies distant objects, it has a very narrow angle of view. As you reduce the magnification and zoom out toward smaller focal lengths, the angle of view likewise increases. You can see this graphically in Figure 3-14.

At the extreme end of the scale—specifically, wide-angle lenses—the image is actually shrunk with respect to what the human eye can see. The angle of view becomes extreme, sometimes even greater than 180 degrees. This kind of wide-angle lens is known as a *fish-eye lens* due to the peculiar effect of the angle of view.

The focal length of your lens has one other important characteristic. Depending on whether you have your lens set to wide angle, normal, or telephoto, you'll get a very different depth of field. As you saw previously in this chapter, a telephoto setting yields minimal depth of field, while a wide-angle setting generates a lot of focusing depth.

2x zoom

FIGURE 3-14   The longer the focal length, the narrower the region a lens can see.

> **TIP**
>
> *The telephoto end of your zoom lens is great for capturing distant subjects, but the additional magnification can create blurry pictures. I highly recommend that you take telephoto images with a tripod, especially if you are photographing in low light, where your camera might choose a slow shutter speed.*

Chapter 4

Flash and Lighting

How to...

- Use your flash for primary lighting
- Fill in shadows with your flash
- Keep from underexposing close-ups
- Use the various flash settings on your camera
- Optimize lighting outdoors and indoors
- Avoid red eye in low-light photos
- Balance your scenes based on the kind of lighting around you
- Use a reflector to fill in shadows
- Take interesting photos at night

Photography is all about light. In previous chapters, I have talked about how to work with the existing light in a scene to control aspects of your photograph such as depth of field. Sometimes, using the light that you already have isn't quite enough, however. That's why photographers spend so much time with flash units, strobes, reflector units, and other gadgets that help enhance or supplement natural light.

In this chapter, I'll talk a fair bit about using the electronic flash. Almost every digital camera made today—with the exception of very inexpensive models—comes with a built-in flash unit. The flash is a way to bring extra light with you and brighten many kinds of pictures. On the other hand, I have found that most people don't really know how to take advantage of the flash built into their cameras, so in this chapter I discuss techniques such as fill flash, red eye reduction, and bounce flash.

Lighting isn't just about using the built-in flash, either. You can use a reflector to spread light around for a more pleasing effect. For better lighting control, you can also play with the white balance built into your camera. And let's not forget about night photography. It's one of my favorite subjects, and in the next few pages I will explain how you can try your hand at this as well. Taking pictures at night can yield some of the most artistic and beautiful images you'll ever see.

The Basics of Flash Photography

These days, most digital cameras have an electronic flash unit built right into the camera body. The flash is designed to fire for a very short period of time and illuminate your scene in one of two ways:

- As the main source of light indoors or in the dark

- As a secondary source of light to fill in shadows when you're shooting in bright light, such as outdoors

In general, your flash will probably know when to fire and can illuminate most pictures without your direct intervention. When your camera is set to the fully automatic exposure mode, the flash will probably come on as needed and not fire when it is not needed. On the other hand, you can probably figure out when you need a flash more effectively than your camera can. For example, there will be situations when you may want your flash to fire when it would probably stay off, and vice versa. That's why your camera has several flash modes to choose from. I'll talk about those a little later, in the section "Master Your Flash Modes."

Stay Within the Range of Your Flash

How far will the light from your flash travel? That's something you need to know if you expect to get the most out of your flash. The flash built into most digital cameras is not extremely powerful; at best, you can expect to get a range of about 20 feet. To find the range of your camera's flash, refer to the owner's manual that came with your camera. You can almost always find the flash range listed in the specifications section of the manual. If you cannot find the range of your flash listed there, assume it is no more than about 15 feet.

The range of your flash also depends on two other factors: the current ISO (light sensitivity) setting on your camera and the focal length setting of the zoom lens. The first factor—ISO—is pretty obvious. The more sensitive the CCD is made to light, the more effective the flash will be. To understand the relationship between focal length and flash range, though, take a look at Figure 4-1. It is an unfortunate side effect of zoom lens technology that when you increase the focal length to telephoto, you typically let less light through the lens than when you are using a wide-angle lens or normal focal lengths. Since there's less light getting through the lens barrel to the CCD at telephoto magnifications, the flash has less effective range.

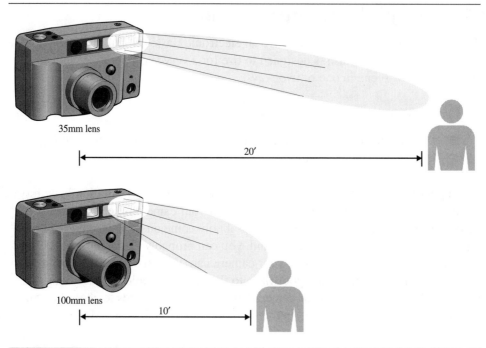

FIGURE 4-1   Because it processes less light, a telephoto lens reduces the effective range of your flash.

If you're used to the great range you would get from an external flash unit mounted on top of a 35mm SLR camera, you might be disappointed by the range from a digital camera flash. It stands to reason, though, that the small flash built into a digital camera could not have the same power as the large flash head, powered by lots of AA batteries, mounted on an SLR.

That means you'll have to be aware of how far you're trying to get the flash to throw light, especially at night or in very dark conditions. If your subject is very far away, such as 25 feet or more, it is unlikely that the built-in flash will have any effect at all on your photograph. In Figure 4-2, you can see that the flash is less effective at increased distances from the subject. In fact, some digital cameras disable the flash automatically when they sense that the lens is focused on infinity or when it is set to a "landscape" scene mode, which focuses on infinity anyway. You might want to check your camera manual or experiment to see if that applies to you.

Getting Too Close

Believe it or not, it's possible to get too close to your subject as well. Some digital camera flash units overexpose the subject when you are within a foot or two of

FIGURE 4-2   These snapshots demonstrate the falloff in light intensity as you back away from your subject at night.

the subject. Since you know about the light-reducing properties of a telephoto lens, you might expect that you can get closer when you zoom in than if you are zoomed out. And you'd be right; with a typical camera, you cannot shoot any closer than about 3 feet when set on normal zoom, but you can shoot to within a single foot if you are zoomed in to telephoto.

As you can see from Figure 4-3, close-up photos are easy to overexpose if you leave the flash turned on. There are a few ways to work around this problem, depending on what your flash unit is capable of doing:

- Turn the flash off completely and shoot with natural light.

- If your flash can rotate or pivot, bounce it off a plain white reflector, such as the ceiling or a reflector card. You'll probably need an external flash unit to bounce, though.

- Reduce the flash's power setting to 50 or 25 percent—most cameras have a setting in the menu that lets you do this.

- Cover the flash with a tissue or gel (available at any camera shop) to reduce its intensity.

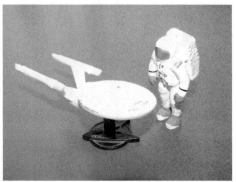

 Your flash may overexpose close-ups if you get too close; natural light was used for the image on the left, but the flash was enabled for the image on the right.

TIP *For many digital cameras, there's an optimum range for your flash photographs. Try to stay between about 5 and 14 feet from your subject. Avoid using the flash in situations where the subject is more than about 15 feet away or closer than 3 feet.*

Master Your Flash Modes

In this digital age, choosing between "on" and "off" is just too easy. Instead, your camera's flash has three or more modes, each intended for a specific photographic situation. Here's the rundown of your options. Your camera may not include all of these features, so you might want to check out your camera manual before you get your heart set on trying all of them out. Your camera should have some, if not all, of these modes:

- **Off**   This one is easy. When you set your camera to this mode, no matter how strongly your camera believes that you need extra light, the flash will not fire. This is handy for situations where you are not allowed to fire a flash, such as in a church or a museum, or when you're too close to the subject and think you might overexpose it. You may also want to turn off the flash in many night photography situations. I'll talk about that later in the chapter.

- **Auto**   This is the standard mode that you'll probably want to leave your flash set to most of the time. When set to Auto, the flash determines whether it needs to fire based on the amount of light in the scene. This is a good mode to use when you don't want to think about whether the flash needs to fire. For typical snapshot photography, just set your flash to Auto.

4

■ **Forced**   This mode goes by many different names depending upon the camera you are using, such as "Forced Flash," "Fill Flash," or just "On." When you set your camera's flash to this mode, it will fire regardless of how much light is available. Why would you want to use this mode? It's most useful as a fill flash: when you're shooting outdoors in natural light, the fill flash can erase shadows that would appear based on the way the sun hits your subject. Fill flash, or forced flash, is great for portraits.

■ **Red eye**   Red eye reduction mode has become extremely popular in all sorts of cameras, both digital and analog. By preflashing the camera flash several times quickly right before the picture is taken, the red eye reduction mode forces your subject's pupils to close down to a smaller size, thus decreasing the chances that the retinas will reflect the light of the flash. When you use this mode, remember that it will take a fraction of a second longer for the picture to be taken; don't pull the camera away as soon as you press the shutter release, or you'll blur the picture. If you're photographing people in a dark room, it is probably worth the extra time it takes using red eye mode. You do not need to use red eye reduction outdoors or in bright light. If the red eye mode isn't completely effective, or if you forget to turn it on, you can eliminate red eye on the PC in an image-editing program—see Chapter 12.

TIP   *Taking pictures at the tavern? The red eye reduction mode can also help reduce the red eye effect in people who have been drinking.*

■ **Low power**   Some digital cameras let you control the power output of the flash. You might be able to reduce the intensity of the flash by 50 percent or more. You can use this mode when you are using the flash to fill in shadows or when you are taking a close-up and a full flash burst would overexpose your subject.

■ **Slow**   In the world of 35mm photography, this slow setting is sometimes referred to as a *rear curtain flash*. Most digital cameras refer to this feature as *Slow Sync*. Of course, that name may not help you understand what the slow setting does. When you set the camera to slow flash, it fires the flash at the tail end of the exposure. This setting is used most often at night, when the exposure is long (such as a second or more), as in the following illustration. What does it do? Suppose you were trying to take a picture of a car driving down the street. With an ordinary flash exposure, the flash fires right away, thus freezing the car at the start of the frame. In a long exposure, you will then see headlights cut through the car and out of the frame. The slow mode, however, saves the flash for the end. In a picture taken with this mode, you will see headlights that travel through the frame and then meet up with the rear of a flash-frozen car. The car is leaving the picture at the end of the exposure, just like it should. Check out another example: in the following illustration, you can see how the kind of flash mode you choose will determine whether the girl will appear to lead or trail the lights she's holding. As you can see, you won't use this mode all the time, but it is indispensable when you need to get a certain kind of long-exposure photograph.

Add an External Flash

Many digital cameras are compatible with external flash units. Your camera can accept a flash if it has a flash shoe on the top of the camera body, which looks like this:

If your camera does have such a mount, check out the camera manufacturer's web site or your local camera store for information on compatible flash units you can attach to your camera. External flashes have these major advantages:

- Greater range for better flash photography in a wider range of environments.

- The ability, with some flash units, to pivot, swivel, and tilt the flash head. By angling the flash, for instance, you can use it to bounce light off of walls and ceilings, which adds up to softer lighting effects.

- Get the flash off the lens axis. Many flash units, with the right bracket adapter, can be held away from the camera. In addition to giving you more creative control over the direction the light is coming from, these lens brackets let you eliminate red eye effects because the flash isn't right in line with the lens.

- Better battery life. Since an external flash has its own batteries, it can last longer and not wear down the camera's own batteries at the same time.

Be aware, though, that all flash units are not the same, nor are they all compatible with all cameras. In theory, pretty much any digital camera should be able to fire pretty much any flash designed for a 35mm film camera, but the advanced, automatic exposure features probably won't work—you'll have to shoot in manual mode, which isn't much fun. It's also possible that an incompatible flash can damage your camera. That's why you should check to see what flash unit is made for your model by your camera's manufacturer.

Add a Slave Flash

It's possible to easily add a flash to your camera even if it doesn't have a built-in flash shoe—by adding a slave flash to your digital camera accessories.

A slave flash might sound like a complex piece of professional photo gear, but it's not. A slave looks like a traditional external flash unit, but thanks to a built-in light sensor, it fires at the same time as your digital camera's built-in flash unit. There's no need to connect cables, and you don't even need to have a digital camera with an external flash "hot shoe" connection. Just turn on the slave flash, and it automatically fires when you take a picture (as long as your digital camera's own flash fires, of course).

Personally, I love the convenience of a slave flash. You can position it anywhere you like—on the camera's hot shoe, on a separate flash bracket, mounted on top of a tripod, or even on a nearby tabletop—and as long as it's pointed at your subject, you'll get good results. In fact, you can use a slave flash to enhance your photos by creatively positioning the flash. Light from the side is less likely to cause red eye in your people photos, for instance, and side light can really enhance otherwise flat scenes. (That said, remember that if you mount a slave too close to your camera, it might exacerbate red eye since the slave can't "pre-fire" the way your camera's on-board flash does. For that reason, you should position your slave some distance from your camera.)

TIP *You can use a slave flash in any situation in which a fill flash or reflector would come in handy—like those described throughout the rest of this chapter.*

Most any digital camera shop should be able to show you a slave flash, or you can look on the Web. I use a $99 model from Phoenix called the D91. You can see it in the following illustration (posing with a Canon PowerShot A75) and find it online at www.pcaol.com.

Improve Your Outdoor Photographs

In my experience, people are more disappointed with their outdoor photographs than any other kinds of images. They complain about the washed-out sky—it was very blue when they took the picture—as well as ugly shadows on people's faces, bad exposure, and highly contrasting and harsh shadows that go through their pictures.

Why do all these problems occur? At the most basic level, it's because your digital camera works very differently from the way your eyes do. When you look around outside, your pupils—the apertures of your eyes—change diameter constantly to adjust to varying light conditions throughout the scene. When you look toward the sky, your pupils close so you see rich, blue colors. Look under a tree, and your pupils immediately open to help you see in the deep shadows that are down there. And then there's the fact that your eyes have a much wider range of exposure values than a camera does. When you press the shutter release on your camera, it has to choose a single exposure level and try to depict the entire scene with that one reading—regardless of how dramatically the light changes throughout the picture. As I mentioned in Chapter 3, it is amazing that we can get good pictures at all. That said, there are many strategies we can employ to get great pictures outdoors.

Beware the Sun

When you take pictures outdoors, always check your watch. By that I mean that there are better and worse times during the day to take pictures. Perhaps the worst time of all is midday, when the sun is directly overhead. The noon sun creates extremely harsh shadows and casts unflattering light for almost any kind of photographic project. People look their worst when you photograph them between about 10:00 in the morning and 2:00 in the afternoon, when the extremely bright, overhead light (particularly in the summertime) can tend to overwhelm a digital camera. If you're shooting on a cloudy or overcast day, though, even midday is fair game since there's no direct sunlight to interfere with your photos.

The alternative? Shoot early or late in the day. Photographers traditionally like the warm colors created by the sun in the late afternoon, but the morning is almost as good. If you are traveling on vacation, for instance, and want to get really great pictures, plan your photo exploits for the early morning hours and then again for late in the day. Heck, it's too hot in the middle of the day to pay too much attention to photography anyway.

If you make a conscious effort to take your best pictures before or after the high noon sun, you're halfway there. You also need to think about the position of the sun in the sky.

In the old days, new photographers were taught to take pictures with the sun to their back. The reason was simple: the sun would best illuminate the subject. Unfortunately, if you were photographing people, the sun would blast that light in their faces, causing them to squint. That made for some mighty ugly pictures. A much better solution is to position the sun over your left or right shoulder. But no matter where you put the sun, don't shoot into it unless you are intentionally trying to photograph a sunset or a silhouette.

Some digital camera experts warn that shooting directly into the sun can damage the camera's sensor, much the way looking directly at the sun can hurt your eyes. The jury is actually out on this topic, but it's better to be safe than sorry—so don't make a habit of exposing pictures with the camera pointed directly at the sun.

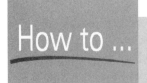

How to ... Shoot Silhouettes

It's easy to photograph a silhouette—in fact, new photographers do it all the time. They just don't always do it on purpose.

The easiest way to photograph a silhouette is simply to position yourself so that the subject you would like to silhouette is arranged against a bright background, such as the sky. Point the camera directly into the sky and slightly depress your camera's shutter release—that locks in the exposure based on the bright sky. Then recompose your picture and shoot. What you'll probably get is a grossly underexposed subject, since the exposure was based on the brighter sky, as in the image shown in the following illustration. If your subject isn't quite silhouetted, you can underexpose the image even more using the Exposure Value (EV) control on your camera. You might also want to use your camera's spot meter (discussed in Chapter 2) to lock the exposure on a bright piece of sky.

You may find that the subject is out of focus because the camera locked its focus on infinity when you pointed it at the sky. If that's the case, check to see

4

if your camera has a separate exposure lock button, and use it. If not, you may need to set the exposure manually (or use the EV control) or focus the camera manually instead. One way or the other, if your subject is too close to focus at infinity, you need to find a way to separate the exposure and focusing aspects of your camera.

Add Fill Flash

While most people think of their camera's flash as something to use at night or in the dark, it's also a great way to improve the look of your photographs in the daytime. Set your camera's flash to its forced flash mode, and use it to shoot portraits and other outdoor photographs. You'll find that the flash fills in shadows nicely, dramatically improving the quality of your images. You'll be surprised, in fact, at how much fill flash can do to improve photos that you thought were pretty good to begin with. Check out Figure 4-4, for instance. Here you can see two portraits—one with a fill flash, and one without. Remember, you'll need to be fairly close for this to work. Stay within 10 to 15 feet of your subject.

FIGURE 4-4   A little fill flash can go a long way.

Reflect Some Light

A second source of light is just the ticket to eliminate shadows, reduce contrast, and even out the lighting in your pictures. Sometimes you can do that with fill flash, and sometimes a small reflector will do the job.

A reflector is often better than a flash because the light from a reflector is softer, and that typically makes better pictures. In other words, it's always better to use natural light, which includes reflecting it, than to use an electronic flash.

There are two ways to get into reflectors: the cheap way and the expensive way. Believe it or not, you don't need an expensive reflector from your local photo shop in order to move light around—you can have a lot of success using a glossy white sheet of poster board. Purchase a sheet of poster board from your local art supply store for a dollar or two to try it out. The problem with poster board, of course, is that it is often difficult to carry around. For a more compact reflector solution, pick up a photo reflector at your local camera store. Personally, I really like PhotoFlex Litediscs. These clever little reflectors fold up so small that you can almost put them in your pocket. Take them out of the bag, however, and they pop open to a variety of handy sizes. I use a Litedisc that measures about 24 inches in diameter (see it in Figure 4-5), and I find that's a great size for most of the things that I want to photograph.

FIGURE 4-5   Instead of using a flash, try asking someone to hold a reflector near your subject. By holding it level with the ground, you can reflect light up into the subject's face.

When you're ready to take a picture with your reflector, you'll probably need some help. It's fiendishly difficult to hold a reflector and take a picture at the same time. So instead of trying some feat of photographic gymnastics, ask an assistant to hold the reflector such that light reflects from the sky onto your subject. Try to hold the reflector to minimize shadows or illuminate the dark side of your subject.

Reflectors serve a second important purpose as well. When you're out in the field trying to take a picture, the wind can sometimes get in the way. You'll notice this most often when you're trying to take a close-up of a light, bendable subject such as a flower. As I talk about in Chapter 5, just a little breeze can create an out-of-focus and blurry macro photo. The solution? Compose your picture so that you can use the reflector not only to add light to the scene, but also to serve as a wind break. That's right, reflectors can block the breeze and give you a more stable picture. See Figure 4-6 for a look at how you can use a reflector this way.

NOTE
A common way to use a reflector is to hold it roughly parallel to the ground, just under a person's face. That throws light upward, into the shadowy areas of the face, giving you softer, more even illumination.

FIGURE 4-6   Reflectors can block the wind as well as reflect light.

Improve Your Indoor Photographs

Indoors, we are often much less concerned about harsh sunlight than we are about having enough light and having light of the proper color. The evil red eye is also the nemesis of many indoor photographs. For common snapshots, there's probably nothing wrong with simply using your flash and leaving the camera in its fully automatic mode. But if you want to get really good at indoor photos, there are a few things you can do to shift the odds in your favor.

Use Window Light

The best light is natural light. Whenever possible, position your subject near a window so that you can take advantage of the natural light pouring into your house. If you want to try the window technique, here are a few tips:

- Avoid using windows where the light streams in directly and thus creates harsh shadows. Instead, pick a window in which you get more diffused, indirect light.

Bounce Your Light for a Softer Effect

If your digital camera has a hot shoe (a rectangular connection on the top of your camera for attaching a flash unit) or an input for a flash synch cable, you can attach external flash units for additional light and control over your images. I love using external flash units because the flash head tilts. That means you can tilt the flash so that it reflects light off the ceiling or a wall, thus diffusing the light and creating a softer effect. Be sure that you're not reflecting light off of colored walls, though, or the reflected light might paint your subject some horrible shade of yellow. You may also want to disable the built-in flash in your camera if you use an external flash. Check the camera's menu system for flash controls. Try it both ways, though, since some pictures can benefit from dual flash units, arriving on the scene from different directions.

- Position yourself with your back to the window and turn your subject to face mostly head-on into the window, with some light spilling over to the side of the subject's face.

- If necessary, fill in the side of the subject's face with a reflector to eliminate shadows. You can also use your camera's flash as a fill flash.

Avoid Red Eye

As I mentioned earlier in the chapter, the dreaded red eye is the effect that happens when the flash reflects off your subject's pupils. You can get this effect with any living subject—although, if you've all seen the *Omen* movies, it looks particularly creepy on dogs. Red eye happens most frequently indoors and outdoors at night because everyone's pupils are wide open to see better in dim indoor light.

Once you understand what causes red eye, it's easy to prevent. Here are the most common ways to avoid red eye:

- **Use the red eye reduction mode on your digital camera.** This is the easiest solution most of the time. When you turn on the red eye reduction mode, your camera triggers the flash several times rapidly right before the picture is taken. When you use this mode, remember the delay between when you press the shutter release and when the picture is actually taken— often, about a second. That doesn't sound like much, but it's enough to make you move the camera and ruin the picture if you're not paying attention.

- **Use an external flash off-camera.** If you have a digital camera with a hot shoe for an external flash, or one that includes a flash synch cable port, you can connect external flash units. The Nikon CoolPix 995, for instance, lets you connect as many as five separate flash units to the camera. The cool thing about using a separate flash is that you can hold it away from the camera. The farther you get the flash away from the camera lens (to the left or right of the camera), the less susceptible your picture will be to red eye, since the light won't reflect directly back to the camera.

- **Photograph people outdoors, or near windows.** If you can arrange your subjects near a bright source of natural light, you can avoid the red eye problem entirely because their pupils will already be closed due to the strong light source.

Correct the Color Balance

The color of artificial light is dramatically different from natural outdoor light. In fact, every kind of artificial light has its own unique properties. And that means that different kinds of artificial light have subtly different colors.

It is because of these variations in color that many indoor photographs simply don't look natural. Your camera has a way to adjust for these different light sources. Called *white balance,* it will help you to make sure that you get natural colors in your pictures regardless of what kind of artificial light you use. If you find that the automatic white balance setting in your camera gives you unpredictable results, then be sure to read the next section, and manually adjust your camera's white balance before every indoor photographic session.

Correct Images with White Balance

As I mentioned above, many digital cameras come with a control for something called white balance. White balance is important because different light sources have different *color temperatures,* meaning that a scene will appear to have a slightly different color tone depending on how it is illuminated.

You have probably noticed this yourself without really even paying attention. You may have seen, for instance, that ordinary light bulbs appear more yellow than the light that streams in from outdoors. And other sources—like candlelight and fluorescent lighting—are certainly a very different color than sunlight.

Photographers and scientists have gone to the trouble of cataloging the different color temperatures exhibited by various light sources. Lower temperatures appear warm, or slightly reddish, while warmer light sources tend to add a blue tone to your pictures. It's not at all unlike the way a flame has different colors at its outside and center. Why? Because those different parts of the flame are different temperatures.

As a point of comparison, this chart shows the approximate color temperatures of several common light sources:

Source	Color Temperature (Kelvin)
Candlelight	2,000
Sunset	2,000–3,000
Tungsten light	3,200
Fluorescent light	5,000
Daylight	5,500
Camera flash	5,600–6,000
Overcast sky	6,000–7,000

If your camera is balanced for one kind of light source (daylight, for instance) and you photograph a scene that has been illuminated by a very different temperature of light (such as tungsten), the resulting image won't reflect the true colors in the scene. What should be white will turn out looking somewhat reddish. Ordinarily, we don't notice this ourselves because, as I've said before, the human brain is very good at interpreting what the eyes see. Our brain adjusts for different color temperatures so that white almost always looks white, no matter what color light we're seeing it in. Of course, cameras aren't quite that smart. And that's why we need a white balance adjustment.

The white balance setting on your camera allows you to specify exactly what the color temperature of the scene is. In many cases, your camera can automatically adjust to conditions—but your camera often guesses wrong and gets the improper white balance fairly often. If need be, you can do it yourself. You'll know that you need to adjust the white balance if your pictures routinely come out shifted to the blue or red end of the spectrum. If your whites are not white—in other words, your camera doesn't do a good job of correcting the white balance—then you need to do it yourself.

If you get in the habit of manually adjusting the white balance, remember to reset the white balance to auto when you are done with each shoot. Otherwise, you might forget that your camera is balanced for fluorescent light when you shoot outdoors, and you'll get very funky results.

Adjust White Balance Presets

Most digital cameras let you choose from a small collection of white balance presets. In addition to automatic white balance selection, your camera probably includes white balance settings for conditions such as incandescent lights, fluorescent lights, an external flash unit, and cloudy or overcast days.

Choose a White Balance Preset

Changing your white balance setting varies from camera to camera, but the process is typically fairly simple. For the specifics on your camera model, check your camera's user guide. In general, though, this is the process:

- Turn on your camera and set it to its normal record mode. If your camera has a separate record mode specifically for manual photography, you'll probably want to set it to manual instead.

- Press the menu button on your camera so that you see a set of menus in the LCD display.

■ Find the option for white balance.

■ Scroll through the white balance options until you find the lighting conditions that best represent your scene.

■ Press the menu button again to turn off the menus. You can now take your picture.

Measure White Balance Yourself

Sometimes these white balance presets just don't get the job done. If you are in a tricky lighting situation, such as a room that has both incandescent light and candlelight, you may need to set the white balance manually based on the actual lighting conditions in the room.

This may sound complicated, but it's really not that hard. Before you start, you'll simply need one additional item: a white surface that the camera can use to set the white balance. Typically, you can get by with a small square of white poster board or typing paper. For better and more consistent results, though, I recommend that you purchase an 18 percent gray card from your local photo shop. Professional photographers use these small gray cards to judge exposure all the time, since the exposure meters in most cameras assume that images average out to about 18 percent gray overall. You can get a gray card for just a few dollars, and you'll be surprised at how handy it is for setting white balance.

So, here is how to set the white balance yourself:

1. Ask your subject or an assistant to hold the gray card with the gray side facing you. Make sure the card is positioned where you're actually going to take the picture, so you are measuring the actual light as it will be in your scene.

2. Turn on your camera and set it to the record mode.

3. Activate the menu system on your LCD display.

4. Find the white balance controls in the menu system.

5. Scroll through the white balance until you find the option to record it yourself. Select this option.

6. You should now see something on the LCD display directing you to photograph a white object. Compose your scene so that the gray card— or whatever you are using to set the white balance—fills the frame.

7. Take the picture and exit the menu system.

The camera will now expose any pictures you take using this new white balance value. Be sure to reset the white balance back to automatic when you're done taking these pictures; otherwise, you may try taking pictures a day or two later in very different lighting conditions and get bizarre results because the white balance is completely askew.

Many cameras set white balance in the way described above, but your camera may do it slightly differently. Refer to your camera's user manual for exact details.

Experiment with White Balance for Creative Effect

Don't think that white balance is used only to get perfectly white whites in your pictures. Certainly, that is the reason most people use this mode. On the other hand, photography is an art, not a science. By changing the white balance values of your camera, you can get some creative results that you might like better than if the white balance were set properly. As one example, I sometimes like the warmer colors I can get by misadjusting the white balance when shooting portraits. By making my subject's face a bit redder, I think the photo looks richer and more lifelike. Try it yourself and remember that photography is all about trying new things.

One of the hardest lighting situations on planet Earth is a school gymnasium. Because of the way gyms are lit, no white balance preset ever seems to work properly. For best results—and to avoid the inevitable yellow cast in your photos—try to arrive early and manually set the white balance with the help of a white or gray card.

Try Your Hand at Night Photography

Taking pictures at night is a rewarding, exciting activity; unfortunately, digital cameras don't always make it easy to do. On the plus side, taking pictures with a digital camera is essentially free, since you're not buying film. So you can experiment to your heart's content without wasting any film.

Not every camera is cut out for night photography. Low-light photography requires long exposure times; if your digital camera is not capable of shutter speeds of one second or more, you will probably have some trouble getting decent night shots. In fact, your camera should have a manual exposure mode so you can dial in the shutter speed by hand. Automatic exposure settings may not give you anything even remotely interesting. If you're shopping for a camera and are specifically interested in night shots, try to get a camera with a bulb setting—that's photography lingo for a shutter that stays open for as long as you hold the shutter release down—or at least a maximum shutter speed of eight seconds. Not all night exposures are measured in seconds, though. I captured this image with a tripod and only about a one-second exposure, something virtually any digital camera should be able to do:

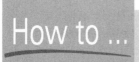 **Take Your First Night Shots**

So, you're ready to take your first pictures at night. I recommend that you choose an interesting locale to begin with. Go downtown, where there are lots of neon store lights and cars with headlights on. Alternatively, try a local carnival or fairground. The idea is to find a location that has lots of interesting lights and motion.

To take your first night pictures, do this:

1. Mount your camera on a tripod. Your exposure times will be a half second or longer; there is absolutely no way you can hold the camera for that amount of time without introducing an incredible amount of blur.

2. Switch your camera to its manual exposure mode, if it has one. Set the aperture to a medium setting, such as f/5.6. Set the shutter speed to 1/2.

3. Point the camera at something interesting. If this is the first time you are trying night photography, I suggest you go to a fairly busy intersection downtown and frame the street and a store or two in your viewfinder.

4. When a car is about to enter your viewfinder, take the picture. You should be able to get fairly instant feedback on how your picture came out by looking at it in the camera's LCD display. No matter how good or bad the picture came out, do not delete it.

5. Now double the shutter speed. Try an exposure of one second, and shoot the same scene again.

6. Take more pictures, varying the shutter speed so you can get a feel for what kind of results your camera gives at night at various shutter speeds. You will very likely find that your camera won't expose a picture for more than a few seconds; many cameras limit the shutter speed to 5 or 10 seconds. That's okay—just work your way up until you hit your camera's maximum shutter speed.

7. If your camera automatically records exposure information for each picture, great. If not, write down all of your exposure information so you'll remember what you did later and learn from your efforts.

 *A camera with a wireless remote control can also be handy for night photography because you can activate the shutter without shaking the camera. If you don't have a remote, then you might want to trigger the camera with the self-timer feature.*

After you've taken a batch of night shots, you can compare your pictures side by side and see the effect of increasing exposure time. As you can see from Figure 4-7, there is no such thing as the "one perfect exposure" in a night photograph. Increasing the exposure means longer light trails and brighter points of light. Eventually, too much exposure time will lead to obviously overexposed images and perhaps digital noise (which I discuss in the next section). But for the most part, the exposure you choose is a matter of personal taste.

 *If your camera does not let you manually choose the shutter speed and aperture, try using its EV adjustment to overexpose your picture by one, two, or even three stops. For example, set your camera to EV −3, focus the camera on the darkest part of the scene, and then shoot.*

CCDs and Noise

Night photography is a little trickier with a digital camera than with a 35mm SLR. Don't get me wrong—film has its own problems. *Reciprocity failure,* for instance, is a phenomenon that affects 35mm film. What it means is that film reacts somewhat unpredictably during very long exposures, such as at night. Film is designed to be exposed to light for a fraction of a second; so if you leave the shutter open for 10

FIGURE 4-7   Longer exposure times lead to longer light trails and brighter points of light.

seconds, the reliable relationship between the aperture size and shutter speed begins to fail. That makes night photography for 35mm photographers something of a guessing game.

> **TIP**   *Don't trust your camera's exposure meter at night. You might want to start with whatever your camera's meter suggests, but you can almost always get more interesting pictures by doubling or tripling the shutter speed suggested by the camera.*

For digital photography, you have a completely different problem to contend with. When you expose a CCD, it gets hot from the electric current surging through its circuits. This heat manifests itself in the form of noise in your final picture. For short exposures, this is rarely, if ever, an issue. You might see some noise in your picture if you set the camera's ISO value to a very high number, but usually the shutter speed is so short that there is little time for the CCD to generate noise in the final image. When you are measuring the exposure in seconds, however, noise can build up quickly. Take a look at Figure 4-8. Here you can see how digital noise affects a picture when the shutter speed is more than a few seconds long.

Some cameras are designed to minimize this noise that occurs with long exposures. The CCD is built directly onto a heat sink to carry excess energy away

FIGURE 4-8   CCDs are not always optimized to take long exposures at night.

during long exposures. Other digital cameras don't have such a feature, however. Instead, there are three ways to minimize this effect:

- Keep the shutter speed as short as possible.

- If it has one, turn on your camera's noise reduction feature—it often does wonders for minimizing digital noise.

- As a last resort, run a noise reduction or despeckle filter on your picture in an image editor after you transfer it to the computer.

Cool Things to Photograph at Night

There are all kinds of things to photograph when the sun goes down, and each one requires a somewhat different technique. Here are some suggestions to get you started:

- **The moon**   When shooting the moon, remember that it is a very bright object. The Sunny 16 Rule (discussed in Chapter 2) may work for you in this situation, but I've found that many cameras get confused by the dramatic variation in brightness with shots like this, so you may need to experiment a bit. If you can get enough magnification out of your lens so that the moon fills up at least half of the frame, you'll need to shoot at a fairly fast shutter speed or even set the EV to underexpose the frame. And be sure to use a tripod. For more details on photographing the moon, see Chapter 7.

- **Sunset**   The sky is full of rich, gorgeous colors around sunset. Base your exposure on the sky itself, not on your subject or anything on the ground. And take a few extra pictures, bracketing your exposure (see Chapter 2 for details) to make sure you get the shot.

- **Dusk**   I have found that photographing lighted buildings and headlight trails works particularly well when you can get the rich blue colors of dusk in the sky at the same time.

Chapter 5   Taking Close-Ups

How to…

- Set your camera to its close-focus mode

- Close-focus a manual-focus camera

- Ensure proper focus when shooting very close-up

- Use the correction marks in the optical viewfinder

- Use optional close-focus lenses

- Interpret diopter numbers

- Configure a tripod for semi-steady macro shots

- Blur the background

- Maximize your depth of field for sharper pictures

- Eliminate reflections from glass display cases

Close-up photography, also known as *macro photography,* is one of the most exciting ways to experiment with your digital camera. It's a whole different world down there when you get within a few inches of your subject; we're used to seeing things from 5 or 6 feet off the ground. But when you're within an inch or so of your subject and it's magnified to several times its normal size, photography suddenly seems like magic.

You might think I'm exaggerating, but macro photography really is a lot of fun. And just because you have a digital camera—not a multithousand-dollar large-format camera—don't think that you can't play along. Certainly, having a digital camera means that you may have to shoot your close-ups in a different way from traditional photographers. Each format has its own unique characteristics, and here in the land of digital photography we will talk about how to get the most out of your digital camera when you are taking pictures in the Lilliputian world.

Capture the Microscopic World

First of all, let's talk about some terminology. When we discuss close-up photography, what we really mean is macro photography. We're not talking about close-ups in the portraiture sense—there are no "I'm ready for my close-up, Mr. DeMille" situations in this chapter. I hope I didn't disappoint you.

Instead, close-up photography is all about photographing the world around us to capture small objects, highly magnified. That usually means getting pretty close to the subject—like within a few inches, as in this shot:

Using 35mm SLR equipment or even larger gear, such as medium- and large-format cameras, you can get incredibly magnified views of small subjects. You could magnify the eyes of a fly to fill up an 8×10-inch print. In digital photography, you typically can't get quite as close as that, though you can take impressive close-ups nonetheless. If you would be happy with getting the fly itself blown up to 8×10 inches, then keep reading.

Coax a Digital Camera to Take Close-Ups

Virtually every digital camera on the market has a close-focus mode. Such a mode exists because the camera lens typically can't focus properly when you get very close—within inches—of a subject. The optics must be rearranged to accommodate such close focusing. How that mode works, though, depends on whether your camera has a fixed-focus or an autofocus lens.

Autofocus Cameras

In cameras with autofocus lenses (and that represents about 98 percent of the cameras on the market today), you usually enter close-focus mode (also called *macro* mode) by pressing a button on the camera body and sometimes spinning a dial or turning a navigation wheel at the same time to make the appropriate selection. A tulip shape typically represents close-focus; you should see a button somewhere on your camera with such a symbol. Can't find it? On a few cameras, the macro mode is buried in the onscreen menu on the LCD.

Tulip

FIGURE 5-1   Follow the tulip on your camera to find the close-focus or "macro" mode.

You can see a typical close-focus button control in Figure 5-1. Often, camera buttons perform more than one function. You might need to press the button several times to cycle through the various modes before the macro mode is actually enabled, or you might need to hold the button down while turning a selector dial.

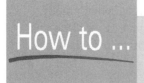 **Ensure Good Focus in Close-Up Mode**

Close-focus photography is a bit temperamental. For starters, the acceptable focusing distance for macro lenses is much shorter than in the normal photo world. You should check your camera manual to discover what the minimum and maximum focus distances are for your camera's lens. Typically, you might be able to get as close as 5 inches or as far away as 3 feet. These numbers vary, though.

Here's what you should do when you're trying to take a close-up photo:

1. Verify the close-focusing range of your camera.

2. Press the macro button on your camera to enter the close-focus mode.

3. Position your camera in front of the subject somewhere inside the close-focusing range.

4. Press the shutter release down half-way to lock in exposure and focus. Look for the camera's visual focus indicator. (Most cameras use a light near the viewfinder to indicate that the image is in focus.)

5. If you're having trouble getting the image in focus, point the camera at an edge or at some sharply defined region of the subject (without changing the distance to the subject). This may help the camera lock onto the subject. Or you can carry a small card with sharply defined black-and-white stripes on it (a business card and a magic marker is all you need). If you're having trouble getting good focus, hold the card right next to the subject and get the camera to focus-lock on that instead. Also, some digital cameras have trouble focusing in low light; you might want to carry an inexpensive light that you can use to illuminate the subject when focusing.

6. When you're ready, take the picture by pressing the rest of the way down on the shutter release.

That's it in a nutshell—the point is that you need to be very sensitive to focus when shooting close-ups, and you may need to reorient the camera slightly to get a good, solid-focus lock. Also, when you do get a lock, make sure that you're actually focused on the right subject. The depth of field is quite shallow at this close distance to your subject, and it's easy to get an out-of-focus image.

When you're in macro mode, it's usually indicated by a tulip somewhere on the camera's LCD display. That tulip is a reminder that you are in close-focus mode, and you will get sharp focus when shooting very close to the subject. (Often, the effective macro range is in the neighborhood of 8 to 30 inches, though some cameras can focus to within an inch or so of the subject.) In addition, some digital cameras require your zoom lens to be within a certain macro range—zoom in too far, and the camera won't be able to focus properly. If in doubt, check your camera's manual.

Fixed-Focus Cameras

Though they are increasingly rare, fixed-focus cameras still exist. If you have one of these relics, I suggest you upgrade to an autofocus camera as soon as possible. Nonetheless, even these models usually include a close-focus mode, though it's harder to use. You might need to slide a manual-focusing dial or lever to get your picture in the proper focus (as in the ancient Canon PowerShot pictured in Figure 5-2), or you might need to position your camera a specific distance from the subject. Some fixed-focus cameras require you to be at a specific distance when shooting macros—around eight inches. As you might surmise, it's not easy to capture good, sharp photos when you have such a rigid focusing distance.

FIGURE 5-2   Old, manual focus digital cameras were hard to use because of their focusing control for macro photos.

   *When you're done shooting in macro mode, be certain to return the camera to its ordinary focusing mode or you'll end up with a memory card full of out-of-focus images!*

Close-Up Enemy No. 1: Parallax

Most digital cameras are of the point-and-shoot variety, as I mentioned back in Chapter 1. Point-and-shoot cameras are models that don't show you an accurate representation of the actual scene in the optical viewfinder. Instead, using the viewfinder is like looking through one window in your house, while someone else looks through a nearby window. You both see essentially the same scene, though they are not identical. If the two of you look to the horizon, for instance, the two scenes are virtually indistinguishable. If you're both looking at a person walking toward the house, though, your two views become increasingly different as the person gets closer and closer.

And that is what it is like when you look through the optical viewfinder and the camera uses the nearby lens to take the photograph. SLR-style cameras don't have this problem, because the optical viewfinder actually looks through the lens right up until the moment of exposure.

The problem, as you have probably guessed, manifests itself when you try to take a close-up with a point-and-shoot digital camera. Since your subject is only a few inches away, the difference in view between the viewfinder and the lens means that you're not even looking at what the lens is about to take a picture of. In Figure 5-3,

5

FIGURE 5-3   You can't trust your window-style viewfinder when taking close-ups because it sees a slightly different scene than your lens does.

you can see the effect of parallax on a photo. The image on the left represents what I saw in the viewfinder; the image on the right represents what the lens actually photographed. That's why many digital cameras have indicators in the optical viewfinder. Called *close-focus marks, parallax marks,* or *correction marks,* these lines show you how to line up the photograph when you are shooting a close-up.

Frame a Close-Up

So now you understand the principle behind parallax and close-up photography. Let's apply this so you can see how to take a close-up photo.

Look through your camera's optical viewfinder. Hopefully, you can see some correction marks. If the lens is located to the right of the optical viewfinder (as it is in most cameras), you should see correction marks on the left side of the viewfinder. Why is that? Well, these marks represent the left edge of the photo when shooting at close distances. Since the lens is off to the right of the viewfinder, you will need to point the camera slightly to the left in order to take the picture you desire. In actual operation, just recompose the scene so the correction marks help frame the left edge of your picture.

You might have correction marks at the top or bottom of the viewfinder as well. If the lens is below the optical viewfinder (as it often is), correction marks at the top of the frame show you how to reorient the camera slightly higher than you would otherwise.

If all this is just a little confusing, take a look at Figure 5-4. Here, you can see how I have oriented my camera to use the correction marks at close distance.

Correction marks indicate left edge of photo when close

FIGURE 5-4   The correction marks help you overcome composition errors caused by parallax.

Correction marks are a guide to help you frame macro photographs. But there are some very important things to remember about them:

- **Correction marks are only approximate.** They help you adjust for parallax error, but they are not perfect. This should be obvious when you realize that parallax varies depending on your distance from the subject.

- **Correction marks work only at close range.** Parallax, by definition, diminishes with distance from the subject. At ordinary distances, you don't need to worry about the marks at all. In fact, if you use them when shooting a subject that is 10 feet away, they will simply introduce composition error in exactly the opposite direction. Remember though, that they are important when using your macro mode.

- **You can avoid using correction marks entirely.** Instead of relying on the optical viewfinder when shooting close-ups, try to use the camera's LCD display instead. The LCD display shows you almost exactly what the lens sees, and therefore there's no parallax at all when using it.

TIP   *Whenever possible, frame your macro shots with the LCD viewfinder. The only time that may not work is in very bright sunlight, when the LCD is too difficult to see.*

Use Add-On Lenses

The macro mode built into your digital camera is certainly a nice start for taking close-up pictures, and you can get some pretty good results with it. But if you yearn for greater magnification than your camera is capable of providing, there is an answer: add-on lenses.

Many cameras are designed to accommodate additional lenses and filters. Of course, SLR-style digital cameras with interchangeable lenses spring directly to mind. Cameras such as the Nikon D100 accept all of the traditional 35mm lenses in the Nikon family, and the Canon D60 works with a whole slew of Canon lenses. Many of these lenses have macro modes that allow you to get excellent magnification.

But what if you're not using a camera like that? Actually, many digital cameras accept add-on lenses as well. These are lenses that snap or screw on to the front of your camera's built-in lens. Sometimes, the manufacturer sells add-on lenses for its own models, such as the Kodak DC 4800 in Figure 5-5. In other cases, your camera may have standard threads on the front of the lens, in which case you can visit your local camera shop or search online for filters and lenses that fit.

5

FIGURE 5-5   Many cameras are compatible with snap-on or screw-on lenses that provide telephoto, wide-angle, and macro capabilities.

You can look online for data on lenses for your camera. First, check out the camera manufacturer's web site for compatible accessories, including lenses. Also visit Tiffen (www.tiffen.com) and Raynox (www.raynox.com). Tiffen is the largest manufacturer of add-on lenses for digital cameras, and it's likely to have something for your camera; Raynox has a variety of macro lenses as well. Last, but not least, camera-depot.com has a great selection of common lenses and filters in stock, and they ship promptly.

The most common close-up lenses for digital cameras look like the ones shown in Figure 5-6. The macro filters in Figure 5-6 have 62mm threads, making them ideal for cameras such as the Olympus e10 and e20n. This set of four, in fact, sells for about $40. Such filters are usually made from a single element of glass and are threaded to screw onto the front of the camera lens, an adapter, or even each other. Of course, the specific close-up filters you get will depend on the size of the lens on your digital camera.

That's right—you can actually combine close-up lenses by threading them together. Adding a +1 lens to a +2 lens, for instance, yields an impressive +3 magnification. For that reason, I suggest getting close-up lenses as a set instead of one at a time. That way, you can combine them however you see fit to get the

FIGURE 5-6   A typical set of close-up lenses

FIGURE 5-7   These images show the differing magnification effect of the Olympus e20n's standard macro mode, plus varying intensities of screw-on macro filters.

magnification you need for a given picture. Check out the picture in Figure 5-7, which shows the effect of four different magnifications: the camera's built-in macro capability, in addition to various combinations of +1, +2, and +4 filters.

NOTE   *If you add too many close-up lenses, you can start to get a vignette effect— that's when the lens and filters get in the way and cut off the corners of your picture. You can see an example of vignetting in Chapter 7.*

TIP   *When combining close-up lenses, put the highest magnification on first, closest to the camera lens. That way, you can remove the lenses in smaller increments to achieve just the right magnification. Also, you may find that some lens combinations cause your images to curve unnaturally, thanks to something called "barrel distortion," discussed in Chapter 7.*

Did you know?

Understand Macro Lens Lingo

With rare exception, close-up lenses, also called *close-focus lenses,* are not described in terms of focal length, as are other lenses. That's because they're essentially just magnifying glasses that go in front of the camera's normal lens. Instead, close-focus lenses are described using the term *diopter.*

A diopter is an indirect measure of focal length. It tells you both how close you can get to the subject and what relative magnification the lens provides. Specifically, the diopter number indicates how close your camera lens can focus with the lens set to infinity and the close-up lens attached, in fractions of a meter. A +2 rating will let your camera focus 1/2 meter away, while a +3 rating focuses at 1/3 meter away, and so on. Believe it or not, these diopter numbers hold true no matter what the focal length of your camera lens. Close-up lenses typically come in a variety of strengths, from +1 to +10.

Close-Up Techniques

As I've already mentioned, taking close-up pictures is a very different experience from taking images at ordinary focal lengths. Though it's not particularly difficult to get really good macro photos, it does take a little more care and a slightly different approach.

First of all, you'll find that your subjects are slightly different in macro photography. Obviously, you won't be taking a lot of people pictures from 2 inches away. There are numerous choices, however. I suggest that you start by taking pictures of things that don't move, such as in the example shown here:

Once you have coins and stamps pretty well in hand, you can move on to photographing insects, flowers, and other mobile or semi-mobile subjects.

In fact, lots of subjects look radically different at close range and magnified than they appear from a human perspective. Some subjects can even take on an almost fractal appearance—that is, their underlying structure can seem to have a nearly infinite amount of complexity, as you can see from these ice crystals on a tree branch, captured on a chilly April morning:

That's why I think macro photos make for some very exciting images. Here are a few subjects you might want to consider trying your hand at:

- Hobby subjects such as stamps, coins, and models

- Wildlife such as plants, flowers, leaves, insects, and butterflies

- Found objects such as rubber bands, paperclips, and fabric

- Snow, ice, and water

A Steady Base

Without a doubt, you should invest in a tripod if you plan to take many close-up photographs. Although you can get away with holding the camera in your hands most of the time, the extreme magnification provided by close-up lenses tends to make even the most subtle shake ruin your picture. In close-up photography, I highly recommend planting your camera securely on the floor, or ground, with a tripod.

You do not need to purchase a large or particularly heavy tripod. Some of the very large tripods that feature separate, expensive head units are designed for the rigors of 35mm photography, where the camera itself can weigh over 10 pounds. Most digital cameras only weigh a pound or two, so, in many situations, a lightweight tripod is sufficient.

TIP

Even if you have a digital camera, the outdoors can be unkind to your photos. If you're shooting in the wind, the heavier your tripod is, the better—especially for a light digital camera. A light camera is more likely to be blown around than a heavy one. If you have a light tripod, you can hang something heavy from the center of the tripod to help stabilize it. Of course, in a strong wind, it'll also be hard to keep your subject still unless you have some means to block the wind.

When you set your camera up on the tripod, you can leave the head unit somewhat loose. That helps you move the camera around and position it with minimal fuss. This is really up to you—try leaving the head a little loose, and if you can consistently get sharp images, work this way. If you find that your images are always a bit blurry and you think it's because you're leaving the head unit loose, then tighten everything up before you take your picture.

Here's a perfect example: In Figure 5-8, you see a bee that I photographed hovering around a columbine. If I had tightened down every knob and lever on my tripod, there's no way I could have caught the little guy as it flitted around somewhat randomly. Instead, the tripod gave me the support I needed, and I left the head unit loose so I could move the camera around to catch the bee at just the right moment.

FIGURE 5-8   A loose tripod head comes in handy when you're taking pictures of moving insects.

Bean Bag Camera Supports

I heartily recommend getting a tripod. The problem with tripods, though, is that they're bulky and are a pain to carry around, and heavier ones always tend to work better than lighter ones. What's one to do?

Well, you can carry a bean bag instead. I'm not suggesting bean bags as the ultimate, full-time replacement for tripods, but I have run into situations when they can steady your camera in a pinch. If you have something you'd like to lean the camera on top of, such as a fence post, a boulder, or even the ground, try putting a bean bag under the camera. It'll conform to the shape of the camera as well as to the shape of whatever you're placing the camera on, and the dense clump of beans in the bag will help steady the camera as you press the shutter release.

And if you don't have a bean bag, improvise. As a scuba diver, for instance, I always have bags of soft weights when I go on dive trips. They're filled with small beads of lead shot, and aside from being a lot heavier, they act a lot like bean bags.

Finally, if you want a bean bag that has been designed especially for photographers, check out The Pod, a bean bag–style camera support with a tripod bolt sticking out of the top. It's available for about $15 from www.thepod.ca.

Keep the Subject Sharp

In Chapter 3, I spent a lot of time talking about depth of field. If there were ever a time when depth of field was important, this is it. The reason? At high magnification in very short focusing distances, depth of field becomes vanishingly small. In fact, it's not unusual to find that the total depth of field in a close-up photograph is only about half an inch. In Figure 5-9, for instance, you can see that only part of the flower is in sharp focus, while most of the image is blurred. Even parts of the flower are out of sharp focus. Or go back and check out the photo series in Figure 5-7. As you move from picture to picture, the magnification gets greater, and you can actually see the depth of field get smaller and smaller in each image.

That said, the focusing range of your camera is always at a premium in close-up photography. Even if you want your background to be out of focus, you often want the most depth of field you can possibly get your hands on, since the background will almost certainly be out of focus anyway.

FIGURE 5-9   It's easy to blur the background in a close-up; the hard part is getting everything you want to be in focus actually in focus.

Here are a few things you should keep in mind to help you control the depth of field in your photograph:

- **Distance**   Remember that the closer you get to your subject, the less depth of field you will have available. So to regain depth of field, back away from your subject. To do that, you may have to remove a close-up lens from the front of your camera if you're using one or more add-on lenses.

- **Aperture**   Another way to increase depth of field is to close the aperture as much as possible. You may need to enter your camera's aperture priority or manual exposure mode to control this.

- **Light**   The more light available, the more you can close the aperture. You can use the camera's built-in flash, an external flash if your camera allows it, or just shoot in situations where there is a lot of natural light.

CAUTION   *Be careful when you compose your picture so that the subject is parallel to the lens, not perpendicular. If your subject has depth with respect to the axis of your lens, part of it will be in focus and part of it will not. When you can, turn the subject or the camera so that the entire length of the object is in sharp focus.*

Mind the Background

The background is an important part of your photograph. In general, you probably want your background to be fairly indistinct. As luck would have it, that is not too hard to do in a close-up photograph. After all, there's precious little depth of field to begin with, so the background will probably be blurry. Here are a few tips for tweaking the background of your photograph:

- **Turn it black.** If you use your flash, you'll throw so much light onto the primary subject that the background—especially if it is more than a few inches away from the subject—will be black. This is a good effect in certain situations, but it doesn't look particularly natural. That's why many professional macro photographers avoid using flash units when shooting flowers in the field.

- **Use a plain background.** You can insert a prepared background—a piece of poster board, for example—between the main subject and a distracting background. If the poster board is far enough away, it'll be out of focus and give you a plain, diffused look. I use big slabs of colored foam board from the local hobby and craft store for this purpose.

- **Blur it out of existence.** As I have already mentioned, depth of field is perhaps your most powerful tool when taking close-ups. You can check how much depth of field you currently have by half-depressing the shutter release. The camera's LCD display will show you the image with the aperture closed to the appropriate level, and that will give you your final depth of field. If you need more or less depth of field, let go of the shutter release and tweak the camera settings. Just check your depth of field over and over in the camera's display until you are happy with the result. I took the image shown in Figure 5-10 with a very wide aperture to blur the background while keeping the monk's head flower quite sharp.

FIGURE 5-10   This image was taken with a very wide aperture and no flash.

Beware of the Flash

You might start to get the impression that I am not a big fan of the electronic flash unit built into many digital cameras. Flashes that have limited range can make your pictures look artificial and can sometimes create harsh shadows. Nonetheless, flash units are admittedly an essential tool, and I don't hesitate to use them when needed.

On the other hand, you should be aware of two key limitations that may be inherent in your camera's flash unit when used in close-up photography:

- **Overexposure** Unfortunately, some digital camera flash units are not designed for very close range. When you're taking a close-up (and you're within, say, a few inches of your subject), most camera flash units won't fire at all (they're disabled in macro mode) or they'll badly overexpose the subject. Most flash units expect the subject to be several feet away and don't react well when the subject is much closer. You can find out very easily if your camera suffers from this problem. Just take a test picture or two and evaluate the results. Of course, there are workarounds to this problem. You can try underexposing the picture using the EV controls on your camera, or try a low-tech solution: lay a piece of thin tissue or some photo gel (available at any camera shop) in front of the flash to diffuse the light.

■ **Blockage**   Some flash units are positioned so that the lens itself blocks some of the light when the subject is too close to the camera. In my book (and hey! This *is* my book!), this is a camera design deficiency, plain and simple. Nonetheless, if your camera is affected by this particular glitch, it's easy to see for yourself. As in Figure 5-11, there will be a huge shadow in part of the picture where the lens got in the way of the flash. Ordinarily, your camera may not suffer from this problem, but it may become prone to light blockage if you add snap-on lenses.

Shoot Through Glass

Sometimes you might want to take a close-up of something that is under a sheet of glass—jewelry in a display case, for example. There's a common problem with this kind of subject, though: light from the sun or overhead lamps can reflect off the

FIGURE 5-11   Some cameras block the flash when the subject is too close; if yours does this, use only natural light to illuminate your subject.

glass and cause unwanted glare in your picture. Not only is glare like this ugly, it can actually make it difficult to see what it is you were trying to photograph under the glass. The solution? Use a polarizing filter. A polarizer does a few nifty things for your photograph, but the most important one is that it eliminates reflections caused by glass and water by blocking polarized light.

Polarizing filters are sold in many sizes and for many digital cameras. It's not a bad idea to carry one in your camera bag for those occasions when it might come in handy. Polarizers are usually two-piece devices that rotate on the end of your camera—you turn the outer layer until the reflections are minimized.

 *You want a circular polarizing filter. You probably won't have trouble on that count, since most photographers today buy circular polarizers. But a less-common linear polarizer simply won't work right for you because it confuses the camera's light sensors.*

That may sound complicated, but it's actually pretty easy. The LCD display on your camera gives you immediate feedback on the effect of the filter. If you can see a reflection in the display, continue turning the polarizer until the reflection is gone (or at least minimized). Keep in mind that a polarizer is most effective when you photograph at a 34-degree angle from the reflective surface, as demonstrated in this illustration:

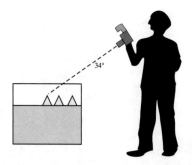

Not sure what 34 degrees works out to be? Just experiment a bit and you'll quickly find the right position. If you use your polarizer properly, you can reduce glare significantly—sometimes completely. In Figure 5-12, for instance, you can see the effect of a polarizing filter. The image on the left is uncorrected; it's what you would get without a polarizer. The image on the right has had its reflections stripped away using a polarizing filter.

FIGURE 5-12   By turning a polarizing filter on the end of your lens, you can minimize the reflections caused by light and glass.

Your Own Macro Studio

It's not always easy to get perfect results from close-up photography. There are so many elements to worry about: wind, lighting, the narrow focusing range, and limited depth of field. Lighting is especially tricky, in fact, because certain subjects look pretty bad when you hit them with an electronic flash. Lots of people try to photograph reflective items such as coins and jewelry, for instance, to sell on ebay.com or post on a web site, and they're disappointed with the reflections from the flash.

If you are excited about macro photography and expect to do a lot of it, you might want to invest in a product called the Cloud Dome (available from www.clouddome.com). This clever little gadget is a plastic dome (it looks like an upside-down salad bowl) that covers your subject and has a hole at the top for mounting your camera. The dome itself diffuses light from the outside, illuminating the macro subject evenly and professionally. I swear by this gadget.

When using the Cloud Dome, you're shooting in a controlled environment. The dome takes care of the lighting, and it even blocks wind if you use it outdoors. The dome securely holds the camera in place, acting like a tripod. All you need to worry

FIGURE 5-13 The Cloud Dome comes with a bracket that fits almost any size of digital camera and creates a virtual studio in which you can make the focus and lighting perfect with little effort.

about is framing your subject and getting the focus sharp. If you need more light than what is getting through the dome, just shine a table lamp or some other sort of light at the dome. You can see the Cloud Dome ready to shoot in Figure 5-13.

On the downside, the Cloud Dome is not inexpensive—in fact, at about $200, it costs an awful lot of money. I've experimented with household items like oversized plastic food containers and lamp shades, though, and haven't come up with anything that works nearly as well as the Cloud Dome. Perhaps the best inexpensive substitute you can find is a small white umbrella.

Chapter 6

Sports, Action, and Active Kids

How to…

- Catch fast-moving subjects despite shutter lag
- Stop the action with shutter and sports modes
- Pan for action
- Freeze kids at sporting events
- Capture wildlife at the zoo and in the woods
- Take beautiful waterfall pictures

Everybody likes motion—even our vocabulary makes that clear. We love "movers and shakers," for instance. We describe fun friends as having animated personalities; the good stuff is always up and coming. Slowpokes, like sloths and snails, on the other hand, have a somewhat less glowing reputation. So, if motion is such a good thing, perhaps we should put a little in our photographs.

But you already know that. Action photography includes capturing sporting events and kids, well, pretty much doing anything, and these are some of the most common photographic subjects. And so you know just how tricky it can be to catch a picture of your kid running around the bases of a softball game. In this chapter, you see how to capture sports, action, and kid photography.

Action Photography Essentials

Action photography is often considered the most exciting kind of photography, but it's also the most demanding. The problem—obviously—is that you're taking pictures of things that are moving. And that means not only do you need a shutter speed fast enough to "stop the action," but you also have to contend with the slight delay between when you press the shutter speed and when the picture gets taken— this is called *shutter lag,* and it's common to many digital cameras. Let's talk lag first.

Avoid the Dreaded Lag

Often, the most common complaint one hears about digital cameras is this: "There's a long pause between when I press the shutter release and when the picture is taken." The result: when trying to take an action shot, the subject sometimes moves before you can take the picture. You may see the picture on the left in the viewfinder, but what you get on your memory card is the picture on the right:

6

 **Capture the Moment**

Most digital cameras have a two-step shutter release. Knowing how to use it is key to taking great pictures.

When you put a little pressure on the shutter release button, the camera springs into action—it locks in the focus. If you continue to hold down the shutter button, the focus won't change; you can then recompose the picture and, when it meets your approval, press the shutter release all the way to take the picture.

For several reasons, you might want to use the focus/exposure lock step without pressing the button all the way down:

■ Focus lock takes a little time—a fraction of a second, but time nonetheless. If you're taking an action shot in which you want to precisely control the instant of exposure, lock the exposure and focus first; then wait with your finger on the shutter until you are absolutely ready to take the picture. Then, all it takes is a hair more pressure to capture the scene more or less instantly.

■ If you want something that's off to the side of your picture to be in sharp focus—and this commonly is the case if you follow the Rule of Thirds—then point the camera at your off-center subject and lock the focus. Then recompose the shot to put the subject off to the side, and snap the picture.

Indeed, while some cameras are better than others, that pause is responsible for more frustration than all of the world's child-safe medicine bottles combined. Older digital cameras had a "shutter lag" that lasted a whole second or more, but even many of the newest digital cameras have some lag—and that's a real problem whether you're trying to freeze a NASCAR rounding the corner or catch your grandson hugging the dog. This, by the way, is a great reason to play with a camera before you buy it, rather than simply ordering it, sight unseen, on the Internet. Only by handling the camera and trying to take some pictures in a store can you see if the camera has an annoying lag between the time you press the shutter and when the picture gets taken.

Shutter lag happens because—invisible to you—digital cameras have a veritable checklist of tasks to perform when you press the shutter release. Not only does the camera need to measure the distance to the subject and lock in the proper focus, but it also has to measure the light, figure out how to balance the colors so whites look white and blue looks blue, calculate the best exposure, and lock in an aperture setting and shutter speed. The camera also has some obscure computer-like "housekeeping" chores to perform, like initializing the sensor chip and flushing buffers that hold data about your picture. You don't have to know what any of that means, just know that your camera is busy doing stuff as you start to take a picture.

If your camera's lag doesn't bother you, fine. You might have a camera with a short lag and, if that's the case, consider yourself lucky. But, if you want to minimize the lag, you can do a few things:

■ The single biggest time-saver is using your camera's autofocus. If you prefocus your picture, you can save valuable milliseconds of lag.

■ If you're more adventurous, you can also try presetting the camera's white balance based on the kind of scene you're shooting. If the white balance is set on auto, it'll have to adjust the colors in the image every time you take a picture, and that takes a little bit of time each time you press the shutter release. Instead, you can use the camera's menu to set the white balance for whatever lighting conditions you're shooting in, such as daylight, night, florescent, or incandescent lighting. Just remember to change the white balance for every new lighting situation you find yourself in.

■ If you try those things and still find lag a problem, you may need to shoot *predictively*—and by that I mean to press the shutter release a heartbeat before you want to capture the photo. Measure the amount of lag your camera has—a half second? A second?—and start pressing the shutter release that far in advance.

- Some digital cameras try to get around the lag problem by offering a "Continuous Fire" or "Burst" mode. When set to that position, you'll capture a series of pictures in quick succession, usually about 1/3 second apart. The presumption is that you'll get lucky and at least one of them will look good. Experiment with that mode and see if it helps you get better action shots.

- Finally, you can try panning at the same time to better freeze your subject. See the section "Panning for Action" later in this chapter.

Stop the Action

If your digital camera is an "all auto" point-and-shoot model, there's not a whole lot you can do to change your camera settings to help freeze the action—your camera is already programmed to try to use the fastest shutter speed it can most of the time. But you definitely can try your hand at panning, as we explain in the section "Panning for Action."

But, if your camera has a shutter priority setting—and many do—you're in luck: shutter priority mode was born for action photography. To freeze the action, you'll usually want to use the fastest shutter speed you can get your hands on—and shutter priority mode makes that easy to do. This is what shutter priority mode typically looks like—either an A or a Tv symbol:

In general, it is recommended that you use the fastest shutter speed available to capture action. To do that, set your camera to its shutter priority mode, and then use the controls on your camera to the fastest—or close to the fastest—shutter speed available. Good speeds for freezing action are 1/125, 1/1250, and 1/500 of a second, or even faster. But if the shutter speed is really slow—like 1/60, 1/30, or, heaven forbid, 1/15 or slower, then it's pretty likely your picture will be blurry—but those shutter speeds are great for panning, which we'll talk about shortly.

What if your shutter speed just isn't fast enough to freeze the action? Bump up your camera's ISO, which we first talked about back in Chapter 2. Many cameras have an adjustable ISO level, which, like the film speed rating it's named after, lets you change the sensitivity of the camera to light. Increase the ISO level to enable you to shoot with a higher shutter speed.

Pan for Action

Another really cool action photography technique called *panning* captures the subject in good, sharp focus, while "holding" the background as a motion blur. See Figure 6-1 for an example of panning used to freeze a child's wild ride at a renaissance festival. This is a great technique to try for a couple of reasons:

- It gives the picture a great sense of motion. Freezing everything can make the picture look too static; panning lets you see that the subject is really ripping through the picture.

- It works well at slower shutter speeds. So, while your camera might usually blur an action shot in a bad way, panning lets you blur it in a good way.

FIGURE 6-1   Panning freezes the subject while blurring the background.

Learning to pan takes a little practice. To create a good pan, you need to twist your body in synch with the motion of the subject as you press the shutter release. Here's how:

1. Position yourself where you can twist your body to follow the motion of the moving subject, without having the camera's line of sight blocked by something else.

2. If you can, set the camera's shutter speed for about 1/30. Feel free to experiment with this, but if you set the shutter speed too slow, you can't capture the subject effectively—it blurs. And, if the shutter is too fast, you won't get the contrasting blur in the background.

3. Twist your body with the motion of the subject and track it for a few seconds through the camera's viewfinder or on the LCD display. Keep the subject centered in the viewfinder, and then press the shutter release and continue tracking the subject for a few moments, even after you hear the picture get recorded. Just like in baseball or golf, ensure that you follow through the motion even after the shutter releases. That way, you don't stop panning in the middle of the exposure. You may need to practice this a few times to get the shot right, but your digital camera gives you the opportunity to practice 'til perfect, for free!

There's another way to show action—hold the camera rigidly in place and let the action scream through the viewfinder as you take the picture, capturing *its* motion, instead of the background's motion. If you're shooting in broad daylight with a reasonably fast shutter speed, you can hand-hold the camera for this kind of shot. If you're shooting with a slow shutter speed in a dark location, though, you might get better results mounting the camera on a tripod. Here's an example of capturing motion in a New York subway station at about 1/15 of a second:

Experiment with Action Mode

Your camera might have something called "Action" or "Sports" mode, like the one on the dial here (it looks like a running person):

If that's the case, consider using it to take these kinds of pictures. Action mode is usually designed to use the highest possible shutter speed available with no additional effort on your part. And that's great.

But, beware—not all action modes work the same way. I've found that some cameras, when set to action mode, disable focus locking. Most digital cameras lock in the focus the moment you apply slight pressure to the shutter release, and I recommend using that technique to help reduce the inevitable shutter lag when taking pictures in fast-changing situations. With some model cameras, though, the lens will continue to autofocus continuously, right up to the moment of exposure, even if you try applying some pressure to the shutter release. How does your camera work? You'll have to experiment with it to see. The easiest way is to put a little pressure on your shutter release button and move the camera around so it has to change focus from a nearby to a distant object. If the focus changes as you move, then give some thought to using the shutter priority mode instead for hectic shooting, such as at a soccer game.

Compose Action Shots

As in all kinds of photography, you can no doubt take some great pictures with your camera's zoom lens set on anything from its wide-angle position all the way up to the photographic equivalent of the Hubble telescope. And your camera's wide-angle setting can, in fact, have a role in action photography. But the essence of many action shots is a highly magnified immediacy—something you can only get with the lens zoomed all the way in to the telephoto position. Try zooming in tight for action shots—check out the difference between these two pictures, and decide for yourself which one is more exciting:

Photograph Kids at Sporting Events

So, you're at a soccer game and trying to get some great pictures of your kid and the team. Here are a few pointers for getting great shots:

- **Stay close to the action.** If you can get close to the sidelines, you won't have to shoot over or between other spectators. Get right on the sidelines whenever possible. Getting closer also means that you don't have to zoom in all the way just to get something interesting in the frame—so your pictures won't be as shaky.

- **Get down to their level.** If you have little ones, get on your knees or on your belly so you're taking pictures from their perspective. Often, they'll be a lot more interesting than photos that look down from 5 feet in the air, which is a towering height to a toddler.

- **Keep the sun out of your eyes.** If the sun is anywhere in your field of view, your pictures will be badly underexposed. Scout out a good spot before the game starts, so that you can keep the sun behind one of your shoulders. If you want to know the basics of exposure, check out Chapter 2.

- **Frame the action tightly.** Whenever possible, try to frame the action as tightly as you can, meaning that only a few players are in the frame at once. If you're including the whole field in your shot, the scene will lack impact and it will be less interesting.

Photograph Animals

Animal photography—whether it's your family pet or a pack of wolves at the zoo—works best when you have a lot of zoom, a fast shutter speed, and a tripod. Try to fill the frame as much as possible, and expect the unexpected—like your subject suddenly darting out of your frame just when you get ready to snap the picture. Figure 6-2, for instance, shows a pair of wolves frolicking that would have been impossible to shoot without a fast shutter and a lens with a long reach.

FIGURE 6-2   Wildlife photography requires many of the same shooting skills as action photography.

Photograph Waterfalls

Have you ever seen those cool running-water shots in nature books and wished you could get the same sort of thing on your next vacation? Well, you can—it's easy to get images like this one:

Here's how:

- You need to ensure that your camera will give you a long exposure, on the order of a half second. The best way to do this is to show up at the waterfall or running stream early in the morning or late in the afternoon, when there's not much light available.

- Be sure that your camera's ISO setting is as low as it'll go, such as 100.

- Set your camera on a tripod. (The long exposure absolutely requires a steady support—but you can use a very small, lightweight tripod.)

- Compose the image and take the shot.

- If your camera allows it, take several pictures, each with a different shutter speed. The longer the shutter is open, the "smoother" the water will look.

Finally, you don't encounter waterfalls every day—so it pays to be prepared when you find one out in the real world. Practice at home! You can simulate a waterfall in your own kitchen. Check out the following pictures, shot in a kitchen sink. The first one was taken with the camera in automatic mode. Then I set the camera to shutter priority mode and dialed the shutter speed to 1/30 of a second. Notice the picturesque way the water rolls off my dirty dishes. Take a few of these sorts of images, and you'll be ready for a real waterfall!

Chapter 7

Pushing Your Camera to Its Limits

How to…

- Take pictures in special color modes such as black and white or sepia
- Decide when to use special color modes on the camera or wait and process images on the PC
- Shoot a series of panoramic photos
- Add wide-angle and telephoto lenses to your camera
- Interpret lens magnification numbers
- Avoid vignetting when using add-on lenses
- Correct for distortion caused by wide-angle lenses
- Take a series of time-lapse photos
- Turn time-lapse photos into a movie

These days, cameras are no longer just cameras. Take a look at the most common cameras in the local computer or camera shop, and you'll find that many models are designed to record movies, take panoramic photographs, record sound, and do a host of other things as well. It seems that camera manufacturers think that if you like a camera, you'll like a camera that washes your dishes and plays music even better.

Most of this book concentrates on how to use your camera to take good pictures. A lot of the extra features that you find on cameras are, in my opinion, usually just gimmicks. On the other hand, every once in a while you may find a useful, creative application for one of the gizmos built into your camera. And that's where this chapter comes in: look here for information about all those other things your camera can do.

And that's not all. This chapter is about pushing your camera to its limits. That means we'll talk about how to do unusual things with your camera, such as use it to perform time-lapse photography.

Get Creative

Your camera may come with photo modes besides the ones that we have already discussed, especially if it's a high-end model. The most common features you'll encounter in digital cameras are additional color modes. By setting your camera to the appropriate mode, you might be able to take pictures in black and white or with a sepia tone.

> TIP
>
> *If your camera does not come with one of these special effects modes, you can always convert your images to black and white or sepia on a computer after you've taken them. Refer to Chapter 13 for information on how to convert images to black and white.*

Using the black-and-white or sepia mode on your camera allows you to capture images that have a somewhat old-fashioned look. Very old photographs, of course, have a brownish tint, called sepia, that comes from the dyes that were used to print them.

You might also want to use the black-and-white mode if your final output is going to be in print, such as in a newsletter. Black-and-white images take up less space on a memory card, so you can typically take more black-and-white images than color images. Black-and-white images also make a strong artistic statement, so people use this mode to be creative. If your pictures will be black and white in the end anyway, you might consider taking them in black and white to begin with.

The downside? If you might want some of those images in color for a different application, it's simply not possible to put the color back in later. If you're not sure how your images might be used, I recommend that you start with ordinary color and save them to your computer's hard disk in that format. Later, you can convert the images to black and white in an image-processing program if necessary.

In summary, here are the pros and cons of using the special effect modes on your camera:

Pros	Cons
Images typically take up less space.	If you later need the original color image, you won't have it.
You get a specific effect immediately without the need to process the images on a computer—convenient if you don't actually own any image-editing software.	If you forget to switch out of the selected mode, you may find a whole memory card full of sepia-toned images.

The Old-Fashioned Look

If you want an authentic-looking old-time photograph, you can get a pretty authentic imitation with your camera's sepia mode. People instantly recognize the brownish hue of the sepia-toned image as something that is quite old—or at least something that's supposed to look that way. But in addition to just using a little sepia color, there are other things you can do to ensure that the image looks more authentic. Try these tips:

- **Pay attention to costumes and props.** If your goal is to take a picture that is set in a specific period, it will look more authentic with the right garb, regardless of whether it is colored sepia or not.

- **Use natural light.** Avoid using an electronic flash, which can get in the way of the picture's look.

- **Fine-tune the picture in an image-processing program.** You can employ tricks like adding digital noise, converting the image to black and white or sepia, and tweaking the contrast to make it feel like an older picture.

Make a Panorama

Panoramic photographs have been around for a long time. Before digital photography came along, there were two ways to make a panorama. Special cameras—loaded with extra-wide film—were capable of taking photos that were much wider than they were tall. In fact, Advanced Photo System (APS) cameras still do this with contemporary film. Unfortunately, APS cameras cannot make very wide panoramas; actually, all you get with a panoramic shot using APS film is a picture in which the image has been cropped to make the film seem wide. In other words, APS cameras simply throw away information across the top and bottom of the picture to give you the impression that you have taken a panoramic photograph.

The other traditional way to make a panorama is to take a series of photographs and connect them, sort of like a collage. This collage technique allows you to make very, very wide panoramas. Unfortunately, you can often see the seams between each photograph, since each print is simply layered, one on top of the other.

Digital photography allows us to make panoramas in an entirely new way. Using a still camera, it is a piece of cake to take a high-resolution photograph that spans your entire field of view from left to right, including your peripheral vision—like the ones in Figure 7-1 that I took from a Circle Line tour boat in New York harbor. Heck, you can keep going around and take a 360-degree photograph. I can't easily show such a picture on the pages of this book, though, because to squeeze a very long image onto the page, it would become so narrow that you wouldn't be able to see what was in the picture. Nonetheless, you can read more about them in Chapter 12.

FIGURE 7-1   Panoramic images allow you to see a picture more or less the same way your eyes see the real world.

The Best Reasons to Shoot Panoramas

People sometimes ask me why they should bother with panoramas. There are two excellent reasons:

■ **Fit more in the frame.** "I can just use a wide-angle setting on my camera's zoom to take the same picture," people tell me. That's simply not always possible, though. Often you can't back up far enough to fit everything in the frame. And when that happens, your only choice to capture it all on film is to take the picture in sections and stitch it together afterward. Hence, a panorama.

■ **Get more resolution.** You might want to print your picture at poster size, but your camera is just three megapixels—not enough to make really big prints. No worries; shoot the picture in sections. When each three megapixel square of the photo is stitched together, it might be ten or even twenty megapixels. There—you have enough resolution to make any size print!

Some cameras boast right on the box that they have this capability. Some cameras don't. Either way, you can make a panorama; so don't despair if it appears that your camera does not have a panorama mode. Creating a panorama on the PC is actually pretty similar to making a collage of prints. The software simply takes a series of photographs and stitches them together digitally so that the seams are essentially invisible.

Before we get there, though, we need to take the initial batch of pictures. Believe it or not, you can get some very nice panoramic photographs even if you are a bit sloppy when you take the original images. For best results, however, you should be as careful as possible when you take your pictures. Just like the old computer axiom "garbage in, garbage out," the better your original images are, the better the final panorama will be.

Have the Right Hardware

You can take a series of panoramic photographs by just holding the camera up to your eye. I've done that myself. In England a few years ago, I made a panoramic photo in front of Abbey Road Studios, where the Beatles recorded virtually all of their music. This was something of a religious experience for me, and I was distressed that I didn't have a tripod with me to make the shot perfect. But I made do with what I had—essentially, my body and an Epson digital camera—and the results were fine.

For the best results, though, it pays to travel with the right gear. To take a good panoramic shot, each image should be taken level with the ground. Remember that there are two different axes to keep under control. The lens needs to be parallel to the ground, and the horizon needs to stay level in each picture. That's not easy to do when you're holding the camera in your hand.

Instead, mount the camera on a lightweight tripod. Some companies even sell special panorama heads for tripods for just this purpose, but I've never felt the need to use one. Instead, I just keep the camera loosened on top of the tripod so I can spin it slightly for each picture.

Get the Right Overlap

Perhaps the single most important step in making a panorama is getting the correct overlap. The software on your PC will need to know how to combine each image in order to make the finished panorama. To do this, you should try to get about 30–50 percent of the scene to overlap between each pair of pictures. If you make sure that some of the scene you photographed in the first image also appears in the second image, the stitching software on your PC will be able to match them and combine them into one wide picture. See Chapter 12 for details.

How do you ensure the right amount of overlap? That's where your camera comes in. Some digital cameras have a panorama mode built in that helps you line up each picture using a series of guide marks.

Switch your camera to panorama mode and look in the LCD display. You should see a set of guide marks like the ones shown here. As you take each picture in your panorama, the guide marks help you keep part of the previous shot in the next picture you are about to take.

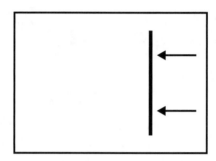

7

If your camera does not have a panorama mode to help you compose each shot, just be sure to include some overlap in each image, using your eyes to estimate distance.

How to ...   Take a Panoramic Series

Ready? It's time to actually take your panoramic series. Here's what you should do:

1. Set up your camera on a tripod in front of the scene you want to photograph. Make sure the camera is level with respect to the horizon.

2. Turn on your camera and set it to the panorama mode. Frame the rightmost edge of your panorama and take the picture.

3. Turn your camera on the tripod slightly to the left so that it is framing the next part of the scene. Make sure, however, that the leftmost 30–50 percent of the first image now also appears in the second image. It is this overlap that will allow your computer to line up the image into one seamless panorama.

4. Continue turning the camera and taking additional pictures until you reach the leftmost edge of your panorama. Or if you are taking a 360-degree panorama, continue taking pictures until you reach the first image with a suitable overlap.

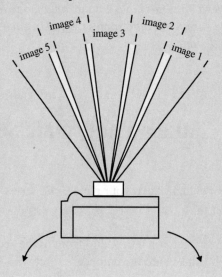

Add Lenses for Different Perspectives

As you've already seen in Chapter 5, you can attach additional lenses to many digital cameras to enhance your photographic options. In Chapter 5, for instance, you saw how to add close-up lenses to shoot macro photographs.

Your options don't end there. There are add-on lenses that cover the spectrum of photographic possibilities. Even if your camera only comes with a 2X zoom, you can probably enhance that with a set of telephoto, wide-angle, and close-up lenses.

The first thing you'll need to know is how you will be attaching additional lenses to your camera. Typically, there are three ways of doing this:

7

- ■ **Threads**   Some digital camera lenses are threaded at the end. If your lens has screw threads, you can probably screw additional lenses directly onto the end. Even so, you may need something called a step-up ring. This is a device that screws onto the end of your lens and provides a different diameter for screwing on the additional lenses. Lens manufacturers typically only make lenses in a few sizes, such as 37mm and 43mm. If your camera has a different thread size, you will need the step-up ring. You can get such an animal at your local camera shop, from a filter company like Tiffen (www.tiffen.com), or a web store like B&H (www.bhphotovideo.com). Your camera's manufacturer may sell a step-up ring specifically for your camera as well. No matter where you buy it, a step-up ring shouldn't cost more than about $10–15.

- ■ **Adapters**   Some cameras do not have a threaded lens, but instead allow you to snap additional lenses onto the end of the camera using an adapter. Usually, you'll snap or clip the adapter onto the end of the camera lens and then screw the add-on lenses onto the end of the adapter. Figure 7-2, for instance, shows a Kodak camera with its lens adapter in place. The camera manufacturer typically makes adapters like these since they are such specialized devices, designed to affix only to specific cameras.

- ■ **Jury-rigged**   Unfortunately, not all camera manufacturers include a way to add new lenses. That may sound like the end of the line, but it is possible to affix additional lenses to your camera using homemade adapters, in some cases with an adapter for a different camera, some tubing, or a judicious amount of tape. Sounds like something a fourth grader might do? Well, lots of professionals resort to this method on occasion, so if you try it, you are in good company. Personally, I've taken pictures just by holding a filter in front of a digital camera lens, and I'm sure many other experimenters have done so as well.

FIGURE 7-2   Lens adapters are a common way to add wide-angle and telephoto lenses to your camera.

Choose Lenses

Be sure to visit your camera manufacturer's web site or your local camera shop to see what kinds of lenses are available for your camera. Even if your camera manufacturer does not sell lenses for your specific model, you can probably get a suitable substitute from a company like Tiffen (www.tiffen.com), which sells a wide variety of lenses and probably has something that will would work for you.

Lenses are typically identified by their X power. In other words, the lens will be marked as something like .5X, 2X, or 3X. This designation tells you what the new focal length will be once the lens is attached to your camera. If it is a 2X lens, for instance, the lens will double the focal length of your camera. Obviously, a 2X lens is a telephoto, and attaching it to a typical digital camera should yield a focal length in the vicinity of 200mm.

If you are looking for a wide-angle lens, shoot for one that has an X power of less than 1. Suppose you purchase a .6X lens. When you attach it to your digital camera, it will reduce the focal length by 40 percent. Zoomed out at a focal length of 40mm, your camera will actually provide a focal length of 24mm, which is quite wide. If you zoom in to your camera's telephoto position, the add-on lens will still work. Now, your usual 100mm will only be 60mm.

FIGURE 7-3   A collection of add-on lenses that all fit common digital cameras

7

You can sometimes purchase add-on lenses in a complete set, such as the one in Figure 7-3.

Add-On Lens Precautions

While add-on lenses are a powerful tool for expanding your photographic options, you need to take some care to avoid an effect known as vignetting. *Vignetting* is what happens when the lens barrel itself gets into the picture, causing the frame to lose its square shape. Subtle vignetting might simply cause the corners of your pictures to be dark, blurry, or rounded off. Extreme vignetting (as in the example in Figure 7-4) can feature a perfectly round vignette; in this case the edge of the lens itself is included in the photo.

You can avoid unwanted vignetting by keeping an eye on the camera's LCD display. If your add-on lens is prone to vignetting effects, zooming farther into the telephoto range will usually eliminate the problem. You can also crop the darkened corners out of your picture or paint over the edges with nearby bits of the picture using your photo editor's clone tool. See Chapter 12 for tips on how to do that.

Distortion is another potential effect of adding lenses to your camera. All lenses have some small amount of distortion; after all, no piece of glass or group of optical elements is perfect. But you'll rarely notice any distortion from your camera's

FIGURE 7-4   This image suffers from a particularly extreme case of vignetting, thanks to an add-on telephoto lens. Reducing the zoom setting will reduce the effect.

principal lens by itself. When you add the equivalent of a big magnifying glass on the front, though, you can start to see some effects. Most of the time, it'll be either pincushion or barrel distortion—vertical lines will bend in or out of the frame instead of being perfectly straight.

Eliminate Lens Distortion on the PC

Obviously, if you can clearly detect distortion in your photos when using an add-on lens, you may want to avoid using that lens. On the other hand, it's possible to remove this sort of distortion from your pictures once they're on the PC. There are utilities available that are designed to straighten such images.

If you're using Paint Shop Pro 8, there's a tool built-in that corrects barrel distortion. Simply open the image with the distortion and choose Adjust | Lens Correction | Barrel Distortion Correction from the menu. From there, you can just experiment with the tool strength until your distortion goes away.

What if you are using a different image editor? As long as it can use standard Photoshop-style plug-ins, I suggest that you try LensDoc, sold by Andromeda Software (www.andromeda.com). *Plug-ins* are small programs that extend and enhance Photoshop and other image editors with additional capabilities.

If you have a picture with obvious lens distortion, here's how to use LensDoc to fix the problem:

1. Load the distorted picture into a graphics program.

2. Start LensDoc by choosing it from the Filter menu. In Paint Shop Pro, choose Image | Plug-In Filters | Andromeda | LensDoc. The LensDoc program should start.

3. Turn off the three green squares by clicking the second button in STEP 2 (the button with three connected green circles) on the LensDoc screen.

4. One at a time, grab the three yellow squares in the image and position them along a line that should be straight but isn't. Avoid positioning the squares too close to each other.

5. When you're ready, click the Correct button. Your image should be straightened (check out the before-and-after versions below).

 *You can increase the accuracy of LensDoc by using the green squares to mark a second line.*

Infrared Photography

Just for fun, you might want to try shooting some pictures in a completely different part of the color spectrum: infrared.

Infrared light is off at the south end of the spectrum, just below the "red" in the ROY G BIV color spread that you no doubt learned in high school. Humans can't see infrared, but photographs exposed to infrared light can look dramatically different, as if you're seeing the world through the eyes of a bat or one of those aliens from the movie "Predator." Trees and plants can glow a bright, luminous white, while the sky is often much more visually turbulent. Indeed, different plants and trees respond differently to infrared, so you can get a spread of infrared effects shooting flora outdoors. Indeed, infrared photography is often like peeking into another world. Best of all, for our purposes, you never really know what you're going to get before you press the shutter release. It's like a photographic grab bag.

Get the Gear

Before you can try your hand with infrared, you need to learn if your digital camera is capable of seeing in infrared. Not all cameras can; some include something called a "hot mirror," which is explicitly designed to block infrared light.

Go grab an infrared remote control, like the one that operates your television or stereo. Point it toward your camera's lens, turn on your camera, and look at the camera's LCD display. When you press a button on the remote, can you see a red light at the end of the remote? If you can, the camera is sensitive to infrared and you're ready to go. If you don't see the remote light up, then your camera has a hot mirror and you can't shoot infrared, sorry.

As you have probably guessed, you need some way to prevent visible light from entering the camera lens when you shoot in infrared. What you need is a filter. Infrared filters are designed to block most or all of the visible light in a scene. All that reaches your camera's CCD is infrared light, which is what your camera will use to take the picture.

Here's the bad news: infrared filters are specialty photographic items and typically aren't available at your local photo store. You may be able to special-order an infrared filter, but it's probably cheaper from an online photo store like Adorama (www.adorama.com) or B&H (www.bhphotovideo.com). Either way, an infrared filter will set you back around $50–75. They come in a variety of strengths, but I've found any one will do. Just be sure to order one that will fit the thread size on the front of your digital camera; if you camera doesn't have screw threads, you may be able to order an adapter.

Pointers for Taking the Shot

When is the best time to shoot infrared photos? In the early morning or late afternoon hours. You can't shoot at night, of course, because there's little or no infrared light available to expose your picture. You'll find out very quickly that infrared photography is dramatically different than visible light photography. The most important difference, of course, is that an infrared filter blocks nearly all of the visible light coming into the camera.

The lack of visible light means that exposure times are much longer than usual. You might find your camera exposing pictures for a quarter-second or half-second in broad daylight—which means that a tripod is essential.

There's so little light that you may run into another problem: it's hard to see through the lens. As a result, the camera's LCD display is very nearly useless for framing your shot. The LCD will be very dark, and you'll have to concentrate quite hard while blocking glare on the LCD to see anything at all. If your digital camera has a window-style optical viewfinder that doesn't get its information from the lens, you can use it to frame the scene instead. Alternatively, you can line up your scene with no filter in place and then screw the filter onto the lens and take the picture. Obviously, you'll need to use a tripod.

Edit Your Infrared Pictures

When you get the images back to the computer, you may find that the infrared shots have a relatively narrow dynamic range. Load your images into an image editor such as Paint Shop Pro and use the Histogram Adjustment tool (I explain how in Chapter 11) to fix the image. After you tweak the image, you can leave the red tint or convert it to a grayscale image.

Connect Your Camera to a Telescope

Folks with SLR cameras—digital or film—can easily connect their camera to a telescope to take extreme-telephoto pictures or even photograph the heavens with the help of a simple adapter that's available from many camera and telescope shops.

Essential Add-On Lenses

Granted, this is a matter of opinion, but there are a few add-ons that I highly recommend keeping in your camera bag. I suggest that you carry these lenses if you like to experiment with different perspectives and focal lengths:

- **UV filter**   If your camera has screw threads on the front of the lens, add a UV filter to protect the lens from bumps, bangs, dust, dirt, and over-aggressive cleaning. A $15 filter can protect your expensive camera investment for quite a long time, making it one of your smartest investments. Throw it away and replace it with a new one about once a year.

- **2X telephoto.** This add-on doubles the magnification of your lens, giving your telephoto more "reach."

- **A .5 or .6 wide angle.** Need to get more in your photo? This add-on lens can help you capture a much wider scene.

- **Set of close-focus (macro) lenses.** Macro lenses let you get within an inch or so of your subject and greatly magnify small objects.

- **Circular polarizer**   Discussed in Chapter 5, this add-on filter lets you cut reflections from glass and water.

■ **Neutral density filter**   This is a translucent piece of glass that fits over the lens. It's designed to reduce the light entering the camera by one or two stops, thus letting you slow the shutter to add more "blur" in action shots (such as the one shown here) or increase the depth of field on a bright day.

If you want to try that with a point-and-shoot camera, you're in luck—companies such as LensPlus (www.lensadapter.com) sell just the sort of adapter you need. LensPlus, for instance, sells a gadget called the LE-Adapter, which acts as a docking port between your digital camera or digital camcorder and other optical gadgets such as telescopes, binoculars, spotting scopes, and microscopes. It works with a wide variety of digital cameras—all you need is a set of threads on the front of your camera's lens to screw on the LE-Adapter.

The adapter comes ready to screw onto cameras with either 37mm- or 52mm-diameter threads. If your camera has a different diameter lens, you can buy a step ring that goes from your camera's threads (the size is usually inscribed right on the front of the lens) to either 37mm or 52mm.

If you go shopping for a step ring, be sure to get the right size. If your camera's lens is larger than 52mm, you'll want a step-down ring. A step-up ring will have threads that go the wrong way, so the distinction is important.

Once you screw the LE-Adapter onto your camera, you then bolt the other end of the adapter onto your telescope, binoculars, or other optical system, and start taking pictures. In most cases, your digital camera should be able to autofocus right through the new optics.

The LE-Adapter works pretty well, as long as you understand that the optics won't necessarily be as bright and as sharp as you're used to with your ordinary lens. A set of binoculars, for instance, may give you a lot of magnification, but the optics aren't designed to take professional-caliber photos. Personally, I've had a blast photographing the moon through my 6-inch reflector telescope, though, and it's a way to capture photos that are otherwise absolutely impossible with your digital camera:

Your results will also vary depending on what camera you own. In testing, I have found that the Nikon CoolPix 4500 works just fine, though Sony DSC P5 suffers from terrible optical degradation. The preceding shot of the moon was taken with an Olympus e10, which you can see in position here:

Take Time-Lapse Photos

If you've ever been impressed by a time-lapse movie of a flower opening or traffic moving on a busy highway, you might want to try it yourself. It's not hard to do, though it's certainly easier if your camera supports time-lapse operations to begin with.

First, a little theory: time-lapse photography is just the process of shooting the same subject over and over with a certain time interval between each shot, so that when you play the images back later in sequence, it's like a movie in which events happen faster than normal time.

If your camera has a time-lapse feature, this is a piece of cake. The control might be on the camera itself (in the menu system) or on your PC. If it's only on your PC, you may need to connect a laptop to the camera to control the time-lapse operation. If the control is on the camera, though, you don't need any special equipment. All you need to do is configure the camera's "interval time," which is the interval between photos.

If your camera doesn't have a time-lapse control, you can still take a series of photos, but you'll have to shoulder more of the work. Specifically, you'll have to turn the camera on, take a shot, and turn the camera off. Then you need to wait the appropriate time period and repeat the process. When you use automatic time-lapse photography, the camera does all that on its own.

The final results can be worth it, though. Figure 7-5 shows a series of photos that were captured with the time-lapse mode of an Olympus e-10 digital camera.

If you want to try your hand at time-lapse photography, here are a few pointers to keep in mind:

■ **Use a tripod.** This is probably obvious, but I once saw someone try to take a time-lapse series by hand. The effect is ruined if each and every image isn't composed exactly the same way.

■ **Choose a subject.** Most of the time, a time-lapse photo series works best—in other words, it looks its best—when you find a single subject that is going to change over time and make it the focal point of your photos. If too much changes in the frame, the image loses its impact. In simple terms, it looks like a mess.

■ **Find the right interval.** This may take some experimentation, but it can make or break your photos. Choose an interval between shots that best highlights the changes in your subject. If the interval is too long, the subject will change too much between shots, and it'll look disjointed and confusing. If the interval is too short, not enough will happen between frames to make a visual difference.

FIGURE 7-5   Time-lapse photography lets you see changes over a long or short period of time.

- **Start fresh.** Make sure that you have plenty of room on your memory card to take your series. You might want to start with a blank card and reduce the resolution of each image to a manageable 640×480 pixels. If you plan to take a lot of pictures, be sure the camera batteries are fresh (so you don't run out of gas halfway through the series), and perhaps start with a large memory card.

- **Use automatic exposure.** Most of the time, make sure the camera is set to automatic exposure. That way, it can react to changing light conditions throughout the day. The exception: if you're taking a series of night shots, configure the camera for the desired manual settings, such as f/5.6 for 8 seconds each.

Movies on Your Camera

These days, it seems that most digital cameras come with some sort of movie mode. Thus, instead of simply snapping stills, you can record a short video that can be played back on the camera or on a PC.

While the movie mode is easy to operate, not all cameras treat movies the same. Some digital cameras have no microphone, for instance, so they can't capture sound. Likewise, some cameras set a fixed length for your movies—say, 15 or 60 seconds—while other cameras will record any length, right up till the point you run out of memory on your storage card. Depending on what kind of camera you have, the movie will either be recorded in MPG, AVI (also known as Video for Windows), or MOV (QuickTime) format. No matter which format your camera records, it should be playable on any PC with the appropriate viewer application.

Finally, when you make a movie, remember that you can often choose the video's resolution—but even the biggest movie will still be fairly small on the computer screen.

Make Movies

Once your time-lapse series is complete, you might want to turn it into a film. There are two ways to do this: by using video-editing software or animation software.

- **Video-editing software**   If you have a camcorder and you make your own home movies, this is a great solution. Just open your favorite video-editing program and import all the still time-lapse frames. Arrange them in the filmstrip or timeline so they each play for some small fraction of a second, and then render the movie. Using this technique, you can save your movie so it plays "full screen" on the PC or on a television, directly from the PC or from videotape.

- **Animation software**   Using a program such as Jasc's GIF Animator (included with Paint Shop Pro), you can arrange the individual stills, configure them each to play for a fraction of a second, and save the finished result as an animated GIF or some other kind of animation file that plays in a small window on the computer screen. This technique is better if you want to upload it to a web site, e-mail it, or just view it on the PC.

Keep Batteries Warm in Cold Weather

You may want to run outside in the dead of winter to photograph snowmen, snowball fights, and freshly fallen snow clinging to the trees. But because they're electronic devices, digital cameras don't function as well in cold conditions as in the heat of summer.

You can prevent most problems, though, just by keeping your camera batteries warm. If the batteries get too cold, the chemical reactions that generate power are inhibited, and they'll simply stop working. Here's what I suggest: carry a spare set of batteries in your pocket, where your body heat can keep them warm. If the current in the first set of batteries drops off due to the cold, swap them out with the ones warmed by your body, and then continue shooting. Since the first set of batteries will recover some of their charge when you stick them in your warm pocket, you can swap back and forth a few times—unless you're shooting in the Arctic where the ambient temperature is 50 below zero.

Did you know?

Carry Spares

I never go anywhere without a spare set of batteries in my camera case. I don't need to tell you how frustrating it can be to run out of energy in the middle of Yellowstone National Park. If you can fit it, I also suggest bringing a charger with you so you can charge your batteries as needed. I am particularly fond of slim-line chargers like the one shown here, since it takes up so little space and can be used to hold a second set of batteries without consuming any more precious space in your camera bag:

In addition, you might want to invest in a set of Instant Power back-up batteries. Instant Power (www.instant-power.com) sells a great emergency-power solution for digital cameras, camcorders, PDAs, cell phones, and other devices. They're disposable fuel cells that provide hours of operation if your primary batteries die. The cells have a long shelf life when left sealed in their pouch, meaning you can put a set in your travel bag and leave them there for months at a time.

Also, it pays to spend a little more money on a smart charger, which can totally charge a set of batteries in 60–90 minutes, rather than the dozen hours it takes most run-of-the-mill chargers. Need to charge anywhere, anytime?

7

Be sure to check out your local camera or computer shop for special-purpose chargers that can charge your batteries using the power adapter in your car or even solar power, like the iSun Solar Power Charger (www.isunpower.com), shown here, which can top off a dozen AA batteries at once via solar power, a wall outlet, or your car's power port:

Part II

Transferring Images

Chapter 8

Conquering File Formats

How to...

- Use image file formats

- Distinguish among formats such as JPG, TIF, BMP, and GIF

- Recognize file extensions on the PC

- View file extensions in Windows

- Understand the value of JPG compression settings on the camera

- Select the best image compression on a camera

- Determine when to use the TIF format to capture pictures on your camera

- Know when to save images in various file formats

- Batch-save a large number of images in a different format automatically

- Choose the best JPG compression level on the PC

Like it or not, working with a digital camera means that you are going to have to learn some of the nuances of your PC. That can be bad news. After all, computers can be a pain in the neck, and Windows, in particular, can be a nightmare. Nonetheless, the pictures stored in your digital camera are not terribly useful to you unless you understand how to work with them. The images are stored in individual files not unlike the document files you'll find on the computer itself—such as word processing files, music files, or the saved game files created by a computer game. In this chapter, we will look in some detail at the image files created by your digital camera. We will talk about file formats, image quality, and what you need to know about all of this to get the best results with your camera. Don't worry, though: this is not a computer class, and we won't go into any more detail than you will actually need to manage your pictures.

What Are File Formats and Why Do I Care?

When you take a picture with your digital camera, the camera's imaging sensor interprets the scene and records a representation of it on the camera's memory card. The scene is essentially a grid, or matrix, of pixels. How many pixels there are depends on the resolution of the camera.

If you were taking a 1-megapixel picture, for instance, the image's resolution would be about 1280 pixels across (the X dimension, or width) by 960 pixels down

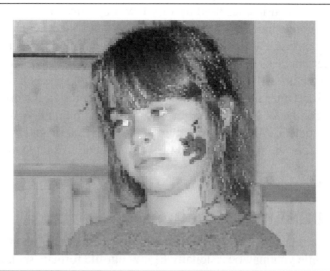

FIGURE 8-1   A digital image is little more than a grid of colored pixels.

(the Y dimension, or height). It would look something like Figure 8-1, in which you can see each individual pixel that makes up the image, assuming you can zoom in far enough. The picture is a sort of paint-by-numbers grid—just add the right color to each of the pixels, and you'll end up with a picture of something.

So far, so good. The problem comes in when the camera tries to save all this data to the memory card. How does it do it? Essentially, the camera needs to save the data in some standardized format so the information will be understandable to software and devices other than the digital camera itself. In the old days of computing, every word processing program stored its documents in a unique file format that was understandable only to that program—a real hassle if you needed to open a document on someone else's PC using a strange word processing program. Likewise, if your camera stored information about the color value of each one of those pixels however it felt like it, odds are good that only the camera would ever be able to understand that information again.

And that is a somewhat long-winded explanation of why we have file formats. By writing the color information about each of those pixels in a standard and predictable way, each picture the digital camera saves can be read by your computer's software, even if the software didn't come from the same company that made the camera.

Digital cameras and graphics programs use more than one file format—many more. In fact, there are well over a hundred file formats in use by image software on computers today. Only about a half dozen are particularly popular—most are really just historical curiosities used by very few programs—but even that small number can be confusing. Why are there so many file formats? Good question. It's not just to confuse everyone. Instead, different file formats exist because some are better at certain tasks than others. Some file formats compress well—in other words, a large picture will only take up a small amount of space on the memory card or hard disk. Other file formats more accurately represent the original image, are optimized for the Web, or are designed to work well on both Windows and Macintosh computers. And most importantly, they were all invented at different times, under unique circumstances, and they simply tend to hang on because some folks still use them.

The Most Common File Formats

As I said earlier, there are really just a few file formats that most people use most of the time. So while you may occasionally hear about file formats such as IFF, IMG, and KDC, you typically need to pay attention to just a very few.

By the same token, you really should get to know the most common file formats and use them when it's appropriate. Here is a quick overview of the most common formats and what they are used for:

- **JPG** Short for Joint Photographic Experts Group (pronounced "jay peg"), this file format is considered *lossy*. That means that when you save an image in this format, some of the data are lost. That's because JPG files are compressed to save storage space. Why do people put up with a file format that sacrifices image quality? The answer is that the JPG format does an outstanding job of preserving all the visual information that the human eye can generally see in a picture. When you save a picture in the JPG format, you'll typically have to zoom in quite a bit to begin to see any artifacts or digital noise caused by the format.

- **JPEG2000** A fairly new file format, called JPEG2000, uses the same basic compression technology as JPG, but it offers better image quality for roughly the same file size. JPEG2000 has a lot of fans, and it's supported by most image editors. On the other hand, digital cameras still use the JPG format—so to use JPEG2000, you'll have to convert the images from JPG to JPEG2000 format on the PC. I'm pretty ambivalent about JPEG2000. It's certainly an improvement over JPG, but unless or until digital cameras adopt this format, I'll stick with JPG.

- **TIF** Short for Tagged Image File format, this format is also very popular, but for exactly the opposite reason that JPG is popular. TIF files can be saved in two different ways: with a small amount of compression or without compression. Either way, TIF files are absolutely *lossless*—they preserve 100 percent of the information about every pixel in the original image. TIF files are also popular because they are used on both the Windows and Macintosh platforms; that makes TIF a good choice if you need to share files with someone who is using a different kind of computer than you.

■ **BMP**   This is the old standard bitmapped file format for Windows users. It can be used for general-purpose storage, for image editing, and as the wallpaper on your Windows desktop, but it isn't generally readable by Macintosh computers. In addition, BMP files are not used on the Internet. That makes this a relatively unpopular format. Another reason that BMP files aren't particularly popular is that they tend to be quite large because the BMP format makes no effort to compress the data. In general, the only reason you will tend to use this file format is if you want to display a digital image as the wallpaper on the Windows desktop. Even then, newer versions of Windows let you use JPG images for wallpaper—relegating the BMP format to the "where are they now" file for most savvy users.

■ **GIF**   Short for Graphics Interchange Format (pronounced either "giff" or "jiff," depending on who is doing the talking), this format was originally developed by CompuServe and is commonly used on the Web, along with the JPG format. GIF has a few advantages over JPG on the Web. For one, you can make the background of GIF images transparent, which comes in handy if you want the area surrounding an irregularly shaped image to be the same as the background of the Web page. You can also make GIF images display in *interlace* mode—that is, in chunks, which means that you can get an overall impression of the picture even before it has fully downloaded. That is a valuable feature on the Internet, since many people still have slow modem connections. If you save a 256-color GIF image, for instance, the file will be dramatically smaller and may not look terribly different from the original full-color JPG. On the other hand, that's not a good practice for digital images—you're more likely to save GIF images at a lower color count if the image in question is a graphic such as a company logo or a hand-drawn picture.

Understanding File Extensions

The many file formats used on computers today are generally referred to by the letters that make up their three-letter extension. Computer files are generally named using a standardized system that looks like this:

filename.ext

The *filename* can generally be almost anything—a random collection of numbers and letters or a word or two that describe the contents of the file. Filenames also use a three-letter *extension* that tells the computer what kind of data the file holds. Here are a few common file extensions:

- **.doc**   Word processing document (usually created by Microsoft Word)
- **.xls**   Spreadsheet document (usually created by Microsoft Excel)
- **.mp3**   Digital music file, commonly downloaded from the Internet
- **.htm**   Web page document

In other words, you and I, as users, control the first half of the filename. The file extension, though—the part that comes after the period—depends on the program that made the file or the file format that the data set corresponds to. If you open a folder on your computer and find a bunch of image files, you can immediately tell what format they are in by looking at their extension, as in the following illustration. For example, an image file named *mypicture.jpg* is saved in JPG format, while another named *pretty-flower.tif* is saved in TIF format.

Windows may not be configured to show you the complete filename including the extension. To turn on the extension view in Windows XP, follow these steps:

1. Open a folder on the Windows desktop.

2. Choose Tools | Folder Options from the folder's menu.

3. Click the View tab so that you can see the Advanced settings in the bottom half of the window.

4. Find the entry Hide Extensions For Known File Types (it's about halfway down the list), and remove the check mark from this selection.

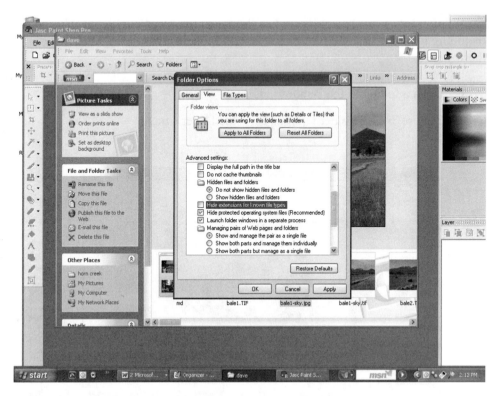

5. Click OK to save this change.

Use File Formats

Now that you understand file formats, you are probably wondering which one you should use on your own system. As in all things, it depends on how you're going to use your images. Let's look at your choices, and I'll make a few recommendations about how you might want to work with and save your images.

On the Camera

Let's start with your camera. No doubt, you realize that your camera saves images in some sort of file format—but which one?

JPG Files

Actually, this is the easy part. Most digital cameras, by default, save their images in JPG format. JPG is a pretty good compromise between quality and file size for most users and in most photographic situations. But what you may not realize is that you have a fair degree of control over how aggressively your camera compresses the

JPG images, and therefore the picture quality. Take a look at your camera, and you will no doubt find that somewhere—whether it is in a menu system or controlled via a button on the camera housing itself—there is a setting for image quality. Note that image quality is quite different from resolution. *Resolution* is a measure of how many pixels are in the image; *quality* determines how much color information can be stored in each pixel and, consequently, how much image quality will be sacrificed.

Most cameras tend to have several quality settings, such as high, medium, and low. I recommend that you stick with the highest setting for your JPG images—the lower-quality settings tend to make for some pretty unsatisfactory images. On the other hand, the highest image quality and resolution setting takes more space on your memory card, reducing the number of images you can keep on a card at once. Which is the bigger deal? Well, consider this: you can always buy another memory card to store extra images, and memory cards have gotten quite cheap. But once saved at a lower resolution, you can never buy back the lost image quality at any price. If you're only using your pictures for low-impact applications such as web pages and e-mail, small differences in image quality may not mean a lot to you. But if you're planning to print your pictures, even a little color fringing or digital noise can make a difference.

Be sure to check your camera menu for details on setting image quality and resolution because every camera is a little bit different. Some cameras make it easy to distinguish between resolution and image quality because they are set with two different controls. Other cameras offer these two controls in a single, somewhat confusing menu selection. You may be forced to work with a camera menu that gives you a choice of SHQ, HQ, and SQ, for instance, where both SHQ and HQ are the same high resolution, but with different amounts of JPG compression. In the illustration below, you can see how a FujiFilm camera on the left limits you to choosing only what resolution you can work with, while the Olympus camera on the right uses SQ and SHQ to distinguish between image quality. Inside each of those selections is the ability to choose a specific pixel resolution. The moral? Read your camera manual to see how to set the resolution and image quality.

8

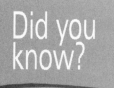

Compression Versus Reduction

In this chapter, I use the term *image compression* a lot. The loss of quality in JPG images, I contend throughout this chapter, is the fault of the file format's efforts to compress the original image.

In reality, there are two techniques used to save disk space in many file formats: compression and reduction. *Compression*, by definition, is simply removing redundant data from a file in such a way that the file can be made smaller without losing any truly unique information. Consider the number 1,000,000,000, for instance. Using data compression, I can represent that value as 1E9. It's the exact same information, but I've managed to write it in far fewer digits on the page. WinZip and other compression utilities used to download programs from the Internet can compress programs without losing any information—otherwise, the original program would never work again after being compressed!

Reduction, on the other hand, is a programming term that refers to making a file smaller by actually sacrificing some data. Small changes in color between adjacent pixels might be approximated, for instance, or numbers might be rounded off with the philosophy of "good enough." With many lossy file formats—such as JPG, MPEG, and MP3—a lot of effort goes into developing mathematical models that can sacrifice data the human brain won't notice much.

The distinction between compression and reduction is a subtle one, though, so I'll mainly use the term "compression" to refer to both techniques.

Lossless Image Files

Many digital cameras have a second file format option—TIF. Remember that the TIF format, unlike JPG, can be used to ensure that the image is absolutely pristine, without any data loss at all. Many cameras have a special setting that you can use to save your images in this lossless TIF format.

You might want to work in TIF if you are shooting a special photograph that you plan to crop, enlarge, and print. Truly professional work may call for TIF images—but even then, a high-res, high-quality JPG may be sufficient. Remember, though, that the TIF format exacts a serious penalty: measured in megabytes, TIF files are so large that you may only be able to fit a very few on your memory card.

If you want to work in TIF format a lot, you should get the largest memory card you can afford. Consider a 256MB memory card in a typical 5-megapixel digital camera. Such a card might usually be able to store about 64 high-quality JPG images. When set to TIF format, though, the same card might only hold 16 images. That's a pretty radical difference, so it's worth asking how significant the difference between TIF and JPG really is. Here's my take: the differences are typically only apparent when enlarged, and even then it isn't always readily apparent. It's most noticeably important when trying to print an enlargement on a good color printer.

There's another issue with TIF: it takes a long time to save these images to memory. Since TIF files are the size of several JPG images, your camera has to spend the time to store the equivalent of several pictures each time you press the shutter release. I've found that it can take anywhere from 30 seconds to a full minute to write each TIF image. Worse, some cameras won't let you take another picture until that one is done getting stored on the memory card.

8

TIP
In general, I suggest that you forget about the TIF mode on your digital camera. It's not worth the sacrifice, since a high-res, high-quality JPG is more than adequate 99.9 percent of the time. Worse, it can take a long time to write a TIF file to memory.

RAW Files

There's one other file format you might encounter with certain digital cameras. The RAW format does TIF one better, storing not just totally uncompressed data, but also storing that data before the camera's processor has had a chance to do anything to it.

What am I talking about? Well, consider this: your digital camera's processor does a lot to each image you snap before it gets stored on the memory card. First and foremost, each pixel of the image sensor can only capture a single color, so the camera's processor combines adjacent pixel information to interpolate the colors you finally see in your finished image. RAW images store the unprocessed, uninterpreted data—and consequently, they don't include the camera's white balance settings or any other tweaks, such as the sharpening filter that many cameras run on images right before they're saved.

In other words, the RAW file is like a digital negative—totally unprocessed, unfiltered, untouched. Some pro photographers use the RAW files because they allow greater creative control over the finished images. But not all digital cameras let you save RAW mode pictures. In my experience, very inexpensive digicams don't have this feature, while better, performance-oriented cameras usually do.

Even then, be aware that all RAW files are not the same. Nikon's NEF format is similar to—but incompatible with—Canon's RAW format, for instance. And some cameras, like a few Olympus models, disguise their RAW mode by simply calling it TIF, so it pays to read your camera's user guide to learn the details.

Many image-editing programs can't deal with RAW files. Unless you have a new application—like Microsoft Digital Image Suite 2006, for instance—the only way to load RAW files from your digital camera is to use the file transfer and conversion software that comes with the camera or to invest in an image-editing program that has special support for your camera's RAW files. Adobe Photoshop offers a plug-in that works with many Canon, Fuji, Minolta, and Nikon camera RAW modes.

On the PC

When you transfer your images to the PC, you'll find them in the same file format that the camera used. There's no magical transformation as they go from camera to computer. But just because they arrive in JPG format doesn't mean they have to stay that way. You can save these images in any file format you like.

NOTE   *When you save a JPG picture in TIF format, you essentially "freeze" the image at its current level of detail and image quality. That way, when you edit and save it again later, you're not degrading its quality like you would by resaving it in JPG format. But remember—just saving an image in TIF cannot restore quality that wasn't there to begin with. Your image will never look any better than it did in JPG format.*

Depending on how important your photos are—and how picky you are about image quality—you might want to convert files that you plan to edit or manipulate into a lossless file format such as TIF. As I have said several times, I have nothing against JPG—it's a great format—but since it is lossy, every time you edit and resave the file, it degrades a bit more.

This is very important! Many people assume that resaving a JPG image doesn't affect the image quality, but that's not the case. Think of it this way: a JPG is nothing more than an approximation of the original that conserves disk space by reducing the total image quality slightly. Every time you save a JPG file, the JPG compression algorithm runs, reducing the image quality again. Each time you click the Save button on a JPG image in an image-editing program, you're making an approximation of an approximation.

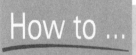 **Change the File Format**

When you open an image to crop it, brighten it, or perform some other minor (or major) editing job, you should save your changes as a new file with a .tif extension. Here's how to do that:

1. In an image editor, choose File | Save As from the menu.

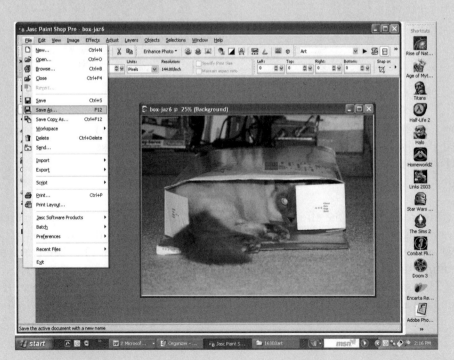

2. In the Save As dialog box, click the list arrow in the Save As Type box, and choose the option for TIF. It is sometimes spelled out as Tagged Image File Format.

3. Change the filename if you desire, and then click Save.

If you no longer need the original JPG file, you can delete it from your hard disk to save space. You might want to keep it, though, in case you want to go back to the original image (prior to the edits you just made).

Figure 8-2 shows the effect of opening and saving the same image a dozen times in an image-editing program such as Adobe Photoshop. Notice that the veins in the leaf are much less sharply defined in the image on the right after it has been resaved multiple times using the JPG format.

That said, don't be alarmed about JPGs that you don't edit and then resave. If you take a picture in JPG format, transfer it to the PC, and then only open it *to look at it,* you can leave it in JPG format because you're not saving it over and over.

FIGURE 8-2   Every time you click the Save button in an image editor, your JPG file degrades a little bit more—the image on the right is a many-times-saved, degraded copy of the original on the left.

Choose a File Format

The TIF format is great if you plan to print enlargements of your images or if you want to preserve an image precisely, without any compression artifacts. Digital images have lots of uses, though, and that's why there are lots of file formats. Here are a few file format tips you might want to keep in the back of your mind:

■ **Web publishing**   If you're publishing pictures on the Web or in a page layout program such as Adobe PageMaker, JPG is often the best choice. But GIF files can have transparent backgrounds, so text can be made to flow professionally around an irregularly shaped image, as you can see in Figure 8-3. I'll discuss Web publishing tools in a little more detail in Chapter 16.

■ **Print publishing**   Creating a newsletter? If you're printing a black-and-white document, such as on a laser printer, it often pays to convert your image to grayscale before you insert it into the page layout or word processing program. There are two reasons for this. First, you can see exactly what you're going to be printing, and viewing it in shades of gray lets you determine whether the image needs brightness adjustment or other edits. Second, you're sending less information to the printer, and the software should work somewhat faster.

8

e world of handheld security, the emphasis is often on ecting the data on the device--to the exclusion of any cern for the handheld itself. In many ways, this tegy is sound: the loss of mission-critical or sensitive can often cost significantly more than the handheld f. But writing off a fleet of $500 Palms seems gious. What organization wouldn't want to be able to ver that hardware investment? rhaps the reason no one talks about vering lost or stolen Palms is because e are few workable recovery solutions lable. all just a matter of time, though. ops, for instance, have been able to modem-based recovery services for s. Absolute Software's CompuTrace, nstance, is a hidden application that des a notebook's hard disk. When ected to a phone line, CompuTrace etly dials home to let you know where it o if thieves try to check their email with your pp, they're exposed to CompuTrace's recovery ice. The problem? No such solution exists for Palm dhelds. may be on its way, though. Last year, federal lation mandated that new cell phones must be pped with technology deigned to locate users placing mergency 911 call, and Sprint has already released a e with an integrated GPS system. Analysts believe

Handspring Treo and the Kyocera Smartphone, should eventually lead to location-aware PDAs that can "phone home" with their exact location when stolen or lost.

One company is already working on just such a product. Wherify is a company in the midst of launching a suite of wireless location services, and the company has set its sights on the PDA recovery market. Right now, Wherify is rolling out a service that tracks and locates our most important resource-- humans--via a GPS-enabled wristwatch. The GPS Personal Locator, designed for children, can transmit its position anywhere inside the United States. The device acts like an alphanumeric pager, can access emergency 911 services, and transmits its location on a continuous basis. Wherify envisions the gadget as an emergency locator for children who get separated from their parents. The system also has a "breadcrumb mode" which allows you to track the position of the wearer via the Internet; this can be used to monitor the whereabouts of a child in the custody of a caregiver.

The system relies on GPS and cell phone technology. Wherify told us that a version of the GPS Personal Locator that works in conjunction with Palm-powered handhelds is coming later this year. There's a downside, though: the current version of the GPS Personal Locator costs $400

| **FIGURE 8-3** | In an image editor, be sure to save your image with a transparent background. Then you can make text wrap around it in your web design or publishing program. |

- **Enlargement printing**   If you want to print digital images at large sizes, such as 5×7 inches or beyond, TIF or JPG is fine, but stick with TIF if you are editing and saving the file first.

- **On-screen display**   The JPG format is perfectly adequate for most onscreen applications, including e-mail, slide shows, PowerPoint presentations, web photo albums, Windows desktop wallpaper, and that sort of thing.

Tweak JPGs

The JPG file format is very flexible. Just as on the digital camera, where you can usually select from several grades of JPG image quality, desktop-based image-editing software usually lets you specify an image quality level as well.

Remember the trade-off with JPG settings: the higher the image quality, the larger the file size. In a program such as Paint Shop Pro, for instance, you can find the JPG controls in the Save As dialog box. With the JPG file format selected, click the Options button, which opens the Save Options dialog box. You should see

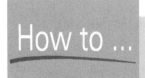 **Batch-Process Your Images**

Some people like to convert their images to TIF (or some other file format) as soon as the images make their way from the camera to the PC. It can be slow and boring to do that by hand—how would you like to access the File | Save As menu item 50 times in a row to save each of your images as TIFs?

Instead, there are various ways to automate the process. If you're using the excellent image management program called ACDSee (www.acdsee.com), you can "batch-process" a slew of images at once. Just select all the pictures you want to convert to another format, such as TIF, and then choose Activities | Edit | Convert from the menu. Choose the file format, and you can even tell ACDSee to delete the original unneeded files when it's done. There's also a batch editor built into Paint Shop Pro 8 (www.jasc.com) and Adobe's Photoshop Elements. Using these programs to batch-process is easy—just choose a list of operations to perform, like cropping, resizing, and adding a filter to your pictures, then select the images you want to modify, as shown here:

8

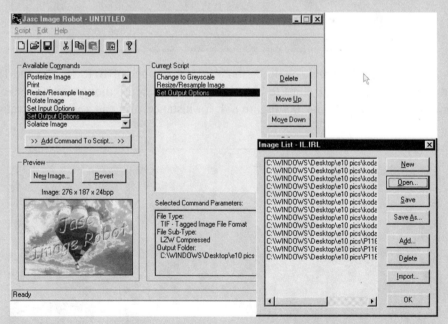

If you work with dozens or hundreds of images at once and frequently need to convert them to another format, investigate one of these programs.

a slider control for increasing the compression level, as shown in the following illustration:

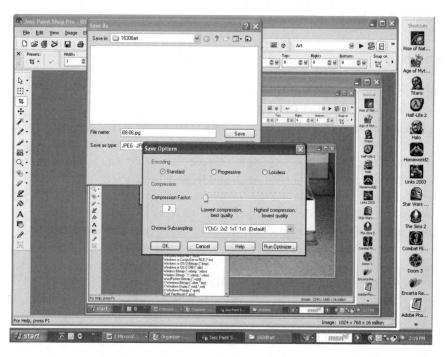

Most people stick with a compression level in the range of 10 to 15. Beyond 15, the compression artifacts start to become quite noticeable, though the file size shrinks dramatically. Check out Figure 8-4, for instance. You can see a conservative

FIGURE 8-4   When you save JPG images, use as little compression as possible to avoid this kind of degradation.

compression of 10, on the left, and an aggressive compression of 50, on the right. The difference is dramatic, especially in the image's background.

My advice: for all my photography, I set my photo editor to the absolute lowest compression/highest image quality and I leave it there. That way successive changes do the very least damage to my pictures possible. Yes, the picture files are fairly large, but they're still just a fraction of what they would be as TIF files.

8

Chapter 9

Working with Digital Film

How to...

- Choose a camera based on its memory card format
- Understand the advantages and disadvantages of various kinds of memory cards
- Use a USB cable to copy images from the camera to the PC
- Solve USB port problems
- Use a memory card reader to transfer images from the camera to the PC
- Delete images from your memory card
- Protect your memory cards
- Recover lost images
- Use a storage device when traveling

Often, you'll hear people describe a digital camera's image sensor—be it the Charge-Coupled Device (CCD) or the Complementary Metal Oxide Semiconductor (CMOS)—as the equivalent of a 35mm camera's film. Heck, I use that comparison myself pretty often. That's because the sensor behaves like film. It's sensitive to light and is primarily responsible for sensing the scene in the same way that the silver halide solution on chemical film records a scene. But, in just the same way that about 50 different people each stake a claim to being the fifth Beatle, many will claim that another component in your camera is "like the film in a digital camera." This is your camera's removable memory, and that's the subject of this chapter.

Removable memory cards like SmartMedia, CompactFlash, Memory Stick, SD, and even the new xD card are just like film in the sense that this is where your images are stored. If you remove the memory card from your camera and hold it in your hand, you're holding your pictures. If you insert that memory card in your PC, you can transfer those pictures to your computer for editing or printing. And, because memory cards can be erased and used again, digital imaging is much more flexible and a heck of a lot cheaper in the long run than 35mm photography. To learn how to get the most out of your computer's digital film, read this chapter.

The ABCs of Digital Film

All digital cameras have to store their images somewhere—it's the *where* that's the big question. There's no single standard way of storing images in a digital camera; almost a half-dozen typical storage schemes are in use by cameras today, so what kind of storage system you want to use might be a consideration when choosing your camera. Almost all cameras use one of the following methods of storing images.

Internal Memory

Although a few low-priced digital cameras use just a few megabytes of internal, nonremovable memory for storing images, this animal is a dying breed. In fact, it's almost extinct. Most cameras include the capability to insert some sort of removable memory. That way, you can insert a fresh memory card when your camera is full of pictures. With only internal memory at your disposal, you can easily run out of storage space and be unable to take more pictures unless you delete a few old images or download your pictures to the PC—something that can be hard to do if you're shooting snapshots on vacation.

9

NOTE   *That said, many cameras come with a few megabytes of internal memory in addition to the removable memory card. That way, if your card gets full, you can possibly snap a few more pictures with just the memory in the camera.*

SmartMedia

SmartMedia—originally known by the somewhat cumbersome name of Solid State Floppy Disk Card (SSFDC)—is the oldest of all memory formats. It's also the thinnest, weighing in at a mere .75mm thick. Because it's so thin, SmartMedia has little on-board "intelligence" and it relies on its parent device (such as your digital camera) to understand how to read and write data on the card.

While this approach makes for a more streamlined memory card, it also poses a potential problem. Older devices, such as 1-megapixel digital cameras, often can't accept larger-density SmartMedia cards. This is because the camera's firmware wasn't programmed to understand those higher capacity cards, which didn't exist when the camera was manufactured. Another problem: SmartMedia cards are wafer thin, somewhat flexible, and have unprotected electrical contacts on the outside of the card. That makes SmartMedia more easily damaged than other kinds of memory. These cards also top out at a capacity of 128MB, so you'll never be able to store a genuinely large number of images on any one card, especially if your camera is a 3-megapixel model. To add insult to injury, SmartMedia writes data quite slowly and comes in two incompatible flavors (3.3- and 5.0-volt versions).

On the other hand, SmartMedia cards are small enough to fit in an adapter that slides into your PC's floppy disk drive or your laptop's PC Card slot, so you can copy images to your PC as if they were stored on a floppy disk. They're also plenty large for 1- and 2-megapixel cameras, especially if you carry a spare card when you go shooting.

Here's the bottom line on SmartMedia cards: I don't like them. Not one bit. Not a lot of digital cameras still use SmartMedia (though Olympus does, unfortunately), and this technology has reached its end of life. In its place, there's a new format, called xD. More about that one in the upcoming section "xD."

CompactFlash

I often call *CompactFlash* the most versatile memory card format on the market. CompactFlash cards are somewhat small, come in a wide range of capacities, and are the most cheaply priced cards to boot.

CompactFlash is the same age as SmartMedia—together, those two formats are the great grandparents of today's mobile storage gadgets. I think CompactFlash is for a good bet for photographers who need to pack a large number of images onto each card. As you can see in the following illustration, CompactFlash is reasonably small (it's about an eighth of an inch thick), yet it comes in capacities up to 4GB— as much storage space as a small hard disk. CompactFlash cards are ideal for high-megapixel cameras and situations in which you can't easily swap out memory cards when the first one is full. (Underwater photography is an excellent example.)

A variation on the CompactFlash format is a small device called the *Microdrive*. IBM's Microdrive is a tiny hard disk packed into the CompactFlash format. Two Microdrives are available: a 340MB and a 1GB card. Not all camera manufacturers certify their cameras to work reliably with the Microdrive, even if the camera accepts the slightly thicker "Type II" CompactFlash cards (which is like the Microdrive), so you should check before investing in one.

Memory Stick

Originally manufactured exclusively by Sony for Sony products, Memory Sticks are slowly starting to catch on. *Memory Sticks* resemble a stick of gum and come in a variety of capacities, from 128MB to 4GB.

Memory Sticks are smartly engineered. They're thin and narrow, like a stick of chewing gum, and they have a "self-cleaning" set of electrical contacts on the end—that means it's hard to damage the Memory Stick, even though the contacts are visible. Thanks to the card's unique shape, you'd have to try very, very hard to insert it into your digital camera incorrectly.

The real appeal of Memory Stick-equipped digital cameras is you can remove the Memory Stick and insert it into any other Sony Memory Stick–enabled device to access your images. Memory Stick products include VAIO laptops, digital picture frames, camcorders, digital cameras, and handheld PCs.

On the other hand, the original Memory Sticks were badly engineered, designed to accommodate a maximum of only 128MB. As a result, Sony recently introduced the *Memory Stick Pro*. Memory Stick Pro cards come in capacities from 256MB to 4GB. Memory Stick Pro is a fast memory format, able to read and write data quickly enough to support DVD-quality video in real time. On the other hand,

9

be careful when getting into Memory Stick territory. Many Memory Stick products can't accept Memory Stick Pro cards—you need to look for the Memory Stick Pro logo on new cameras. Older Memory Sticks work fine in new Memory Stick Pro products, on the other hand.

Secure Digital (SD)

The newest kind of removable memory is called *Secure Digital* (and more commonly referred to by the acronym *SD*). SD is a modern take on the removable memory card problem and offers your digital camera high memory capacities in a footprint about the size of your thumbnail. SD cards are similar to MultiMediaCard (MMC) cards (both share the same overall dimensions, though SD cards are slightly thicker than MMC cards), and most mobile devices are designed to accommodate both formats interchangeably. The principal difference is data encryption: SD cards enable vendors to deliver copyrighted data to the end user while ensuring it can't be illegally copied.

Here's the important part: SD cards, thanks to their small size and reasonable price, are pretty much the standard storage card today. Both Palm and Pocket PC use them in their PDAs, and they are finding their way into most digital cameras and camcorders as well.

xD

When it became clear that the SmartMedia card was ready for the Old Memory Card Home, Olympus and Fuji collaborated on a new memory card format, which they dubbed *xD*. The xD card is SmartMedia's more modern successor, and it appears in several Olympus and FujiFilm cameras. Here's my opinion: the xD card carries the "price premium" you'd expect from a new product line, yet it offers few advantages over other, established memory formats such as SD. xD is certainly the smallest memory card format on the market—which means it can be used to power some very tiny cameras—but it might be a format to avoid for the time being. If I were buying a new digital camera today, I'd pass on an xD model and get one with an SD, CompactFlash, or Memory Stick slot.

Floppy Disk and CD-R

Older Sony digital cameras used the floppy disk drive as a form of image storage. The advantage: floppy disks were ubiquitous. There were no confusing image transfer procedures because you just pulled the floppy out of the camera and inserted it into the PC's floppy disk drive. On the other hand, the floppy disks held only 1.44MB of data—a tiny amount compared to any other memory card format—and were also fairly slow. Those disadvantages added up to cameras

9

Memory Card Glitches

I've heard from readers who complain that their memory cards sometimes seem to "die." If it's stopped working, what's the real problem?

First, remember that some memory cards are pretty delicate. They're wafer-thin, and some have important electrical contacts exposed right on the surface. If you've damaged a card, which isn't altogether out of the question, it's now a really, really small coaster. Throw it away with the knowledge that you can replace it for just a few dollars.

An engineer from a memory card company has told me other possibilities exist as well. It seems that using the same memory card in multiple devices can change the formatting or fill the header information on the card with gibberish, rendering it unable to store digital pictures. So don't use the same card in your MP3 player and digital camera. If you end up with a dead card, you can try to revive the card by using the Format command in the camera's menu system (format it for Fat32). But, if that doesn't work, you're probably out of luck.

that simply couldn't take high-resolution images, and they suffered from a long lag between when the image was taken and when it was written to memory. Such cameras are largely relegated to the dustbin of history, but Sony now sells cameras that write pictures to a recordable CD. These cameras suffer from many of the same limitations as the floppy disk models. They're slow, clumsy, and oversized. My advice? Avoid them.

Choose a Memory Card Format

As mentioned, memory devices vary dramatically in size. In Figure 9-1 you can see the relative sizes of the most common memory formats.

Worth noting is this: in at least a few cases, you needn't choose between different memory storage formats anymore. Some camera makers include both CompactFlash and SmartMedia slots in some of their cameras. Not only does that mean you can pick a camera on features and not worry about whether you like SmartMedia or CompactFlash better, but you can also insert two memory cards in the camera at once and switch from one to the other when one card fills up. The Olympus E-20n (see Figure 9-2) uses just this system, eliminating the traditional confusion over competing memory card formats.

FIGURE 9-1   Relative size of various removable memory cards

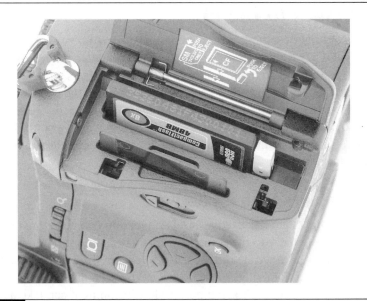

FIGURE 9-2   Most cameras use just one kind of memory, though some models—like the Olympus e-10 and e-20n—accept both SmartMedia and CompactFlash cards for more flexibility and storage space.

With all that said, what kind of memory card should you use? In general, I'd say choosing a specific kind of memory card isn't nearly so important as picking other camera features, such as zoom, optical quality, and useful exposure modes. Of course, I'd definitely avoid cameras based on floppy disk, CD-R, and SmartMedia storage systems. I'm also inclined to avoid xD-only cameras, because those cards cost a bit more than comparable SD and CompactFlash memory. Memory Stick (not Memory Stick Pro) cameras are a bit limiting as well because you're forced to use cards that hold only 128MB or less.

There's little compelling reason to prefer CompactFlash or SD. In my experience, CompactFlash cards are generally the cheapest on the market, and they're also available in higher capacities right now. But history has proven that prices drop and capacities go up for most memory cards, so don't get too hung up on that.

Bottom line? Buy a camera based on other features, and only use the kind of memory card it has as part of your last-look criteria.

Transfer Images to the PC

No matter what kind of digital camera or removable media you use, eventually you need to get your pictures from the camera to a computer, where you'll be able to edit, print, and distribute them. Your digital camera comes with software for transferring images and a cable that you can use to connect the camera to your PC. For many users, this in-the-box solution is all they'll ever need. These days, the de facto standard for transferring images is via USB, though if you find a very old digital camera, it might come with a serial cable. And some high-end pro digitals use FireWire (also known as IEEE-1394).

Transfer Images with a USB Port

In the old days, most cameras used a serial connection cable to transfer pictures from the camera's memory to the computer. That's because most computers—both PC and Macintosh—have serial ports, so camera makers were assured their cameras would work with your computer, no matter what kind you had.

On the downside, your PC's serial port is slow, meaning it can take a long time to copy images from the camera to the computer. The serial port is also kind of stupid. It doesn't know when something is plugged into it, so you have to manually start the software needed to copy images. If you already have a device in the serial port, you might have to disable its software in addition to removing the device. Most computer manufacturers recommend you shut off your PC before you insert and remove cables from the serial port, so that also entails a lot of rebooting.

 *If you're in the market for a new camera, you'll find they're virtually all USB based. You still come across a lot of used cameras with serial connections, though (like on eBay), and I emphatically recommend you avoid them.*

These days, USB is the standard connection system for digital cameras for two good reasons: it avoids most of the headaches associated with serial connections, and it transfers images a lot faster than the old, slow serial ports.

Not only is USB *hot swappable* (which means you needn't power off your PC to insert or remove the USB cable) but, typically, it'll automatically recognize your camera when you connect it and even launch the appropriate transfer software automatically.

In addition, USB ports transfer data at up to 12 Mbps. That's something like 50 times faster than data transfers with the pokey old serial port. In reality, transfers never reach that theoretical maximum speed, but it's a lot faster than serial nonetheless.

Did you
know?

USB 2.0 Versus USB 1.1

The vast majority of computers and digital cameras use a standard called USB 1.1. You might hear about a new form of USB called USB 2.0, though, and it can be a bit confusing.

USB 2.0 is dramatically faster than its older cousin. Instead of 12 Mbps, which is the speed of USB 1.1, USB 2.0 runs at a whopping 450 Mbps. So, if it used to take 5 minutes to transfer your digital images to the PC's hard disk, USB 2.0 will be able to do it in about 10 seconds. Pretty cool, huh?

Unfortunately, for USB 2.0 to work, you need a computer with USB 2.0 ports (most new PCs sold in the last year have them) and a digital camera that's USB 2.0-compliant as well (most digital cameras are still built around USB 1.1). If you use a USB hub to attach lots of USB devices to your PC, that must also be USB 2.0. If any one of those parts is USB 1.1, your image transfers will happen at the regular 12 Mbps speed.

On the plus side, USB 2.0 is 100 percent compatible with USB 1.1, so you can mix and match gear—just remember that if any piece of the puzzle is USB 1.1, all the data is transferred at the slower USB 1.1 speed. USB 2.0 is a big step forward, but not everyone can take advantage of it.

9

USB Glitches

Although USB is susceptible to fewer problems than serial ports, it can occasionally annoy you. The main problems? A lack of power and bandwidth, which can rear its ugly head when you try connecting a lot of USB devices to your computer. Consider these tips:

- **Add more ports.** Most PCs come with only two USB ports. If you have two USB devices connected to your PC, you're already out of ports. Solve that problem by buying a USB hub from the local computer store. A USB hub typically turns one USB connection into four, as you can see in Figure 9-3.

- **Power the ports.** While some USB devices can get power from the USB port itself, many require more power than the USB port can deliver. That's why it's a good idea to use a *powered hub*—that's a USB hub that you plug into AC power. If your USB devices seem to work erratically or if you get warning messages in Windows, be sure to use a powered hub and keep the hub plugged in.

FIGURE 9-3   Belkin's powered USB hub is just one of many options for connecting more USB gadgets than your computer's limited array of USB ports allows.

■ **Distribute your bandwidth.** Your PC probably has two USB ports (though newer computers are beginning to come with more), each of which can transfer up to 12 Mbps of data. If you attach a hub to one of those ports, those four new ports in the hub still have to share the original 12 Mbps of data. If you put four data-hungry devices (a digital camera, a video webcam, a joystick, and a speaker set, for example) on the same hub, they can overtax the USB hub and make it perform erratically. So, if you have a bunch of USB devices, I suggest you put a hub on each port and try to move devices around so the most power-hungry ones aren't all connected to the same port.

Transfer Shortcuts: Use Memory Card Readers

Just because your camera comes with a serial or USB cable, that doesn't mean you have to use it. *Memory card readers*, also called *memory adapters*, are gadgets that let you insert a memory card and read images from it like a floppy disk, and they let you easily transfer images to the computer without messing with any cables at all. Using memory adapters has several advantages:

■ You can conserve camera battery power because the camera isn't used in the transfer.

■ You don't have to get to the back of your computer to connect or disconnect cables.

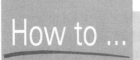 **Connect Your Camera with USB**

If you have a USB-enabled camera and PC, the transfer process is easy. Here's a general overview of how to do it:

1. Start by installing the software that came with your camera. You need to install the software before you plug in the USB cable and the camera for the first time.

2. Connect the USB cable to your computer's USB port and to the camera. You needn't turn off your computer to do this, even if you have to disconnect an existing USB device to free up a port.

3. Turn on the camera and set it to its transfer mode. Connect the camera to AC power if you can.

4. The computer should automatically recognize the camera and start the transfer software. If you haven't installed the special software that came with your camera, Windows itself will usually display a wizard and offer to copy your pictures to the computer. Go ahead and let it do the work for you if you like. If you installed your camera's software, it might have its own picture import wizard; either method works just fine.

■ Transfers might be faster with an adapter.

■ You can avoid confusing transfer software because adapters let you drag-and-drop images directly to a folder on your hard disk.

Choose a Memory Adapter

The kind of memory adapter you choose depends largely on the kind of removable memory your camera uses. In general, they're all more efficient than connecting your camera with a cable.

■ **Desktop single-format card readers**   For $15 or $20, you can get a USB card reader that accepts whatever kind of memory card your digital camera uses. You can get readers for CompactFlash, SmartMedia, SD, Memory Stick, and even xD. The downside? If you ever need to read a different kind of memory card—such as from a second camera or a digital music player—you'll need to buy a second card reader, which will eat up a second USB port and more desk space.

- **Desktop all-in-one readers** Just like cameras that are starting to accommodate more than one kind of memory card, readers are becoming more flexible as well. Universal readers can accommodate six or more kinds of memory cards, making it easy to read and write to cards for your digital camera, MP3 player, and PDA all from the same device. I use my 6-in-1 universal card reader from Dazzle all the time. These multicard readers are almost as inexpensive as single-format readers, usually costing $30 or $40.

- **Internal card readers** For the ultimate in convenience, you can find card readers that fit in one of your PC's empty drive bays. Y-E Data (www.yedata.com), for instance, sells an excellent 7-in-1 reader that packs six kinds of memory card slots into a floppy disk drive. Replace your existing floppy disk drive and have access to any memory card (except xD) right from your PC.

Memory Card: Fact and Fiction

I've met people with some interesting misconceptions about digital film, so let me try to dispel some myths.

Removable memory cards are nothing more than digital storage for your camera. That means memory cards aren't designed to store images of a certain size. Some people mistakenly believe that if they want to store images of a larger or smaller pixel size, they need a different memory card. Memory cards are completely standardized and interchangeable, and they don't particularly care what you store on them. In fact, you don't even have to put digital images on them at all. They'll hold sound files, text documents, and more. Your camera won't know what to do with files like that and, consequently, they'll ignore such files, but you can store anything on a memory card.

Differences exist among memory cards, though. The principal difference is speed—cards are rated at speeds like 2x (slowest), 4x, and 8x (fastest). The faster ones write data faster and are a good choice if you value speed when taking pictures. They're also good for high-megapixel cameras because large files take longer to record. On the other hand, faster cards cost more, and the speed benefits generally aren't measurable unless you have a digital SLR— many other digicams don't take advantage of the faster performance.

9

Care for Your Memory Cards

After you finish transferring images from the memory card to your PC, you no longer need those images. You can delete them to make room for more pictures. You can do this in any one of three ways: you can delete them via the PC, use the camera's controls to delete them, or reformat the card. If your memory card is inserted in the PC via some sort of memory card adapter, using the PC doesn't waste camera battery power, and that's a good reason to do it that way. If you don't have that luxury, a good idea is to plug the camera into its AC adapter so you don't drain your camera's batteries.

To delete images from your memory card via the PC, you can usually just select the files and press the DELETE key on your keyboard. It's just like deleting any kind of file from your PC's floppy or hard disk. But, if you want to format your memory card, only do it on your camera—not on your desktop PC.

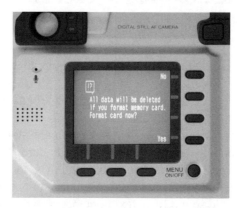

To delete images using the camera's interface, you'll have to navigate the camera's menu system. Typically, you'll have the option of either deleting a single image or all the images on the disk at once. Be careful—this operation can't be undone.

NOTE *If you have some important images on your memory card and you don't want them deleted, you can usually use your camera to protect them. Check your camera's menu system for a feature called "protect" or "lock." That way, you can delete all the images on your memory card, and those specially protected images will remain until you explicitly unprotect them. In general, though, I suggest moving special images to your PC where you'll be less likely to accidentally delete them.*

In addition to deleting images from your memory cards, you should take other precautions to ensure your cards live a long and fruitful life. After all, memory cards can be expensive. Keep the following tips in mind:

- Avoid putting memory cards in direct sunlight.

- Don't put memory cards in your back pocket or other places where they can get bent or crushed. That's particularly true for SmartMedia cards and floppy disks, which can break at moderate force.

- Keep your cards empty whenever possible. All memory cards look alike, and the last thing you need is to put a memory card in your camera while you're on vacation only to discover it's still full of images you never saved to your PC from last time. Transfer images to the PC promptly, and then format or erase the card.

■ Never write on memory cards or put any kind of sticker on them to track their contents. That can damage the card or the camera.

Recover Lost Pictures

Have you ever accidentally deleted an important file, noticing it was gone an instant after you sent it irretrievably to the trash? All you can do is shout, "d'oh!"

The same thing can happen to pictures on a memory card. Thankfully, when you erase a card, the files aren't necessarily gone right away—the memory card simply "forgets" it's holding data. If you need to get back lost images, there are several programs to choose from. All are inexpensive and work very well:

■ **ImageRecall**   www.flashfixers.com

■ **Photorecovery**   www.lc-tech.com

■ **Digital PhotoRescue**   www.objectrescue.com

These simple programs (such as ImageRecall, shown in the following illustration) recover deleted images, movies, and other data from removable memory cards. And they all work with any kind of removable media, from SmartMedia and Compact Flash to Memory Stick and SD Cards.

No matter which program you choose, they all scan the contents of your card, restoring lost files to a folder on your PC's hard disk. I've tried all three, and they work. In fact, a friend of mine once sent me a card he believed was corrupt—after he filled it with pictures, the PC reported no images were on board. I used ImageRecall to get a batch of photos back. My friend was quite grateful.

Just remember, if you plan to run a photo recovery program on a memory card, do it before you use the card for anything else. Adding new data to your card can damage "deleted" pictures already on the card, lowering the odds that you'll get anything useful from the recovery process.

What are the odds you'll ever need one of these programs? Pretty low, I suspect. But if you do find yourself with a dead memory card or lost pictures, it might be worth a try.

Travel with Pictures

It's one thing to travel with a memory card or two and a digital camera—it's quite another thing to have so many memory cards that your pockets jangle when you walk. But if you're traveling for a while, such as on a vacation trip, how can you have enough memory space to take all the pictures you need without running out of room? Instead of taking a half dozen 256MB memory cards, I have a better solution: take a storage device that you can use to transfer your pictures to, and then erase your card and start anew.

Several gadgets are on the market that can store your digital images while you're on the road. These devices have memory slots to accept images from your memory cards and securely store your images until you can get home and transfer the data to your PC. Here are some you might want to consider:

- **Portable Digital Image Backup (www.ezpnp.com)** This is my favorite gadget. It's a portable CD recorder that accepts AC power or AA batteries. Insert your memory card and press the Record button—the contents of the card will be written to a folder on the CD-R, after which you can erase the card and continue shooting pictures. I like this device because, compared to a portable hard disk, a CD-R is essentially indestructible—it won't break from rough handling.

- **eFilm PicturePad (www.delkin.com)** This handheld, battery-operated gadget stores massive amounts of digital images and includes an LCD display that lets you preview your images while you're still on the road.

- **Nixvue (www.nixvue.com)** Nixvue is a company that offers both kinds of storage devices—CD-R–based and hard disk–based solutions. The *Vizor* records images to disk, while the *Vista* is a portable hard disk with an integrated LCD. The *Digital Album II* is a hard disk without the LCD display, but it has video outputs for connecting to a television.

Chapter 10

Finding and Organizing Your Pictures

How to...

- Use the My Pictures folder

- Organize your images in Windows

- Transfer, rename, and categorize your images to reduce clutter

- Browse images visually with your favorite image editor

- Search for images more easily using keywords

- Use the Picture and Fax Viewer to see pictures without opening an image-editing program

- Estimate file size for TIF and JPG images

- Archive your pictures on CD-ROM

- Install a new hard disk for additional storage

- Back up your photos

In the previous chapter, we talked about how to get images from your camera or its memory card onto your PC. That's a good start, but if you're anything like me, you need some help getting it all under control. Digital images proliferate like bunnies and can be hard to organize. After just a few months, in fact, you might discover that your computer's hard disk is essentially full, and the unorganized mess within is largely a ton of poorly named, hard-to-decipher digital images that don't do anyone any good.

In this chapter, we'll talk about the essentials of getting your stockpile of digital images under control. You have a lot of things to consider: naming and arranging your images, using special software to better arrange and organize your images, and understanding the relationship between image size and file size so you can predict how much space you'll need. And, because you might eventually need to add on to your PC's storage capability, we'll talk about how you can archive your images on media such as CD-ROMs and additional hard drives.

Organize Your Digital Pictures

Keeping your hard disk organized is essential if you hope to find your digital pictures. In a sense, then, part of this chapter is a tutorial in managing the lives of your digital photos.

I know a lot of people who don't worry too much about organizing their hard disks. They just download images from their camera to some folder on their hard disks and assume they can find what they need later. The problem? The images from your camera typically have fairly obscure filenames, like pic00012.jpg or dsc0012.jpg (see Figure 10-1). It's impossible to determine the contents of

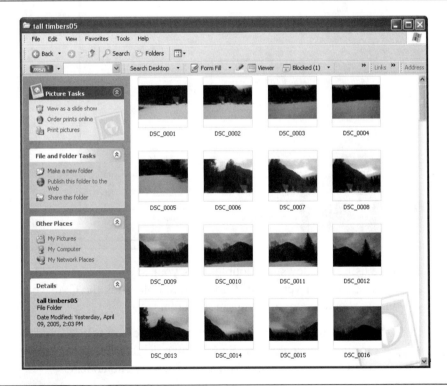

FIGURE 10-1   Your digital camera's code-like naming scheme for images is of no help when you want to find a specific picture.

an image from such an arcane filename. Imagine having hundreds or even thousands of files like this on your hard disk and you start to get an inkling of the problem.

To create folders to store your images in Windows, do this:

1. Click Start and then click My Computer. You should see a window that displays all the devices and drives connected to your PC:

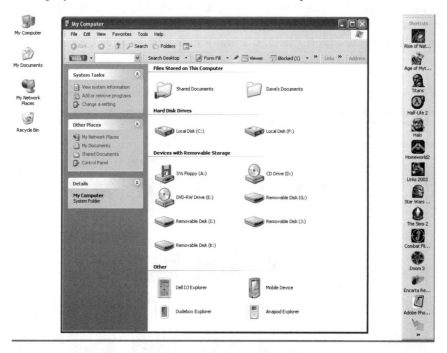

2. If you're using Windows XP, double-click your My Documents folder. If you have an older version of Windows, double-click the C: drive. A window should open, revealing more folders.

3. If you don't see a folder called My Pictures, the default folder Windows supplies for images, you can create your own. Right-click on an empty space in the C: drive's window. You should see a menu appear.

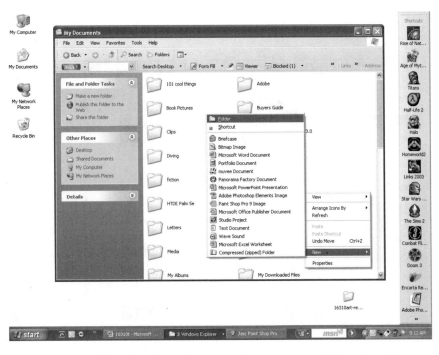

4. Choose New | Folder from the menu. A new, empty folder should appear in the C: drive window.

5. Now it's time to rename the folder. The New Folder text under the folder is highlighted. Type **My Pictures** and press ENTER. You should see the name of the folder change.

 *If you click on the desktop before you have a chance to rename the new folder, just right-click on the folder and choose Rename from the menu. Then type the new name of the folder.*

You can store your images anywhere, but I think that a My Pictures folder is a great place. It's easy to remember, and many image-editing programs will automatically look here for pictures.

Now that you have a main folder for storing your images, you might want to create subfolders, which are folders inside your main folder (like My Pictures) that let you organize your pictures more precisely. As you can see in Figure 10-2, I tend to organize my images into myriad folders that help me find specific images by category, event, purpose, and genre.

10

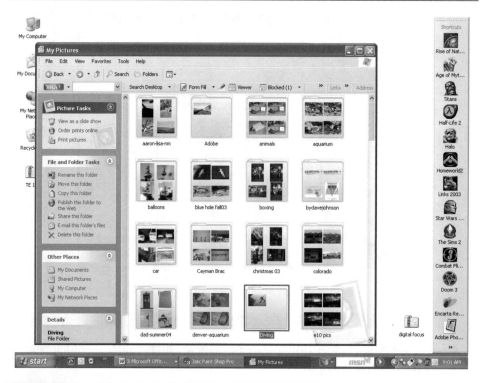

FIGURE 10-2 The more subfolders you use, the easier it can be to find the right image in a pinch.

Rename Images

Now that you have a basic organizational system for arranging your images, it's time to think about filenames. I suggest that when you transfer your images to the PC, you immediately rename them and categorize them into specific folders. Don't put this off till later! If you transfer images and opt to rename them later, you'll end up with a few batches of photos with obscure filenames that need to be renamed. If each batch has 20 or 30 pictures in it, that's a lot of work. The task will eventually get too daunting.

Here's an easy strategy for renaming your images:

1. Open the folder in which your newly transferred images are stored.

2. If you're using Windows Me or Windows XP, you should be able to see a preview of the image in the folder. If you can't, choose View | Filmstrip

or View | Thumbnails from the folder's menu. Look at the first image and decide what you want to name it.

3. Click the image, pause, and, after a second, click the image's name. Don't simply double-click, or the image will open. If you did this step properly, the filename should be ready to edit. Type the name of the file and press the ENTER key.

If this technique doesn't work for you, right-click the image and choose Rename from the menu.

4. Repeat the process with the other images in the folder.

5. When you're done, you can drag images into an appropriate subfolder in the My Pictures folder and delete the empty temporary folder.

If you want a better view of a picture in the folder, you can always just double-click it. Windows will display it in the Windows Picture and Fax Viewer, as shown here. You can use the scroll wheel on your mouse to zoom in and out when in the viewer.

10

If you're using an older version of Windows, you don't get the fancy image preview tools that Windows Me and Windows XP users see. Instead, you can access the contents of each image as you rename it by using the Quick View tool from the menu. Just right-click each picture and choose Quick View from the menu. Then close the Quick View preview of your image and rename the photo.

Finally, keep in mind that if you install certain programs, they can replace the built-in Windows picture viewer with their own picture viewing utility. If you install ACDSee to manage your images, for instance, it'll substitute its own image viewer.

If that happens to you, you can always reset Windows by right-clicking a photo, choosing Open With | Choose Program, and then setting it back to the Picture and Fax Viewer. Don't forget to click the option to always use the selected program.

Faster Renaming

Ideally, you'll rename all your photos as you transfer them to your PC; that way, it's a bit easier to find them whenever you need a specific image. But let's be honest, sometimes that's just a bit too much work. If you simply want to change the name of your files from totally indecipherable (like P7281775) to something that reflects the overall theme of the batch (like Summer Vacation), then you can do that as well.

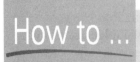

Preview Pictures with the Picture and Fax Viewer

Windows comes with a built-in photo viewer that makes it easy to preview your images without opening a dedicated image-editing program. Using it couldn't be simpler—just double click on any photo icon, and the Picture and Fax Viewer automatically starts.

Don't forget that there is a slew of handy tools at the bottom of the viewer. You can use the Next and Previous buttons to advance through a folder full of pictures, for instance. You can also launch the pictures in a full-screen slideshow and zoom in or out for a better view. Most conveniently, you can rotate pictures that were taken with the camera on its side by 90 degrees.

What of the "fax viewing"? If you have a multipage TIF file, the kind of files made by fax software, it will open automatically in the Picture and Fax Viewer as well, and you can use a special set of tools in the program to change pages and "mark up" the fax with special annotations.

Select all the photos in the folder. You can do that by choosing Edit | Select All from the folder's menu, or you can click the first picture in the folder, scroll to the last image, and click again, holding down the SHIFT button on your keyboard. *SHIFT-selecting*, as it's called, lets you choose all the files between the first and last click in a single action.

Only want to select a few images? Use the CTRL key on your keyboard and click to CONTROL-select only certain images. Or, select all the images and use the CTRL key to deselect the images you don't want!

Right-click one of the selected images—it doesn't matter which one—and choose Rename from the menu. Type a new name and press the ENTER key. Your pictures will all be given the new name, with a number in parentheses so you can tell them apart.

Locate Images

Even with a rigorous set of subfolders, it can get difficult to find specific images on your hard disk. My hard disk contains many hundreds of images, for instance, and even with descriptive filenames and lots of aptly titled subfolders, it can be a challenge to locate "that picture of the two wolves frolicking in the fallen leaves" I took two years ago. It's akin to finding a needle within a stack of other needles.

Filenames and folders are great, but there's no substitute for looking at your images. That's why I'm going to show you how you can catalog your images with a visual tool—software that lets you view your pictures directly, all at once, and open the one you need without delay.

Locate Your Images with Your Image Editor

Many popular image editors make it easy to find your photos visually with some sort of thumbnail-based file browser. My two favorite image editors—Corel Paint Shop Pro and Adobe Photoshop Elements—have such a feature. These are far more powerful than simply rooting through folder in Windows, because these programs display all of your images in a single view—something Windows can't do if you use more than one folder to manage your pictures. These programs also include powerful ways to sort, group, and organize your images for easy reference.

Use Paint Shop Pro's Image Browser   One great reason to use one of these programs is the capability to browse your images visually. Paint Shop Pro's Browse tool, shown

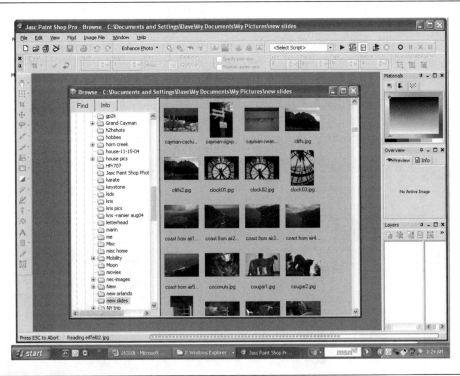

FIGURE 10-3   Paint Shop Pro lets you browse your hard disk visually.

in Figure 10-3, lets you see the images on your hard disk graphically, with each image represented by a thumbnail. That means you can use Browse in two ways:

- If you want to edit or print an image, you can use the Browse tool to find an image visually, without needing to know the filename.

- If you just want to review your images, you can use the Browse tool to see your image thumbnails.

Here is how to use Paint Shop Pro's Browse tool:

1. Start Paint Shop Pro.

2. Choose File | Browse from the menu. The Browse window should appear.

3. Use the folder tree on the left side of the window to find the folder you want to look in. When you click the folder, thumbnail images will appear on the right. To view images in My Pictures (where Windows XP commonly stores images), for instance, you would click its folder on the left, under Desktop, and click to see all the subfolders stored within.

4. To open an image in Paint Shop Pro, just double-click a thumbnail or click-and-drag it to the Paint Shop Pro workspace. The image will open, ready for editing, printing, or just viewing at a larger size.

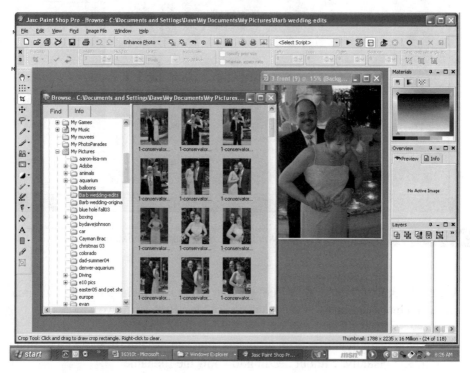

5. You can continue opening additional images from the Browse window. Close the Browse window when you're done with it.

 *You can right-click image thumbnails in the Browse window to perform many common operations, such as print, rename, and rotate.*

Use Photoshop Element's Image Browser   If you use Adobe Photoshop Elements, you'll find a similar browse tool under the hood of that program as well. Just choose Window | File Browser, and you'll get access to all the folders on your hard disk

To give your action photos a sense of motion and activity, use your image editor's Motion Blur filter. To control the effect, add the blur in a separate layer and then use the Eraser tool to blend the two images together. Read about this technique in Chapter 13.

Shoot at night

Night photography is very rewarding and can be done with any kind of digital camera—even a point-and-shoot, all-automatic model. For best results, use a tripod and turn off the flash. The longer the shutter remains open, the brighter the lights will appear in the picture—which can lead to interesting light trails when you shoot moving subjects. See Chapter 4 for details.

Your camera's macro mode (usually indicated by the tulip symbol) lets you take bigger-than-life photos of small objects such as insects, stamps, coins, flowers, and jewelry. Remember that the depth of field is very shallow, so careful focusing is a must. Chapter 5 has more information.

When you master tools like selections and layers, you can do all kinds of special effects easily—such as replacing the ugly gray sky in your photos with one from a bright, blue day. Here, I simply used the Magic Wand to select the uniform gray sky, copied the blue sky image, and then pasted it into the selection. Read more about these kinds of techniques in Chapter 12.

Punch up your photos with the histogram

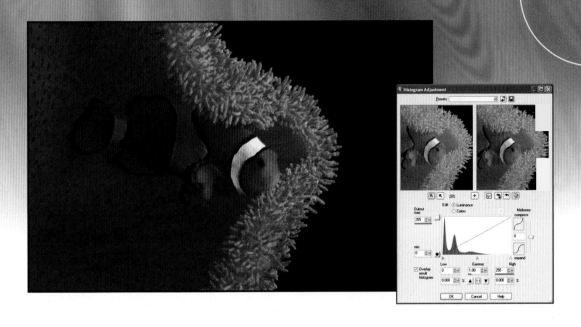

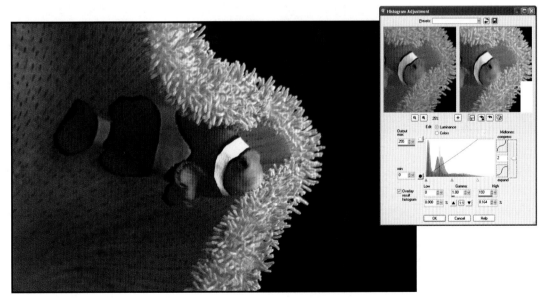

The histogram displays your photo's exposure in a graph. You can use this graphical display to see if your picture is badly under- or overexposed, and even to improve your photos after you transfer them to your computer. Learn how to do this in Chapter 13.

See the world differently

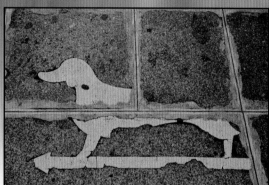

We often fall into the trap of taking the same kinds of pictures over and over. Think differently and try to capture photos with unusual subjects, perspectives, or composition. Instead of freeze-framing your kids, for instance, try including motion. Look for unusual photos in everyday objects such as signs on the street. And don't forget that framing is important—remember the Rule of Thirds. Or try taking a bizarre portrait in a mirror. Learn more in Chapter 3.

While you're experimenting with your image editor, go all out for some wacky special effects. In this photo, I've erased the houses and sky and replaced them with a different background. I also painted the grass a lusher green and then used layers and feathering to disintegrate one of the young actors. Read all about it in Chapter 13.

Redesign reality

Don't like the way your town looks? Then rebuild it on your PC with your digital photos. It only took me about five minutes to combine this cityscape of Seattle—which showed a distant, underwhelming view of Mount Rainer—with this zoomed-in, dramatic shot of the same mountain. Learn how to make images like this in Chapters 12 and 13.

in a drop-down window. Navigate to your My Pictures folder (it's probably in My Documents) and you can surf around your images.

Be sure to notice that you can go "up" to the previous folder via the small Up Folder button atop the screen, and you can choose other, recently chosen folders from the folder drop-down menu as well.

When you're ready to work with an image, you can double-click to open it or just click-and-drag it to the Photoshop Elements workspace.

Use Photo Organizing Software

If your collection of digital images is large enough—and by large enough, I mean you have more than a hundred or so photos—you might feel constrained by the file browsers in programs such as Paint Shop Pro and Photoshop Elements. If you have a few thousand images in your library, consider a dedicated photo album program.

What does a photo organizer do for you? Well, instead of trying to remember in which of dozens of folders you've potentially stored a particular photo, photo organizer software shows you your entire photo library at once. And a variety of organization tools make it easy to narrow down your search and find exactly the picture you need quickly.

10

I have become a huge fan of photo organizers. So many times I hear people tell me, "I wish it were easier to find a photo on my computer"—but they haven't given their pictures logical names, have dispersed photos across two dozen folders, and don't have any way to locate what they need aside from just browsing each folder by hand. That's hard work.

Instead, get a photo organizer. You have a number to choose from, though; here are my favorites:

- **ACDSee**   www.acdsee.com

- **Extensis Portfolio**   www.extensis.com

- **Adobe Photoshop Album (included in Photoshop Elements Premier)**   www.adobe.com

- **Microsoft Digital Image Library (included in Digital Image Suite)**   www.microsoft.com

- **Corel Paint Shop Photo Album**   www.corel.com

Using any of these programs, you can search for images visually, by keyword, or by filename. You can drag-and-drop images directly into your editor for modification or printing, and you can generate web pages based on your digital image thumbnails automatically, with little effort. A long-time favorite among digital photographers is ACDSee, which combines ease of use with powerful cataloging tools and some basic image-editing features.

Portfolio, on the other hand, is the most sophisticated of these programs, and is probably a good bet only for photographers who are truly serious about organizing their images and have many thousands of pictures to keep track of. Portfolio has the capability to automatically update its database with new pictures as they're added to your hard disk with no intervention on your part, and a small browser program sits in your System Tray, ready to find images at a moment's notice. Although it's the most expensive program in its class, Portfolio is the best for those who work with tons of photos, if for no other reason than its automatic update feature. With other programs, like Photoshop Album, you'll need to tell the program to locate new pictures every time you add some to your PC from a digital camera.

Adobe's Photoshop Album (available separately or included with Photoshop Elements) is also pretty cool, and works well for most users. Photoshop Album uses a clever drag-and-drop keyword system. Instead of painstakingly typing the same keywords into each of your picture's Properties boxes over and over, you create a bunch of "tags" and then drag them onto pictures that should match that particular criteria. In this way, you can quickly create a few dozen common tags (such as "family," "kids," "pets," "vacation," and so forth) and associate multiple tags with each image. When you want to find a picture of your kids on vacation, select those tow tags and click the search button—it's that easy. The program also has a great calendar-based search feature that lets you locate images according to when they were taken, just by dragging arrows around on a timeline.

My personal favorite is Digital Image Suite Library (included with Digital Image Suite), from Microsoft. This program has a simple but powerful keyword painter—just select the keywords you want to assign to a picture and then click the pictures to assign them. You can also filter the view by keyword to narrow down your search. And the program has a great hover preview—whenever the mouse finds its way over a picture in the thumbnail view, a larger preview pops up so you can see more details in the photo. I highly recommend getting Digital Image Library, even if you don't use the editor program that comes with it.

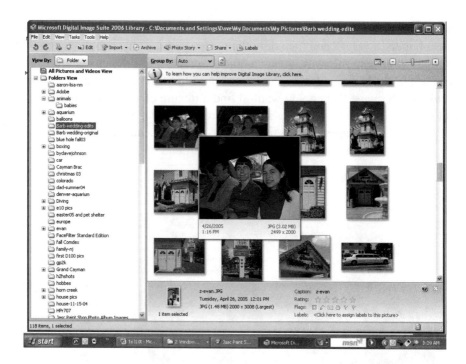

Use Keywords

A *keyword* is a term you can use to identify the contents, theme, or style of an image. Suppose you have this witty picture, for instance:

May contain peanuts.

You might want to associate the following keywords with this image: **peanut**, **funny**, **macro**. When you search for all your pictures that have the word "funny" or "peanut" in their description, this image should appear in the list. Keywords are a manual operation, though. You need to decide what keywords to use and enter them all by hand in whatever program you use that supports this feature. But if your cataloging software supports keywords, a little effort up front can make it quite easy to find that proverbial needle in the haystack.

Estimate File Size

So, you save a lot of images on your hard disk. How many can you pack in before you need more storage space?

That isn't necessarily an easy question to answer. That's because the most common file formats, like JPG, don't always save an image to the same file size. The size that any particular image takes up on your hard disk will vary, depending on how much color information is stored in the image. A single-color image, such as a graphic that's plain, solid blue, will compress dramatically to a miniscule size, while a complex image won't compress as efficiently. Nonetheless, you can make some ballpark estimates that will help you keep track of storage space if you want to.

Calculate TIFs

You might remember from Chapter 8 that some file formats—particularly TIF—are considered lossless. That means that no matter how many times you open and resave a TIF picture, no loss of data will ever occur; the picture will always look exactly the same as the day you shot it. That's because the image isn't being compressed in a way that destroys information in the original image. Every pixel is preserved forever (unless you intentionally edit the picture to change those pixels, of course). The most common lossless file formats are BMP and TIF files. To figure out how much space either of these files will take up, consider this handy-dandy chart:

Picture Size (in Megapixels)	Picture Dimensions (in Pixels)	File Size (in Megabytes)
2	1600X1200	5.8MB
3	2018X1536	9.4MB
5	2560X1920	14.7MB
8	3504X2336	24.5MB

10

The rule for figuring the file size of a TIF is pretty simple. To apply it to any picture, regardless of how many megabytes it is, just multiply the height and width of the picture (in pixels), then multiply that by 24, and then divide the result by 800,000. You'll get the file size, in megabytes. I doubt you'll have to whip out the old calculator very often, though—just know that TIF images tend to make big files that you generally need to measure in the double digits.

Calculate JPGs

That's all well and good but, most of the time, you'll probably have your digital camera set to shoot in the lossy file format known as JPG. JPG files can be adjusted to compress more aggressively—that makes the files smaller but the quality lower— or compress less for bigger, higher-quality files.

There's no easy equation you can use on JPGs, because the compression varies not only according to the image quality setting you use on your camera, but also according to the amount of color information, sharpness, and overall complexity of the picture. Nonetheless, I'll take a stab at it. Consider a typical 5-megapixel picture. Here's what sizes you would get at varying levels of JPG compression (remember that saved as a TIF, this picture would be almost 15MB):

Compression Level	Approximate Setting (in an Image-Editing Program)	File Size (in Megabytes)	Comments
Low	1	2.93MB	Great for "archive quality." Virtually identical to the original TIF.
Medium	15	816KB	Adequate for routine use.
High	50	221KB	Not recommended.
Insanely high	75	126KB	Picture has such obvious defects that you wouldn't ever use this setting.

What does this say about how you should store your images? In general, high-quality JPGs are good enough for most applications, and they take up a mere fraction of the space TIFs or BMP files would consume. When you can, use the JPG format, and your hard disk will thank you. Be careful about using too much JPG compression, though. I recommend sticking with a fairly low compression level, or your image quality will suffer.

Archive Images

Eventually, your collection of digital images could grow too large for your hard disk. If that's the case, you have a few choices:

- Delete nonessential images from your hard disk.

- Archive the images on another storage device, such as a CD or DVD.

- Add another hard disk for additional storage space.

Deleting images is the easiest route, but it has the least potential. You probably want to save most of your images forever, so you might not want to use deleting as a routine housekeeping option. Instead, consider archiving your images to another device. If you have a CD-RW or DVD-R/RW drive, you can copy dozens or hundreds of images to a disk (depending on the file size) that will last more or less forever. CDs do degrade over time, but they will last for a hundred years or so—longer than the ink on many kinds of photographs. To be sure your images are protected, you can duplicate your CD or DVD every few years—or, more realistically, transfer the images to whatever technology is popular then, like nuclear bionic laser holographic kneepads. Or whatever.

A *CD-RW drive* is a kind of CD drive that can write to blank disks, while *DVD writers* come in several varieties—the most common of which is DVD-R/RW and DVD-RAM. Most of these drives come with software like Adaptec's Easy CD and DVD Creator (www.adaptec.com), shown in Figure 10-4, or perhaps Nero (www .nero.com). These programs let you simply drag-and-drop image files from the hard disk to the CD and then "burn" the disk, a process that takes a few minutes to copy all the data to the CD. After it's done, the CD-R is playable in any computer with a CD-ROM drive.

If you have Windows XP and a CD-RW drive, you don't even need any additional software—just open a folder with images and select the images you want to copy to CD. Then click Copy to CD from the Picture Tasks pane on the left side of the folder. After a few moments, you'll see a balloon in the System Tray that says "You have files waiting to be written to the CD." Place a blank CD in your drive and open My Computer. Right-click the blank CD and choose Write These Files to CD. It's a bit more complicated than using a program like Roxio or Nero, but it's free.

10

FIGURE 10-4   CD burning software makes it easy to copy blank images to a CD.

When you archive your images onto CD, be sure to use CD-R, not CD-RW. The two media are quite different, and CD-RWs are generally not readable on other PCs. In addition, data copied to CD-RW can be deleted, so it's possible to accidentally overwrite your images later. To be safe, always use CD-R media, which are cheaper anyway. On the DVD front, the same is true of DVD-R and DVD-RW; use DVD-R, which is cheaper, can't be erased, and is more universally compatible.

Add Extra Hard Drives

One other option you might consider is adding another hard disk. Hard drives get cheaper and bigger every year, and these days 200GB drives are neither unusual nor particularly expensive. Some people install a second drive and dedicate it for images, video, music, and other multimedia files.

To see if your PC is a good candidate for a second hard disk, shut it down and open it up. Many computers have tool-free cases that you can open easily; other PCs

Did you know?

Pixel Potential

If you photograph a plain white background, in JPG format it'll take up almost no space at all on your memory card or computer hard disk. That's because the JPG format stores information about the change in color information from one pixel to another, and if the image is all white there's little changed data to record. But what about a TIF? The same picture stored as a TIF will be much larger, because the file holds a space for all 24 bits of color data in each pixel. The TIF format isn't concerned about the colors in the image; instead, it's preoccupied with the potential colors that could be in the image. Even though every pixel is white, the TIF format has enough room to store any color in each and every pixel. TIF files compress quite nicely using a ZIP program, though, so you can save a file in TIF format and "zip it up" to e-mail it to someone.

require a small screwdriver to remove the side of the case. In either case, once the PC is open, check to see if there's a spare bay to mount the hard disk. You can mount it in one of the drive bays or perhaps on the bottom or side of the case, where there are some mounts for exactly that purpose. If there's somewhere to put a hard disk, it's easy to install yourself.

TIP
If you don't want to mess around inside your PC, you can add an external hard disk instead. These days, USB 2.0 (discussed in Chapter 9) and FireWire (also known as i.Link or IEEE1394) hard disks are fast, inexpensive, and install in just minutes by doing nothing more than plugging in a cable. I highly recommend these sorts of external drives.

Once you've found somewhere to put the drive, follow these basic steps:

1. Ensure that the PC is turned off and you are fully grounded before proceeding. You can purchase a static grounding mat or a strap that attaches to your wrist at any local computer shop. Alternatively, you can ground yourself by touching the metal cage surrounding the computer's power supply as long as the computer is plugged into the wall outlet. If you leave the computer plugged in for grounding purposes, be absolutely sure the computer is turned off before you open it and start working.

10

2. Remove the new hard disk from its packaging and review the instructions that came with it.

3. Configure the hard disk depending on how you're installing it and the sort of PC you have. If your computer is new, it might use Serial ATA (SATA), a faster, smarter, more modern way to connect hard disks. You can only connect one hard drive to each long and thin SATA cable, which dramatically simplifies the installation process. These drives are a snap to attach. If you have an older PC with a traditional, wide ATA ribbon cable, you usually need to set the hard disk's jumper on CS (cable select).

4. Mount the drive in the PC. Connect the power cable and data cable to the hard disk.

5. Without closing the case, turn on the computer. When the PC starts to boot, display the BIOS screen (usually by pressing the DELETE or F1 key as your computer starts to boot) and check to see that the computer recognizes the hard disk. If it doesn't, make sure you have set the jumper properly, that it's connected to the correct IDE channel, and that the power cord is fully inserted in the hard disk.

6. If all is well, shut down the PC and seal the case.

7. Finally, use the software that came with your hard disk to format the drive and prepare it for operation in Windows.

Protect Your Pictures Using Backups

There's one problem with using a hard disk to store your digital photos: eventually they all fail. No matter how new, fancy, or expensive your hard disk is, a day will inevitably come when it stops spinning. Hopefully, you'll buy a new computer and transfer all your data to its fresh, new hard drive before that happens.

But if you keep your computer for a very long time—say, more than 5 years—the odds increase that your hard drive may fail while you're still using it. And when that happens, all your pictures—unless they're also backed up somewhere else, like on another hard disk or on a CD-R—will be lost and gone forever. That's why I'm a big advocate of using some sort of regular backup system in your computer.

Use a Backup Program

One easy solution is to get a backup program that can run routinely and automatically at a set time each day or week. I like a program called Casper XP, which you can download from www.fssdev.com. When you run Casper, you can tell it to automatically run once a week (say, every Friday evening at 9:00 P.M.) and back up automatically to a second hard drive on your PC. It's pretty painless. (If you prefer, you can also use a program like Nero or Roxio to back up your hard drive, since those programs come with many new computers.)

Install RAID

Once you get past the initial setup, using a RAID drive is even easier. What, exactly, is RAID? RAID stands for Redundant Array of Inexpensive Disks. It is a combination of two or more hard drives, controlled in such a way that they act as one virtual drive. Long used just by large businesses, RAID systems have traditionally been too expensive and complicated for normal folk like us. That has changed, though, and RAID now offers a way to painlessly and securely back up 100 percent of your data (including digital images) in real time, with absolutely no effort on your part. No more delayed backups, tape rotation schemes, archives of CD-Rs, or forgotten data files. And unlike a backup solution like Casper, the backups happen continuously, so there's no worry of not getting a backup made because the PC wasn't on during a scheduled backup. In many ways, RAID is the perfect backup solution.

There are many flavors of RAID, usually referred to as "RAID implementations" or "RAID levels." Large businesses have about a dozen RAID levels to choose from, each designed for some specific purpose. RAID 6, for instance, delivers "independent data disks with two independent distributed parity schemes." If you need that, you'll want to find a good book on RAID—I can't help you. I don't even know what that sentence means.

But more typical users, like you and me, can choose from three handy RAID levels. RAID 0 is called a *striped array*, and it writes alternating blocks of data across two separate hard drives. The result? Two 120GB hard disks will appear as a single 240GB hard disk in Windows, for instance. And because the data is being distributed across multiple channels, data access is much faster than if you

10

had a single, large hard disk drive. The downside, of course, is if either drive fails, 100 percent of your data is irretrievably lost unless you maintain a separate backup solution. RAID 0 is the most vulnerable way imaginable to store your data. And that's not our goal.

Instead, you want RAID 1. This *mirror array* treats two identical hard drives as a single drive and writes the same data twice, once to each physical drive. While there's no performance advantage like you get with RAID 0, there's no penalty, either. That's in stark contrast to mirroring data to a second drive using backup software, which uses system resources and slows your PC in a noticeable way. If one drive ever fails with a RAID 1 array, your PC continues functioning as if nothing ever happened, and all your images are preserved. Of course, you're warned during the PC's boot sequence if the RAID array isn't running perfectly, so you know it's time to replace the bad drive.

The final option, RAID 0+1, is the most expensive solution. Using an array of four drives, RAID 0+1 stripes data to one pair of drives, while duplicating everything on the second pair. The result: higher overall performance, while also maintaining a real-time backup. The downside, of course, is that you must purchase four identical hard drives.

To install a RAID system on your PC, you'll typically need a RAID controller card and two or perhaps even four *absolutely* identical hard disk drives—they should be the same brand and model number. Installing it isn't difficult, but if you aren't handy inside a PC, you might want to take it in to a shop for the surgery.

NOTE   *If your RAID 1 hard disk is ever infected by a nasty virus or gets corrupted, both drives will be equally affected—so it isn't a bad idea to conduct periodic backups of your hard disk in addition. What RAID does is ensure you'll never get stung by a physical failure of your hard disk—and that's very reassuring, to say the least.*

Part III

Editing Images

Chapter 11

Quick Changes for Your Images

How to...

- ■ Determine what the system requirements are to edit images on a PC
- ■ Choose an image-editing program
- ■ Open and edit images in Paint Shop Pro
- ■ Change the resolution of digital images for e-mail, web, and other applications
- ■ Change the number of colors that can be displayed in an image
- ■ Save an image in a different file format
- ■ Crop images to improve composition
- ■ Crop and copy an image into a new file
- ■ Create an irregular crop
- ■ Rotate images taken with the camera on its side
- ■ Fix a crooked image
- ■ Change the brightness in an image
- ■ Correct the color balance in a picture

One of the most exciting advantages of using a digital camera is the flexibility and control it gives you for tweaking and improving your images. Don't like your composition? Change it. You can crop your pictures just a little to subtly improve their appearance or radically change the look of a picture by turning its orientation from landscape to portrait. You can fix a crooked horizon, resize an image for e-mail, tweak the colors in or brightness of an image—it's all up to you.

These are things that, until recently, you needed a darkroom and a whole lot of practice to do right, and every attempt would cost you money in photo paper and chemicals. These days, you can experiment endlessly. It never costs you a penny until you're ready to print the final result because it's all done with pixels on a computer screen. As long as you're careful not to save over the original file, you also never have to damage or change the original image.

In this chapter, we'll get started with image editing. This is the place to turn to for the most common kinds of corrections—simple things you can do to your images without learning a whole lot about the art and science of image editing. For more sophisticated things you can do to edit your images, check out Chapters 12, 13, and 14, which get into the topic a little more deeply.

How Much PC You Need

You're probably expecting me to tell you that you should have the fastest PC you can afford—a 10 GHz Pentium 5 is just about right. Aside from the fact that computers haven't gotten that fast yet, you don't need quite that much speed. To be perfectly honest, you *should* work with the fastest PC you can afford. Image editing, especially with high-megapixel images, is a horsepower-intensive task. The more computer you have pushing pixels around, the more fun you'll have. A slow PC might frustrate you because it'll take a long time to perform editing operations and it'll even take a while to redraw the screen.

Here's what I think you should have, as a minimum, to do image editing without getting an ulcer:

■ **Pentium 4 processor**   I used to do image editing on a sluggish 200 MHz Pentium (now known as a Pentium Classic), so it can obviously be done. But it's slow. Really slow. A much better configuration: you should have a Pentium 4 processor to push all those pixels around.

■ **512MB of RAM**   This is the minimum, and many less-expensive PCs come with this amount of memory, but here's where spending a little extra can really pay off if you can afford it. If you can upgrade to a full gigabyte of RAM (which costs about $100, and you can install it yourself if you want to), image editing will seem much faster, even on a slower processor. That's because high-megapixel images occupy lots of room in memory, and if they can't fit there, Windows stores parts of them on the hard disk. That can make something as simple as a screen redraw drag on forever. Is there value in having a gigabyte of memory? There sure is—if you have several large images open at once, your system won't slow down as it would with less memory. On this count, you're in luck: many new PCs come with 1GB of memory to start with.

■ **200GB hard drive**   They're really cheap now, so you should have lots of room to store your images. The bigger the better, but unless you also want to make digital video, you probably don't need a monster 400GB hard disk. Your best bet: get a pair of matching 200GB or 300GB hard drives, so you can automatically back up the data on one drive on to the other, which can become your built-in backup drive. I talk about this at the end of Chapter 10. A second hard disk or a disk burner (like CD-RW or DVD-RW) for archiving old images can come in handy as well.

11

Choose an Image Editor

Before you can get started editing images, you need an image-editing program. Any one will do, at least at first. For the most part, all image editors give you the capability to do certain things, such as:

- Resize and crop your images

- Select specific regions of a picture and apply changes just to those instead of the entire image

- Apply "paint" to your image, using a set of brushes and other paint tools

- Add text and other graphics

- Delete parts of the image, which you can use to crop and change the composition

- Combine multiple images into a new composition

- Use tonal controls to change aspects of your image, like the brightness and contrast

That's certainly a quick overview of image editing, but the point is that a lot of image editors are around that can get the job done. Which one is for you? Well, you might want to start with a free one. If your digital camera came with an image editor of some sort, you might want to give it a spin and see if you like the way it works.

Ultimately, though, you might be dissatisfied with the bundled software and decide to invest in a better program. If you investigate, you'll find that many programs specialize in either automatic or manual tools.

Automatic tools generally include wizards and automated processes that change your image for you without giving you a lot of control over what happens. These tools can adjust the colors and brightness in an image, remove red eye in flash photography, and perform a host of other minor miracles without any real input from you. The downside, of course, is this: the final result isn't always what you expect and, often, such automated attempts to fix your photos don't quite hit the spot. Use them with care, and always remember you can use the Undo button to revert to the original image. Automatic features are generally aimed at novices who don't want to learn the ins and outs of an image-editing program, but want immediate results.

If you're reading this book, I suspect you're probably more interested in getting your hands dirty, so to speak, with a more manually operated set of editing tools. These features give you more control and power, but of course you have to master

FIGURE 11-1   Photoshop is an outstanding program, but its sheer number of features can be intimidating.

11

the interface before you can see improvements in your images. Perhaps the most famous image editor of all time is Adobe Photoshop, seen in Figure 11-1. The downside of this program is that it has a somewhat steep learning curve. Another alternative is Photoshop Elements. I like the way Adobe has combined the best parts of Photoshop with a simpler interface that's designed for ordinary folks, not graphics professionals. Elements is a good program that combines both automatic and manual tools for the enthusiastic photo editor. (You can download a trial version of Photoshop Elements from www.adobe.com.)

But if you ask me, Photoshop Elements not the best choice. Personally, I use and recommend Paint Shop Pro from Corel (www.corel.com). This image-editing program has about 75 percent of the features found in Photoshop, but at a fraction of the cost and with a much simpler interface. It's very similar to Photoshop Elements in terms of overall capabilities, but is even easier to use. Throughout the rest of this book, I'll generally use Paint Shop Pro to illustrate techniques. Remember, though, you can use any software you like, but the actual mouse and keystrokes will differ somewhat depending on what program you choose to use. (You can download a trial version of Paint Shop Pro from the Corel web site at www.corel.com.)

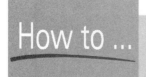 **Open an Image in Paint Shop Pro**

Because I'm going to spend a lot of time in Paint Shop Pro over the next few chapters, let's take a quick look at how to use the program. Start Paint Shop Pro by choosing it from the Windows Start menu. You can open an image in Paint Shop Pro in three ways. Use whichever method you find easiest:

■ Choose File | Open from the main menu, and in the Open dialog box navigate your way to the image you want to open. Double-click the file, or select it and click the Open button.

■ Choose File | Browse from the menu. The Browse window appears, which shows a set of thumbnails in the right pane and a directory tree of your hard disk on the left, as shown in the following illustration. When you select a hard disk folder, its contents appear on the right. Just double-click an image to open it. The Browse window remains open in case you want to open more images in this way.

■ Open the folder containing the image you want to open directly and drag the image file from the folder to the Paint Shop Pro window. If Paint Shop Pro isn't on top, you can do this instead: drag the image file out of the folder and hold it over the Paint Shop Pro button in the task bar at the bottom of the Windows desktop. Don't let go of the file yet; just hold it there for a few seconds. Paint Shop Pro should pop to the front. Finally, just move the file up to the Paint Shop Pro window and let go.

NOTE

Throughout the rest of this book, I've mainly used Paint Shop Pro to illustrate how to perform many common image-editing tasks. You can use an older version of Paint Shop Pro or another program entirely, but remember that the menu items and tool locations are somewhat different.

Tweak the Picture's Format

Much of the time, you'll only need to make minor changes to your images to get them into e-mail, on the Web, or into other documents and applications. In the next few sections, I'll show you how to make changes to the file itself, such as resizing and changing the file format.

Shrink Your Images

As Jebediah Springfield, founder of the animated city in *The Simpsons,* once said, "A noble spirit enbiggens the smallest man." If *The Simpsons* founder can make up a word, so can I—so this section is all about de-biggening your pictures.

Why would you want to do that? Well, high-res megapixel images are great, but they're just too big for many applications. Suppose you want to post some images to a web site, for instance. Or, say you want to e-mail some pics to friends and family. A 3.3-megapixel image, which measures about 2048×1536 pixels, is just too big for these kinds of applications. If you e-mail a 3.3-magapixel image to your friends, you'll lose friends fast. Files that big tend to clog e-mail pipelines and can take quite a while to download.

What you need is to de-biggen your images. In other words, shrink them to a manageable size that others can appreciate—to a size smaller than the computer monitor, for starters, so people can see your image all at once without panning around.

 A few digital cameras have the capability to resize images even before they're transferred to the PC. You should check your camera manual to see if there's a way to automatically make a duplicate, e-mail-size copy of images you want to share. That way, you can skip this de-biggening step when you want to e-mail or upload your pictures.

How small is small enough? I suggest that for web-based or e-mail images, you shrink the file so its longest dimension—either length or width, depending on the orientation of the image—is no more than 600 pixels. Here's how to do it:

1. Open Paint Shop Pro and load the file you want to resize.
2. Choose Image | Resize.

3. Because you want to make the image a specific pixel size, make sure Pixels is selected on the right side of the Resize dialog box. You could also change the size of the image based on percentage or print size, but you don't need those options now.

11

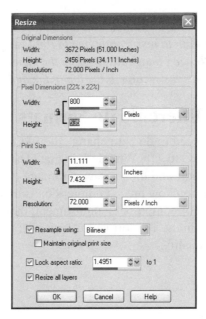

4. Make sure the options Lock Aspect Ratio and Resize All Layers are set (you can find these options at the bottom of the dialog box). Also set the Resample Using option to Smart Size. This tells Paint Shop Pro to use the best algorithm for resizing the image to generate the best final result.

5. Finally, enter the new dimensions for your image. You only need to enter the height or the width, and because the aspect ratio isn't changing, Paint Shop Pro will fill in the other number for you automatically. Assuming you started with a 1024×768-pixel image, enter **600** for the width, and you'll see the height change to 450 pixels. Just remember, though, that the second number will automatically be set to keep the picture in proper proportion based on the starting size of the image.

6. Click OK to resize the image.

7. You should see the image shrink on the screen. You can now save your image over the original—destroying the original—or save it as a new file so you retain the original's larger pixel size. To overwrite the original image, choose File | Save from the main menu. To save the image as a new file, choose File | Save As and give the image a new name.

You might have noticed that you can also make images bigger using this procedure. Avoid increasing the size of your images, though, because all you can do is stretch and manipulate the pixels already in the images. The result is generally unattractive, especially if you enlarge the image too much.

Most image editors have features similar to those I'm discussing for Paint Shop Pro. If you want to resize an image in Photoshop Elements, for instance, choose Image | Resize | Image Resize from the menu and enter your changes in the Pixel Dimensions section at the top of the dialog box.

Save Images in Different File Formats

Something I commonly need to do is to change the file format of some of my pictures—usually from JPG to TIF. Why do I do that? Usually, to preserve image quality. Every time you edit and then resave an image in JPG format, it loses a little quality (depending on how much compression is used in the resaving). TIF is immune from that kind of compression punishment, though, so as soon as I start to edit an image, I save it in the TIF format to "lock in" (as they say in the zip-lock bag industry) the image quality.

Why don't I just take pictures in TIF format right from the start? Well, even though my digital camera can take images in TIF format (as most can), it's not a very useful feature. Even with a large memory card, I can only take a few pictures in the huge, space-consuming TIF format, and it takes an enormous amount of time (a minute or so each) to save a TIF to the memory card. Because the image quality difference between TIF and high-quality JPG is quite small, I take the pictures in JPG format and convert them to TIF afterwards, when they're on the PC, if I plan to edit them. It's a compromise, but a sensible one.

> **NOTE** *Just looking at a JPG file doesn't affect the image quality. You can open the file in an image editor, view it, and close it again without affecting quality—just don't make any changes and click the Save button. If you don't plan to edit an image, you can safely leave it in JPG format.*

You might want to change image file formats on the PC for a number of reasons. Here are some of the most common reasons:

- To convert a JPG to TIF to preserve image quality before repeated edit-and-save sessions.

- To convert a TIF to JPG to save disk space or to make an image small enough to upload using the Internet.

- To import an image into a program that doesn't support the file format the image is currently in.

- To save an image with features unique to the image editor you're using, such as with masks or layers intact. If you save an image in Paint Shop Pro as a PSP file, for instance, you can retain special characteristics, making it easier to finish editing later.

For a more in-depth discussion of file formats, check out Chapter 8. Saving images in different file formats is easy, though. Just follow these steps:

1. Open the image in Paint Shop Pro.

2. Choose File | Save As from the main menu.

3. In the Save As Type drop-down menu, choose the file format you need.

11

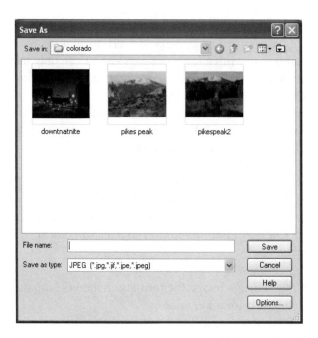

4. If necessary, click the Options button to fine-tune the file format. Depending on the file format you have chosen, the Options button lets you specify the amount of image compression, the number of colors the image will be saved in, and other properties. Remember that the more compression you use on a JPG image, the lower its visual quality will be.

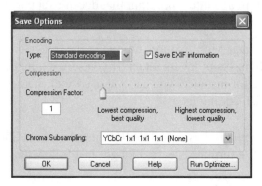

5. Click OK to save the file.

After saving the file, you'll have two copies—one called myfile.jpg and one called myfile.tif, for instance. You can delete the older file, or if you might still need it, keep both copies. Of course, when you look at two files with the same name but with different file extensions on the Windows desktop, telling them apart can be hard. If in doubt, right-click the file and choose Properties from the menu. Verify the file extension before you possibly delete the wrong file.

One-Step Photo Enhancement

Even advanced image editors with lots of manual controls often give you easy, one-step tools for improving your images. Personally, I'm enough of a purist that I usually avoid these features. Sometimes, though, I'll try the quick-fix approach to see if it helps the image. If it does, great! I can save the image and get on with my day. If I don't like the results, the Undo button is one mouse click away.

What am I talking about? Check out Paint Shop Pro, which has an Enhance Photo button in the Photo toolbar at the top of the screen. Click it, and select the One Step Photo Fix menu item to make Paint Shop Pro run a slew of corrections on your picture, including color balance, contrast, and sharpness. You can also run these corrections one at a time by choosing them from the menu under Enhance Photo. Either way, they let you quickly optimize a picture with little to no effort on your own part.

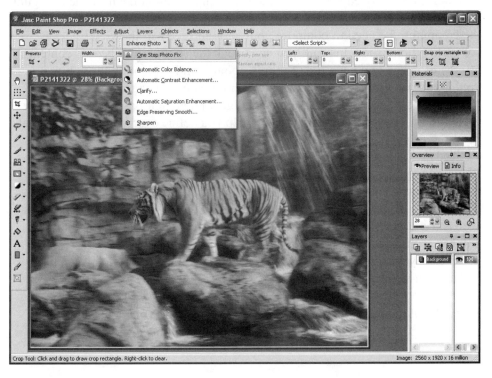

11

 *If you have Adobe Photoshop Elements, you can take advantage of a few Auto levels in the Enhance menu.*

Improve Your Composition

In the world of 35mm photography, editing your composition isn't always easily done. To crop an image or change its composition, you typically need your own darkroom or a local photo shop with which you can work closely to dictate crop marks and reprint photos to your personal specifications.

Of course, exceptions exist. In many photo stores, you can insert your picture into a kiosk and the image is then scanned and displayed onscreen. You crop the image on the screen and print the result minutes later. These image-editing stations are just big, in-store versions of the image-editing software you have on your PC.

In other words, you don't have to drive across town and pay money to do it in a store anymore. Now you have the tools to do it yourself at home.

Crop Your Image

I wouldn't be surprised if this were the single most common edit made to digital photographs. Because you can crop and recompose your images so easily on the computer, the need to compose your shot perfectly in the viewfinder is somewhat diminished. Instead, you can tweak the shot to your heart's content afterward, when you have time to think about it and evaluate your options. And if you want to make a print of your photo, you'll have to crop it at least a little anyway, since the proportions of a digital photo don't precisely match the proportions of a print, and cropping will help you define exactly the way the final print should look.

And as you can probably guess, the more megapixels your camera can shoot, the more cropping you can do. If you have a 2- or 3-megapixel camera and intend to mount your shot as an 8×10-inch print, you can't throw away many pixels. But if you have a 5- or 6-megapixel camera, you have lots of extra resolution to work with and still get great 8×10 prints. You can discard a fair bit of your photo and still have sufficient resolution to print an enlargement.

Even if your shot is close to perfect to begin with, a little cropping can likely make it better. Here's how to do it:

1. Load an image into Paint Shop Pro. Adjust it so you can see the entire image onscreen at once. To do that, you might need the Zoom tool,

shaped like a magnifying glass. Click it, and then click on the picture with the right mouse button to shrink it or the left button to enlarge it, until it comfortably takes up most of the screen. If you're not looking at a 100 percent magnification of the image, though, realize that the image you see might be ever-so-slightly distorted from the actual image.

Even without using the Zoom Tool, you can roll the scroll wheel on your mouse to change the image's zoom level.

2. Click the Crop tool, shaped like the thick frame.

3. Do you want to crop the picture to a specific print size? Click the Presets menu in the Tool Options palette at the top of the screen. Choose the crop size that you want from the menu, such as 5×7 inch or 8×10 inch, and click OK.

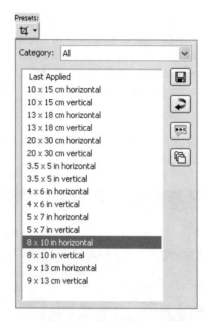

4. If you are cropping to an arbitrary size, click in the image, and, holding down the mouse button, drag the Crop tool until you've drawn a rectangular outline around the part of the image you want to keep. If you are cropping to a preset proportion, the crop box will already be in the image.

5. To move the crop box within the image, move the mouse inside the box, so you see the mouse pointer change into a four-way arrow. Click and drag the box around the image.

6. To change the size of the crop box, hold the pointer over the box outline. You should see a two-way arrow. Now click and drag to change the height or width of the box.

Resize crop
marks

7. When your crop box represents the picture as you want it composed, click the check mark button in the Tool Options Palette at the top of the screen. The image will be immediately cropped down to size, and you can save it as a new file or save it to replace the older image. Compare the original and cropped versions of this picture:

TIP

By default, the Tool Options dialog box is docked to the toolbars at the top of the screen. If you don't see it, it might not be activated. Choose View | Palettes | Tool Options. It should now appear onscreen. Notice that this important dialog box changes depending on which tool you select.

Crop by Copying and Pasting

Not all image-editing programs have a Crop tool. In fact, even in Paint Shop Pro there's another way to crop—one you should learn. In this alternative approach, you select and copy a portion of the image, and then paste it into a new image document. Here's how to do it:

1. Load an image into Paint Shop Pro and configure it so you can see the entire image.

2. Click the Selection tool (which looks like a dotted rectangle). Be sure the Selection Type is set to Rectangle in the Tool Options dialog box.

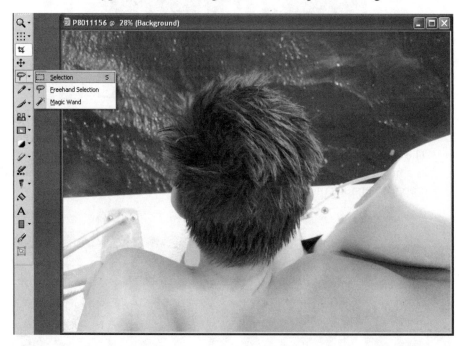

3. Draw a rectangle around the part of the image you want to keep. Note that you can't move or resize this selection rectangle in the same way you did with the Crop tool. If you don't like the result, right-click in the image to undo the selection, and then try again.

4. When your selection is complete, choose Edit | Copy from the menu. This copies the selected region into the Windows clipboard.

5. Choose Edit | Paste | As New Image. The selected region should appear in a new image window, which you can then save to the hard disk.

The Cut, Copy, and Paste tools are just like the ones in Microsoft Word and other programs, though you have a bit more in the way of options. These tools let you grab a selection—some part of the image—and paste it in a variety of ways. You can paste the content of selections elsewhere in the same image (which lets you add a second copy of yourself to a photo, for instance), in another photo (so you can shake hands with Elvis, for example), or even into a new, blank image.

Special Effects with Irregular Cropping

Why would you want to use this process instead of the Crop tool? You might want to create several new compositions, for instance, all based on the same original image. When you crop an image, the original data disappear. With the Selection tool, though, you can keep going back to the original image and copying different, even overlapping, parts and pasting them into new files. This is a way to make an unlimited number of new compositions based on a single photograph.

You can also make irregular crops with this technique—something that's not possible with the Crop tool. What do I mean? Check out Figure 11-2, and you can see I created an image by creating a crop of connected geometric shapes.

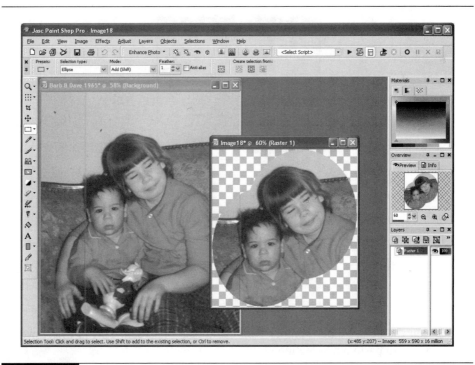

FIGURE 11-2   The Selection tools let you work with irregular shapes.

How does this work? It's easy—just try this out:

1. Load an image into Paint Shop Pro and choose the Selection tool.

2. Draw a rectangular selection in the image.

3. Hold down the SHIFT key and add another selection to the image. The SHIFT key is a modifier that combines selections in the image.

4. Hold down the CTRL key and drag another rectangle in the image. Make sure this rectangle intersects at least part of one of the selections already in the image. The CTRL key is a modifier that removes overlapping selections from the image. You can use the CTRL key to take the edge off a rectangle or even to turn a selection into a "donut" by giving it a hole!

5. Keep adding and removing selections until you're happy with the result. Choose Edit | Copy from the main menu.

6. Now you need to create a new home for this image. Choose File | New from the main menu. In the New Image dialog box, make sure the width and height of the new image are at least as big as the selection you just made, and then click OK.

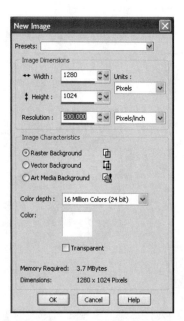

You should see a new, empty window appear onscreen. This is where we're going to paste our selection.

7. Before we do that, let's paint it. Click on the Fill tool (the overturning paint can).

8. Click on a color from the color palette in the upper-right side of the screen. Now click in the empty white image, and you should see it fill up with the color you just selected.

> **TIP** *Left-clicking paints with the program's foreground color; right-clicking paints with the background color.*

9. Finally, it's show time. With the new image window still selected, choose Edit | Paste | As New Selection. The irregularly cropped image should move around under your mouse pointer. Decide where you want it in the new image, and then click. It will pop into the new image, with the strange shape clearly visible against the colored background.

That little exercise only scratches the surface of what you can do with selections in Paint Shop Pro (and other image-editing applications). Here are a few other tricks you can try out:

■ **Create a vignette crop.** Have you ever seen oval-shaped images? This is easy to do with the Selection tool. Choose Ellipse from the Tool Options dialog box after you choose the Selection tool. When you make your selection in the image, it will be in the form of an ellipse that you can customize, depending on how you drag your mouse.

11

■ **Feather the edges.** When you paste an image into another image, you can smooth the transition from the selection to the background using the Feather tool in the Tool Options dialog box. The larger the number, the more feathering you'll get. Be sure to select the Feather tool before you select your region, though, or it won't have any effect. In the following, you can see how I used a feather value of 40 to get a very fuzzy edge to this picture of my musical hero, Kristin Hersh, posing with some of her kids:

■ **Invert your selection.** One cool trick you can try is to create a selection in your image, and then choose Selections | Invert from the main menu. You should find that you got the exact *opposite* of the selected region. It's an easy way to select everything except the middle of an image, for instance.

■ **Paste a selection into another image.** Using the layer technique you'll learn about in Chapter 13, you can take a portion of two images and combine them in interesting ways. Consider the following image, for instance. I cut the bird from one picture and then copied it into a picture of the mirror as a separate layer.

Rotate Your Perspective

Not all your shots are going to be plain old, horizontal shots, especially if you took my advice in Chapter 3 and went nuts with camera position and perspective. If you have images from your camera that are sideways—you took the pictures sideways, so you have to turn your head to look at them on the PC—you should fix those images right away. It's a snap.

Some image editors, like Paint Shop Pro, even have one-step procedures for rotating your images to the left or right by 90 degrees. Here's what you need to do to fix a sideways (landscape-oriented) image:

1. Load the sideways image in Paint Shop Pro and decide which way it needs to be rotated—right (clockwise) or left (counterclockwise). Let's assume we need to turn the picture clockwise.

2. Choose Image | Rotate | Rotate Clockwise 90. The image immediately spins accordingly.

3. The image should rotate so it's oriented properly. If you made a mistake, choose Edit | Undo and try again.

TIP *If your image editor doesn't have such a one-step rotate tool, it probably still lets you rotate by an arbitrary amount. You can even do that in Paint Shop Pro; choose Image | Rotate | Free Rotate and then specify how much you want to rotate the image in the Free Rotate dialog box. Typically, you'd click Left or Right, make sure the button for 90 is selected, and then click OK.*

You can also reorient your image in other ways. If you took the picture with the camera upside down, for instance (and stranger things have happened, trust me), you can choose Image | Flip from the menu. Likewise, you can flip it left to right, giving you a mirror image of the original shot, by choosing Image | Mirror.

Level a Crooked Picture

Nothing is quite as annoying as a crooked picture, especially when the horizon or some other straight line is visible in the image. A crooked shot can ruin an otherwise great picture. Even if the horizon is only off a little, it can be annoying, but you can use the principle you learned in the last section, on rotating sideways images, to fix this annoyance. Here's what you need to do:

1. Load the crooked image into Paint Shop Pro.

2. Click the Straighten tool, which lives in the second cubby from the top of the toolbar on the left side of the screen. You'll see a straight line appear in the middle of the picture.

3. Grab the line and position it so that it lies directly across something in the picture that should be straight horizontally or vertically, but isn't. The horizon or a telephone pole are good examples.

4. Click the check mark in the Tool Options palette to make the change. You should see the picture spin a bit to its new orientation, like this:

5. Inspect the result. If you aren't satisfied, choose Edit | Undo and try again with a different angle of rotation. When you're happy, save the file.

 *Don't apply rotation on top of rotation or the image quality will suffer. Undo the first rotation completely to get back where you started, and then apply a different rotation angle to get where you're going all at once. Any rotation effect will degrade the image slightly, but compounding rotation on top of rotation can wreck the image fairly quickly.*

When you're done rotating your image, be sure to crop it down a bit because the rotation probably introduced some unwanted background color in the corners of your picture.

Improve the Color and Brightness in Your Image

Fixing elements such as bad color or poor exposure requires the most artistic skill, so I saved them for last. These edits can be done, but it'll take some practice before you can make your images look right. Don't worry about that, though; time in your image editor is free, and if you stick with it, you can fix some badly mangled shots!

Set the White Point

Ask a serious photographer what's most frustrating about digital imaging, and you'll get a short list of major gripes: the shutter lag when taking pictures, limited dynamic range, and goofy white balance. We've already talked a bit about all of these shortcomings, and we discussed white balance adjustments in Chapter 6. Often, your digital camera will miscalculate your white balance and give you an image with a pronounced color cast. What does that mean? Not only won't there be a true white or black in your picture, but all the other colors will be a bit off as well.

Thankfully, you can fix the white balance of your photos in almost any image editor. You need to have a white point control and a swath of space in your picture that's white, black, or gray.

In Paint Shop Pro, load an image with something of a color cast and locate a part of your image with pure white or black, and then zoom in on it. Next, choose Adjust | Color Balance | Black And White Points. The Black And White Points dialog box should appear. Assuming you want to use a white region of the image to correct your photo, click on the rightmost dropper in the dialog box, directly above the white color box (or use black instead, if you like).

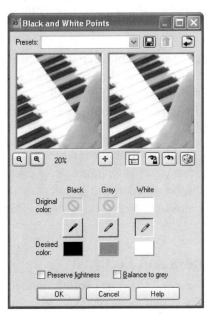

11

Click the dropper in your image directly in the white region. Preview the change, and if you like the results, click OK to save your changes.

Incidentally, the process in Photoshop Elements is similar. To open the white point control, choose Enhance | Color | Color Cast. You needn't specify white or black in Elements. The program will figure it out. Click in the image, and then click OK to accept the changes to your image's color balance.

Brighten Gloomy Shots

Everyone has a stockpile of overly dark images. The flash didn't reach the subject, or perhaps the camera underexposed the subject because of a bright background. Back in the first part of the book, I told you how to avoid those kinds of problems in the lens when you take the picture, but you can also repair some of the damage in post-processing.

You can adjust the brightness in an image in three primary ways:

- You can use the Brightness control (in some programs, it's called *luminance*). *Brightness* raises or lowers the entire image's luminance value indiscriminately, whether or not all areas need it. On the other hand, if only one portion of an image needs to be brightened, you can select it using the Selection tool, and then add Brightness. When part of an image is selected, operations you perform on the image occur in the selected region.

TIP   *Use the Selection tool to add or remove brightness only where it's needed.*

- Alternately, you can use the Gamma control. *Gamma* affects the midtones of an image more than the extreme bright and dark regions, which means you can brighten a dark skin tone without washing out a dark shadow nearby. Gamma affects a limited range of brightness in the image so you can better target your changes.

- Finally, and the best way to tweak the brightness of an image, is by inspecting the histogram. The *histogram* is an intimidating-looking display that tells you the distribution of lights and darks in an image. It can be a powerful way to correct your shots—as long as you're willing to invest a little time to learn how to use it.

Correct with Brightness and Contrast

Let's start with the Brightness and Contrast controls, though I suggest you don't rely on this technique often. Play with it, certainly, but I recommend you get familiar with the other two techniques, the gamma and the histogram (both discussed shortly), and use them.

The process for changing brightness in an image is similar, regardless of software, but we'll use Paint Shop Pro, as usual, for our example. Here's the general procedure:

1. Load the offending image into Paint Shop Pro.

2. Choose Adjust | Brightness And Contrast | Brightness/Contrast. The Brightness and Contrast dialog box appears.

3. Use the Brightness slider to adjust the image. You can see the effect of the change in your image immediately by clicking the Proof button, which is shaped like an eye. Auto Proof, to the left of the Proof button, leaves proofing on all the time, so updates are made constantly as you work the slider.

4. Typically, you'll also need to change the contrast in proportion to the brightness to keep the image from getting washed out. Experiment until you see the result you want.

5. When you're satisfied with the results, click OK. Your image will be updated with the new brightness value.

Better Corrections with Gamma

As I mentioned, the Gamma control is often a better remedy for fixing an overly dark or an overly bright image. Personally, I tend to reach for the Gamma control first. I've found it's often the midtones in a picture that need enhancement, and the Brightness control tends to wash out dark regions and increase the intensity of the highlights—overexposing them. The Gamma control, on the other hand, doesn't

11

affect the brightest and darkest parts of an image, so you can't wash out shadows with this tool, for instance. So, as a general rule, you should see if gamma gets the job done.

To tweak the gamma, choose Adjust | Brightness And Contrast | Gamma Correction, and then move the sliders. (The Link control keeps all three colors in sync, which is the most common way to use this tool.) Unless your image is poorly exposed, you shouldn't need to change the gamma value above 1.5 or below .5.

Fine-Tune Images with the Histogram

The most precise and powerful way of correcting your images is with the histogram. The histogram is a graph that shows the relative amount of information stored in each color channel in your image, or in plain English, it displays how many pixels are dark and light in your image. The left side of the graph represents the darkest part of the image, while the right side is the lightest. A graph like the one on the left in Figure 11-3 has good overall exposure with no clipping in the shadows or the highlights, while the one on the right is badly overexposed in places, and the mountain looks "blown out."

Specifically, what you're looking for in a histogram is to make sure that the curves rise from the horizontal axis and fall back to the horizontal axis within the range of the graph. None of the curve should be "clipped," or cut off, at the extreme right or left side of the graph. In Figure 11-3, you can see that the curve on the left is well behaved, while the curve on the right ends abruptly on the right side. That's why the picture is overexposed.

FIGURE 11-3   The picture on the left is well exposed, though the one on the right is overexposed because information has been "clipped" from the highlights.

We can use this information to tweak the brightness and contrast.

Most good image-editing programs, like Paint Shop Pro, Photoshop, and Photoshop Elements, have a handy tool for adjusting the light levels in your image using the histogram chart and a few sliders. In Paint Shop Pro, it's found at Adjust | Brightness And Contrast | Histogram Adjustment. If you're using the full version of Photoshop, it's found in Image | Adjust | Levels. Finally, Adobe Photoshop Elements puts this control in Enhance | Brightness/Contrast | Levels.

No matter which program you use, this tool works more or less the same way. You simply want to move the sliders under the histogram to set the white and black points, stretching and optimizing the distribution of brightness information in the image. Paint Shop Pro throws a Gamma control into the same dialog box, which is treated separately (as the Curves tool) in Photoshop.

Suppose you have an image like the one in Figure 11-4. Here's how you would correct the image using the Histogram Adjustment tool in Paint Shop Pro:

1. Because the histogram curve drops off before reaching the right side of the graph, that tells us there are few pixels with very bright colors. Consequently, you should drag the white point slider to the left to meet the point where the graph ends. That sets this point in the image as white, and it should brighten the image. You should see the graph stretch as you drag the end points.

2. Do the same for the black point, if necessary.

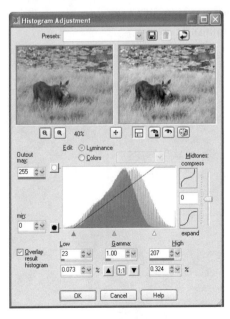

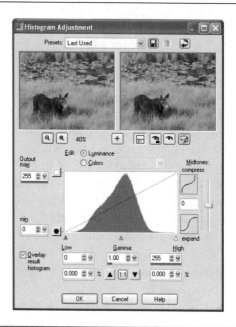

FIGURE 11-4   The Histogram Adjustment tool is a precise way to adjust brightness and contrast.

3. Now use the gamma slider, if needed, to adjust the overall brightness level in the image's midtones.

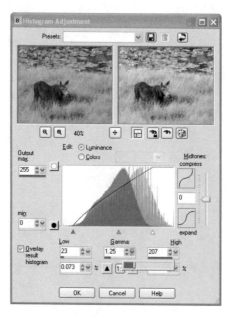

Brightness Only Goes So Far

You need to know the ugly little secret of brightness and gamma control. You can only take it so far because you can't add detail to an image that wasn't there when you originally took the picture. A black shadow, for instance, will only become gray as you continue to increase brightness—you'll never see the authentic Bigfoot creature that was hiding in the thicket of trees. That's why it's important to start with the best exposure you can, although you can always try enhancing it afterwards. You can sometimes salvage an otherwise throwaway image.

I use this histogram adjustment technique on many of my pictures. I suggest you try doing the same. It only takes a few seconds and can improve almost any shot.

Add Snap to Your Colors

You can add life to washed-out, flat, or bland pictures in a few ways. One way is to use the Contrast control. Because bland pictures are often a result of low contrast, you can increase the contrast in the image and make the scene look much punchier. To do that, simply find the Contrast control and work the slider. In Paint Shop Pro, you can find the contrast in Adjust | Brightness And Contrast | Brightness/Contrast.

Contrast can also work the other way to good effect. Want to create some artificial fog? Just reduce the contrast in a picture by about 50 percent, and the image seems obscured by a dense fog.

Another way to improve your image is with the Saturation tool. Saturation increases or decreases the intensity of colors in an image, much like the saturation control on your television. Too much saturation can make the picture look like it was taken on Mars, but it can add life to an otherwise bland picture.

Do you have a people picture that's a little too red? This doesn't happen often, but it can occur when you take indoor pictures in artificial light. Back off on the saturation slightly to get a more natural skin tone.

11

In Paint Shop Pro, the Saturation control is found in Adjust | Hue And Saturation | Hue/Saturation/Lightness. Experiment with the Saturation tool—it's fun. You can bleach all the color from your picture by reducing the saturation to zero, for instance, or hyperactivate the colors by going in the other direction.

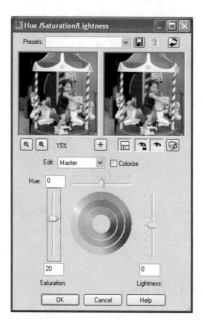

Don't forget that programs like Paint Shop Pro also have automatic controls for many of these tweaks. You can find an automatic contrast adjustment, as well as an auto saturation tool, under the Enhance Photo button in the toolbar.

Correct the Color Balance

Quite often, the colors in some pictures won't come out quite right for some reason. Some cameras, for instance, tend to shift the whole image toward one end of the color spectrum under certain lighting conditions. You can change the color balance in an image in many programs as easily as sliding three controls marked Red, Green, and Blue.

To fix out-of-synch colors, open the color balancing tool in your image-editing program. In Paint Shop Pro, you can find it at Adjust | Color Balance | Red/Green/Blue. You'll see a dialog box in which you can slide the three primary color controls to the left (less) or right (more) to bias the colors in your photo. For best results, use your program's color balancing tool conservatively and be sure to preview your work before clicking OK. You'll rarely need to change the colors in your image by more than about 15 percent.

If your image is too blue, however, you won't necessarily get the effect you're looking for by backing off on the blue slider. Use this chart to fine-tune your image, where x is the amount you move the slider:

Problem	Solution
Too red	Decrease red by x, and then increase both green and blue by $x \div 2$.
Too green	Decrease green by x, and then increase both red and blue by $x \div 2$.
Too blue	Decrease blue by x, and then increase both red and green by $x \div 2$.

Easy Color Correction with Variations

A better solution—unfortunately unavailable in Paint Shop Pro—is usually called the color variations control. Adobe Photoshop and Photoshop Elements both offer this powerful feature. Let's take a quick look at the Color Variations tool in Photoshop Elements because it's so useful.

If you have Photoshop Elements, open it and load an image. Then choose Enhance | Variations. You should see something like the screen in Figure 11-5.

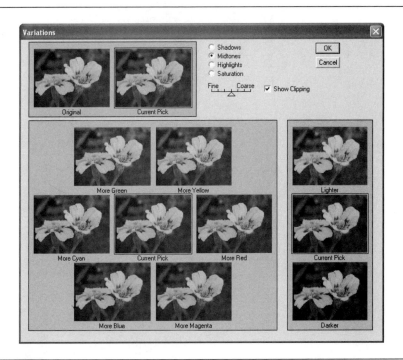

FIGURE 11-5   Use the subtle variations in color to fine-tune your picture, adding or removing just the right amount of color cast.

Here's how you use this busy little dialog box:

1. Start by tweaking the brightness. If you want to make the image darker or lighter, click the appropriate thumbnail on the right side of the screen. All the images will immediately change to show you the effect of the change. (The Original thumbnail at the top left will remain the same, so you can compare your changes to it.)

2. Next, decide what color channel you want to change. If you want more red in the image, for instance, click the box marked More Red. The change will appear immediately.

3. Continue tweaking the image until you're satisfied with the result. At any time, you can revert to the original by clicking the Original thumbnail.

Chapter 12

Cleaning Up Your Images

How to...

- ■ Sharpen blurry images
- ■ Blur the background to enhance apparent sharpness
- ■ Use the painting tools in your image editor
- ■ Choose foreground and background colors
- ■ Make selections based on color, region, and by hand
- ■ Remove ugly red eye from flash photos
- ■ Eliminate distracting objects with airbrushing
- ■ Repair tears and scratches on photos
- ■ Combine a series of photos into a panorama
- ■ Use adjustment layers to improve your pictures
- ■ Replace the sky in your photos

In the previous chapter, you learned some easy and fast techniques you can use to gussy up your images—stuff like how to rotate or resize your images, correct bad colors, and even save them in different file formats.

But you can do so much more. In this chapter, we'll go one step beyond and learn how to fix your images with techniques that actually change reality. For example, you'll see how to remove red eye caused by flash photography, how to sharpen (or blur) a picture, and how to airbrush away distracting elements from a scene and move elements around within a picture.

This chapter is filled with techniques that sit between what I would call elementary quick changes and special effects. We're not adding Elvis to your holiday pictures, but we're certainly going beyond color correction. Strap in and have fun with your images and your favorite image editor!

Sharpen Blurry Pictures

I know what you're thinking. Wow! I can sharpen my blurry pictures! Technology is great!

Well, let me begin by saying that as great as digital imaging is, you can never add detail or information into a picture that wasn't there to begin with. That's why I'm always amused when I see a movie in which the spy takes a surveillance videotape and enlarges the image enough to read the phone number on a piece of paper across the room. No matter how much they enlarge images in the movies, those Hollywood computers always seem to sharpen the focus perfectly.

With that said, there is some hope for your *slightly* blurry images. You can sharpen an image in two ways: a direct way, using the Sharpen tool in your image-editing program, and an indirect way, which amounts to blurring the background so your subject doesn't look quite so bad. I'll show you how to do both.

As you might have guessed, you can combine those two techniques by doing both. But keep in mind that sharpening also can increase the digital "noise" and degrade the overall look of the photo.

Use the Sharpen Filter to Enhance Your Pictures

The easiest way to sharpen an image is with the Sharpen tool. What the Sharpen tool does is increase the contrast between pixels, making the image seem sharper, as you can see in Figure 12-1. If the camera jittered madly while you took the picture, though, no amount of sharpening will hide the result.

FIGURE 12-1   A little sharpening can add an almost subliminal "punch" to your digital images—especially ones destined for print.

12

Sometimes, adding a little noise to a slightly blurry picture can make it look sharper—and, indeed, the Noise tool has roughly the same effect as the Sharpen tool, only noise tends to happen everywhere in the picture, while most Sharpen tools try to be more selective by only working around edges within the scene.

In most graphics programs, a few different kinds of sharpening filters are available. These are the most common options:

- **Sharpening** This affects all the pixels in your image indiscriminately. Sharpen More is a common alternative, which is somewhat more intense.

- **Edge Sharpening** This effect only increases the contrast along edges in your picture, where a lack of sharpness is most obvious. It is usually more effective than the Sharpening option, and it's less damaging to the rest of the image.

- **Unsharp Mask** Yes, it has a weird name, but this variation of Edge Sharpening adjusts the contrast of pixels that neighbor an edge, in addition to the edge itself. This is the most common sharpening filter and, in fact, it's pretty standard practice for photographers to run the Unsharp Mask filter on most images that they scan into digital format from a slide or print.

In Paint Shop Pro, the Sharpen, Sharpen More, and Unsharp Mask filters are available from the Adjust | Sharpness menu.

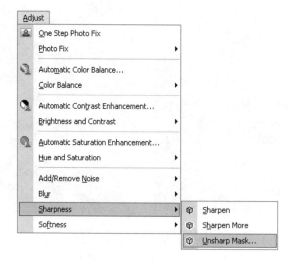

Which one should you use? Not all programs offer all three filters, but if you have a choice, Edge Sharpening is almost always more effective than the plain old Sharpening filter. Unsharp Mask works best of all, but it sometimes takes some tweaking on your part. You'll generally get to set at least three options, as you can see here:

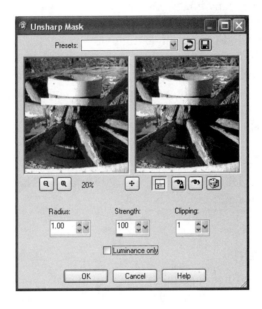

■ **Strength**   Sometimes called Amount, this is the intensity of the sharpening effect.

■ **Radius**   This determines how many pixels around the edges are also affected by the filter.

■ **Clipping**   Sometimes called Threshhold, this determines how different the pixels need to be before they're considered an edge.

TIP   *Start with 100 for Strength and 1.0 for Radius, and then watch the way the filter changes as you change the Clipping setting. A Clipping of 0 is the most harsh effect; beyond about 30, changing Clipping has no real effect on your image. Likewise, raising Radius beyond 1.5 rarely has an attractive effect on your image.*

12

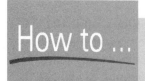

Undo a Big Mistake

Paint Shop Pro, like many image editors, has an extensive undo history you can use to fix a major boo-boo. Unlike most image-editing programs, though, you can selectively undo just a single thing in the middle of a long procedure. So if you decide you didn't like a filter you applied 10 minutes ago—before a whole bunch of other hard-to-reproduce changes—don't fret. You can undo just the filter and keep everything else exactly the same. Do this:

1. Open the History palette by chooing View | Palettes | History.

2. Scroll down until you find the step that you want to remove and click it.

3. Click Undo Selected from the top of the palette. The image will revert to an earlier state.

Blur to Sharpen

Using the Sharpening filter is certainly one way to make your image look sharper, but there's another, more subtle, and more "artistic" way to enhance the apparent sharpness of your image—blur the background. This process works best when you're photographing something that's quite distinct from the background, like a portrait.

To blur the background of your image, you'll need to isolate the subject so the blurring only happens in the rest of the picture. Once your subject is selected, you need to invert the selection so the Blur filter happens to everything except the subject. Finally, you can run the Blur filter on your image. In Paint Shop Pro, you can find Blur by choosing an option from the Effects | Blur menu. Once you've blurred your background, turn off the selection and save your image.

That's the quick overview. Here's how to pull off this feat of digital trickery in Paint Shop Pro:

1. Load a slightly blurry portrait that you'd like to sharpen.

2. Select the Freehand Selection tool from the fifth cubby in the toolbar on the left side of the screen and set the Selection Type to Smart Edge in the tool

palette at the top of the screen. Set the Feather value to about 5—that way the transition from the subject to the background won't be abrupt.

3. Trace the outline of the subject's face or body, being careful to stay along the edge.

4. When you have completely selected the subject, choose Adjust | Sharpness | Unsharp Mask to sharpen the subject but not affect the background, and then click OK.

5. Next, choose Selections | Invert from the menu. This "flips" the selection so the subject isn't selected, but everything else is.

6. Choose Adjust | Blur | Blur More. You should see the background blur slightly. If you're not happy with the result, blur it again. In fact, you can repeatedly use the blur effect until the background is sufficiently blurred.

7. Finally, when the image is complete, choose Selections | Select None.

Hopefully, the subject now looks better, especially in comparison to the background. Compare the two images in Figure 12-2, for instance, for a look at this effect in action.

12

FIGURE 12-2   Blurring the background can simulate a shallow depth of field—great for portraits—while also giving the impression of a sharper subject.

Did you know?

Simulate a Shallow Depth of Field

You wanted to take a picture with a sharp foreground and a shallow background, but your automatic camera settings didn't cooperate. Well, it's easy to simulate the out-of-focus effect that a wide-open aperture gives your background by using the select-invert-blur technique you used in the "Blur to Sharpen" exercise to give the subject more apparent sharpness. You'll need to heap on liberal amounts of blur for this technique to work, though. You can run the Blur filter several times until you get the effect you like.

Paint on Your Pictures

Some of the techniques we'll be discussing through the rest of the book require a little, well, painting. And if you take a look at your image editor—especially a full-featured one like Paint Shop Pro or Adobe Photoshop Elements—you'll see a complete set of painting tools. These digital gadgets enable you to change the colors in an image on a pixel-by-pixel basis. How do they do that? Take a look at Table 12-1; there you can see the most important tools in Paint Shop Pro's Paint Tools Palette. These are fairly typical tools as image editors go. You'll find their equivalents in most other programs.

Tool	Description
	Pan This tool is used to move image windows around within Paint Shop Pro. It's a safe default setting to use because it won't do anything to your image if you click in the picture.
	Zoom You can use this tool to zoom into the image by left-clicking and to zoom out by right-clicking.
	Crop This tool lets you cut out unwanted bits of your picture.
	Selection This tool lets you select portions of an image for further editing.
	Freehand Selection This tool provides a powerful way to select portions of an image.
	Magic Wand This tool selects a region for editing based on color. Because photos have lots of similar colors, you can click on a region and the wand will select everything nearby that's of a similar color. It's an easy way to select, for instance, a person's face, the sky, or a sandy beach.
	Dropper This tool determines the color of the currently selected pixel and makes that the current foreground color for painting and editing.
	Paint Brush This is just what it sounds like. It lets you paint on the image, not unlike the way you'd paint with a real brush. It's a lot more flexible than a real brush, though, because you can change features such as the size and shape of the brush, as well as the amount of paint that you can spread at once.

TABLE 12-1   Highlights from the Paint Tools Palette in Paint Shop Pro

12

Tool	Description
	Airbrush You can configure this tool to splatter paint on your image like an airbrush.
	Clone Brush This tool lets you paint with pixels found elsewhere in your image, effectively cloning a part of your picture as you paint.
	Scratch Remover This automated tool erases scratches from scanned photographs.
	Eraser This tool lets you paint with the currently selected foreground and background colors.
	Flood Fill This tool pours paint into a region. The currently selected color will run right up to whatever color edges exist. As with the Magic Wand, this tool allows you to set the color tolerance.
A	**Text** This tool lets you write text anywhere in your image, in any color and any font.

TABLE 12-1   Highlights from the Paint Tools Palette in Paint Shop Pro (Continued)

Paint Shop Pro stores several tools in each slot of the toolbar. Click the arrow next to each tool to see all the available options.

Choose Colors

So, let's say you want to do a bit of painting. We'll keep it simple: you just want to paint a solid-colored rectangle in the middle of an image. Before you do that, though, you'll need to know how to select colors in Paint Shop Pro.

Every imaging program has two important colors: the foreground color and the background color. These are usually displayed prominently on the screen (as in Figure 12-3) for easy access and reference.

The foreground color is the color you'll paint with when you use the left mouse button. The background color can often be used by painting with the right mouse button. The Eraser is one of many tools that use the background color. Note, the Eraser doesn't really erase anything; it just paints the background color (which can sometimes look like you're erasing).

In Paint Shop Pro, you can choose a color directly from the color palette by moving the mouse over the palette and clicking on the color you like. A left click selects the foreground color; a right click sets the background. You can also set

Color palette

Foreground color

Background color

All tools

FIGURE 12-3 The color palette is an important feature in most image editors because it lets you select colors for painting and editing.

these colors directly from an image; to do that, select the Dropper and click with it on the part of the image you want to grab the color from.

12

TIP
Because colors can change from pixel to pixel in a digital image, you'll have better luck with the Dropper by zooming in for a close-up view of the region before you select a color with the Dropper.

Apply the Paint

Once you've selected colors to serve as the foreground and background colors, it's time to lay down some paint. In Paint Shop Pro, do this:

1. Click on the Selection tool and make sure that the Selection style is set to Rectangle in the Tool Options dialog box.

2. Click and drag the Selection tool in the image to create a rectangle.

3. Click on the Flood Fill tool.

4. Set the fill style to solid color. To do that, make sure the solid round icon is selected (see Figure 12-3). Also select None in the Tool Options Match Mode menu.

5. Finally, click inside the selection with the Flood Fill tool. You should see it fill with a solid color—the same one you selected in step 4. If you like, right-click in the selected rectangle as well. You should see it change to the background color.

 *To paint freely anywhere in the image (as we're about to do in the rest of the chapter), you need to get rid of any selections. As long as a selection is in the image, you'll only be able to paint inside it; that's a powerful tool for making sure you only affect specific parts of the image. To turn off the current selection, choose Selections | Select None.*

 *A faster way to eliminate selections is to right-click the image with the select tool still active.*

Paint More Accurately

You've got the basics of painting down—selecting colors and clicking in the painting. But what if you want to paint a precise set of pixels? The rectangular Selection tool won't get the job done. Instead, you can rely on a few other tricks:

Paint Brush

For lots of close-in, delicate detail work, the old-fashioned Paint Brush is all you need. Select the Paint Brush, and you'll see you have a variety of options in the

Tool Options palette. Of particular importance is the Size slider: by changing the size, you're specifying the number of pixels to be affected every time you click the image with the brush. To test this tool, select it and then click and drag in the image. You can paint by drawing freehand lines or just dab the screen to make small dots of color.

Magic Wand

If you want to change the color (or perform some other kind of edit) on a region of the image that's somewhat similarly colored (such as a person's face or, in the case of the following illustration, someone's shirt), use the Magic Wand to select all the like-colored neighboring pixels. You can make the wand more or less sensitive to color changes by moving the Tolerance slider. To test this tool, choose the wand and click in a region of your image that has a somewhat consistent color. A selection region will appear; you can then use Flood Fill or the Paint Brush in this area. You can hold down the SHIFT key and continue clicking to select a larger area of somewhat similar colors.

12

Freehand Selection

The Freehand Selection tool is a great choice when you want to select part of the image, especially when the part of the image you want to select is irregular in shape and hard to select any other way. Perhaps the most powerful way to use the Freehand Selection tool is to set it to Smart Edge mode. Here's how it works:

1. Select the Freehand Selection tool, as shown in this illustration, and change the Selection Type to Smart Edge in the Tool Options dialog box.

2. Find a region that you want to select. Ideally, it should have a fairly well-defined outline because the Smart Edge tool will snap to high-contrast changes in the image.

3. Click the edge of the region and move the mouse pointer. You should see a box extend away from the point you clicked.

4. Following the outline of the region, click again on the edge some short distance away.

5. Continue clicking with the Smart Edge setting as you work your way around the region. When you reach your starting point, double-click to close the region into a complete selection.

Repair the Evil Eye

Back in Chapter 4, we talked about how to avoid getting red eye into your pictures. Red eye, of course, is the phenomenon that occurs when the camera flash reflects off the subject's retina because the pupils are wide open in a dark room. If you have red eye, either because you didn't take the necessary precautions or because you've just scanned an old picture that has red eye, you can correct it on the PC fairly easily.

Use Automatic Red Eye Removal

First, check to see if your image-editing software has an automatic red eye removal feature. Some red eye removal software is completely automated: just draw a box around the eyes, and the software does the rest. Paint Shop Pro, for instance, has a great semi-automated process for eliminating red eye:

1. Open a photo that includes someone with a case of evil eye.

2. From the menu, choose Adjust | Photo Fix | Red Eye Removal. You'll see the Red Eye Removal dialog box.

3. Move the image on the right around by dragging it with the mouse pointer until you see a red eye in the middle of the frame. (Don't try dragging the left side around because then you'll start to draw new eyes.) Once you can see the eye, zoom in until it fills much of the frame.

12

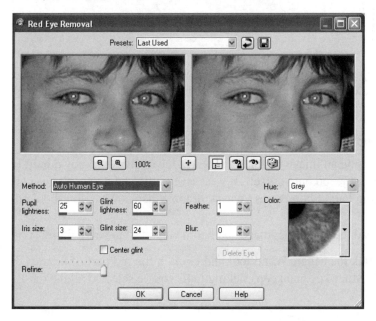

4. Make sure that the Method is Auto Human Eye and select the proper hue for the person you're correcting. Then pick an eye color. Once everything is ready, click in the dead-center of a red eye and drag the mouse away from the center until you've covered the red with the new eye. You can resize and reposition the eye if needed.

If your subject's eye is squinting or not perfectly round, try changing the method from Auto Human Eye to Freehand Pupil Outline so you can trace it more accurately.

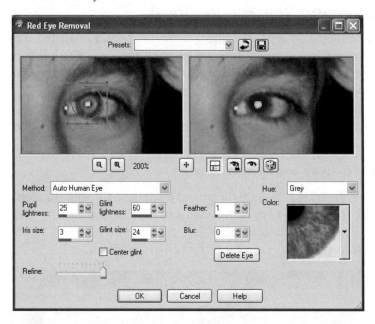

5. Repeat the process for the other eye. When both eyes are finished, click OK to close the Red Eye Removal dialog box and keep your changes.

Remove Red Eye the Old-Fashioned Way

If you're using an image editor that doesn't have red eye removal built in, you'll have to take the red out yourself. It's easy, actually, and it doesn't even take a steady hand. Using Paint Shop Pro as your workhorse, here's what you should do:

1. Load the offending image and zoom way in so the eyes fill most of the screen.

2. Click the Magic Wand tool and click in the red part of the eye. Hold down the SHIFT key and keep clicking until you've selected all the red in one eye.

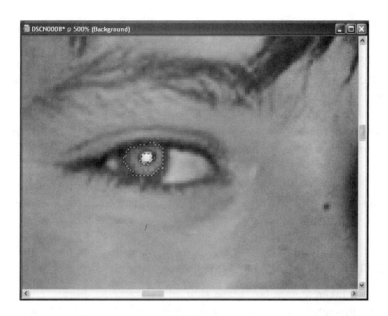

TIP *If the wand grabs too much of the image—parts of the face outside the red, for example—then the tolerance (found in the Tool Options palette) is set too high. You might need to adjust it to 15 or less.*

3. With the red area selected, select the Paint Brush or Flood Fill tool, and then choose a dark color, like black. Click in the selection to paint over the red.

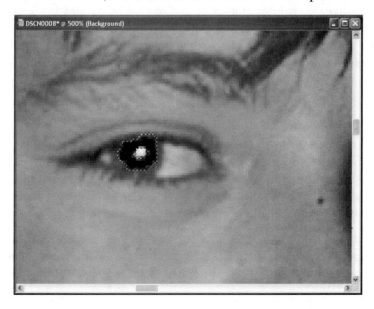

12

4. Choose Selections | Select None from the menu and evaluate your work. If you can still see red around the fringes, you can take the Paint Brush and change the remaining red bits on a pixel-by-pixel basis. To do that, you might want to reduce the brush size to just a few pixels. (The size setting is found in the Tool Options dialog box.)

> **TIP** *Be sure to leave the white spot in the middle of the eye, or you'll have created a portrait of a space alien.*

Notice that you don't have to do a perfect job to create a convincing eye—the detail is so small in most pictures that simply eliminating the red is enough to dramatically improve the picture.

Airbrush Away Distractions

Have you ever taken a great landscape shot only to realize—far too late to reshoot the picture—that a telephone pole is in the middle of what should be serenity? Or a tourist in a loud shirt is right behind your family shot that you wanted to frame? Don't worry—this section will show you how to eliminate those kinds of distractions with a little digital airbrushing.

The tool at the heart of this magical process is the Clone tool. This handy feature, found in most image editors, lets you copy pixels from one region of your image to another. That means you can "airbrush away" distracting aspects of a picture—like power lines, hot spots, and so on—by duplicating a similar or nearby part of the image (see Figure 12-4). Typically, smaller and more-isolated distractions are easier to airbrush away than larger ones (or objects that cut through the main part of your picture); but if you're patient, you can get great results from a surprising number of photos that you thought you'd have to throw away.

To use the Clone tool in Paint Shop Pro, just do this:

1. Click the Clone tool in the tool palette. It looks like a pair of paintbrushes.

2. You'll need to find a region in your image that's similar to the area you want to cover. If you want to airbrush away a power line that runs through the air, for instance, you can look for a nearby patch of sky that's similar enough so you can paint over the power line with it.

3. Set the source for your cloning operation. In Paint Shop Pro, position the mouse pointer over the area you're going to steal color from and either right-click or hold the SHIFT key and click.

FIGURE 12-4   Paint away distractions with the Clone tool.

4. Move your mouse over to the area you want to airbrush and start painting. Don't try to cover the blemish all at once; paint a little, pick up the mouse, and paint again. This reduces the chances that a recognizable pattern will appear as a result of your painting.

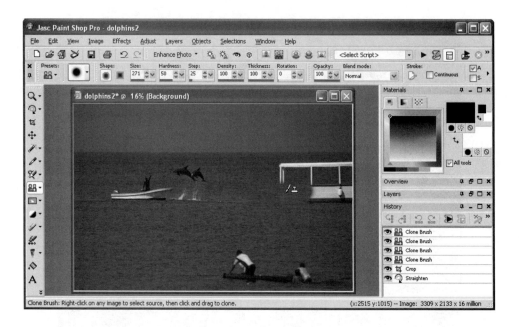

The Clone tool has two different modes. In one mode, when you pick up the brush and paint elsewhere, the source stays where you put it: this is called Nonaligned *mode. If you pick up the brush and start painting elsewhere, and the source moves the same relative distance from where you first started, this is the* Aligned *mode. Some pictures work better with one mode or the other. Experiment to see which is best in each situation.*

The Clone tool works best in small areas because if you paint over too large a region, you can start to tell something is wrong with the area you're cloning to.

By the way, there's another way to solve this problem. If your blemish is small enough, just try using your image editor's Scratch Remover tool. It won't give you good results all the time (sometimes it'll look like the picture is "smeared" around the area where the tool did its work), but often this is the fastest, one-step way to improve your photo.

Clean Up Old and Damaged Pictures

An unexpected benefit of digital imaging and editing has been the capability to restore old pictures—heirlooms and keepsakes you might have written off as too badly damaged to be of much value anymore. Some of the techniques I've already mentioned can be used to fix these old prints on your PC. First, of course, you'll need to scan these images into the PC. Afterward, it's just a matter of applying digital editing techniques to repair them.

Remove Picture Scratches

After a particularly bad moving experience a few years ago, one of my wedding pictures got a few nasty scratches because of the way the glass broke and slid down the print. The image was essentially irreplaceable, so I turned to digital editing to make a repaired duplicate. You can take several approaches to fixing scratches, depending on where they are in the image, how prominent the scratches are, and their relative size with respect to the rest of the image:

- **Copy, paste, and feather.** In some cases, you can select and copy an undamaged area of the picture that's similar in color and overall texture to the damaged portion, and then paste it over the damaged area with a liberal amount of feathering to smooth the edges. This is particularly effective in fairly uniform backgrounds, such as the sky.

- **Use the Clone tool.** Another alternative—and the more common solution—is to use the Clone tool (see the previous section on airbrushing for more details). Select the Clone tool and use a nearby, similar, but undamaged, section of the image to paint over the mar. Remember to use short, dabbing motions to paint, or you'll introduce an undesirable pattern into the image.

- **Use the Scratch Remover.** You can use the automated scratch remover found in many image editors. Paint Shop Pro's Scratch Remover (it looks like a trowel) lets you drag a selection box over a long, straight scratch. It then removes the scratch by painting over it with nearby colors automatically. This technique doesn't work well for wide scratches or scratches that curve or bend—it's off to the Clone tool for those.

Remove Dust, Dirt, and Digital Noise

Your images can be filled with little specks that come from grainy, high-speed 35mm film, from bad scans, or from using a digital camera in very low light. Whatever the reason you get specks on your image, most image editors have a Despeckle tool. In Paint Shop Pro, choose Adjust | Add/Remove Noise | Despeckle.

Did you know?

Let Someone Else Do the Work

Sure, after reading this book, you can do almost any kind of image edit yourself. But there might be times when you'd like a professional to do it for you instead. Or, perhaps you think a professional-quality edit might make a good gift for a friend. In either case, check out a web site called Image-Edit & Art (www.image-edit.com).

This site offers professional tweaks and changes to digital photos for a small fee. Here's how it works: you upload the digital image you'd like to change and pick from the site's extensive list of services. Red eye removal, color adjustment, blurred backgrounds, restoration, wacky caricature filters. . . they're all here. Within a day, the folks at the site e-mail you a price quote. If you choose to pay, it takes a few days to get the work done. They do nice work, but let me be clear: there's almost nothing they do that you can't do yourself, especially if you're armed with this book and a decent image editor. That's why I think that buying a gift certificate (yes, they sell gift certificates) as a holiday gift for your digital-imaging neophyte is a better use for the site.

Come to think of it, you should give a copy of this book to all of your friends and relatives who own digital cameras for the holidays! See that? Now I'm even giving you handy gift ideas.

Stitch Photos into a Panorama

A panorama is an image, such as the one in Figure 12-5, that's wider than the ordinary images produced by your camera. Panoramas are typically used to take landscapes because they provide the wide, sweeping vistas that look so impressive. You can take a panorama of anything, though—a school play, a tall monument, the inside of your home, or some other scene. The key to making something into a panorama with a digital camera, though, is that you'll need to take two or more images and "stitch" them together on your PC. That means the scene shouldn't change much between photographs or you won't be able to match the photos. (For example, you shouldn't wait so long that different people wander in front of the subject from one picture to the next, or try to combine daylight and nighttime versions of the picture.) So, if you're taking a landscape, for instance, the same cars, people, and other objects shouldn't move as you rotate your camera and take successive shots.

FIGURE 12-5   You can connect a number of images to make a wide (or tall) panoramic shot.

I first talked about panoramas back in Chapter 7. In that chapter, I explained how you can use your camera to take the panorama's raw ingredients—the individual shots. In this chapter, we'll pick up where we left off and talk about how to stitch those together on the PC.

As mentioned in Chapter 7, taking a panorama involves two steps: photographing the scene and stitching the images together afterward. When shooting the pictures, keep these tips in mind:

12

- **Take a series of pictures that overlap.** Try to get 30 to 50 percent of each image to overlap into the next picture to make it easier to stitch them together. Scenes with lots of movement are poor candidates for panoramas because the computer needs to look for similar regions in common from one picture to another. A little movement is fine, but the scene should essentially be static.

- **Keep each image's perspective identical.** To do this, you'll need to keep the camera's rotational axis the same. In plain English, that means you need to take all the pictures from the same location. Don't drift a few feet from side to side as you photograph, and take the shots on a tripod if possible (though you can get superb results just holding the camera in your hand).

- **Avoid using a wide-angle lens.** This can distort the images and make it difficult to line up edges.

Now it's time to make the panorama. While it's technically possible to sometimes combine pictures into panoramas by hand, it's quite difficult and it won't always work very well. Instead, you really should purchase a panorama program that automates the entire process for you. Don't worry, though: many inexpensive programs are available that can do the stitching for you. If you're interested, check out any of these:

- **Microsoft Digital Image Suite**   www.microsoft.com

- **Adobe Photoshop Elements**   www.adobe.com

- **Corel Paint Shop Photo Album**   www.corel.com

- **Ulead COOL 360**   www.ulead.com

- **ArcSoft Panorama Maker**   www.arcsoft.com

Using any of these programs, all you need to do is drag-and-drop the individual images into the panorama canvas, and the software does the rest. These programs are designed to match the edges between the pictures automatically, and they typically do a good job even with wide-angle lenses and other technical difficulties.

My favorite panoramic stitching program is without a doubt Microsoft Digital Image Suite. This program doesn't even require you to add the pictures in any particular order—just throw them all into the canvas, and the panorama feature will figure out what order they go in and create a stunning panorama (see Figure 12-6).

The Resolution Advantage

Not all panoramas are photographed just to take wide, scenic landscapes. Sometimes, you might want to photograph a subject in sections so you can get more pixels for a high-res print.

What am I talking about? Consider a situation in which you want to make a 20×30-inch poster-sized print, but your 2-megapixel camera doesn't have remotely enough resolution to make a large picture. You can still get the shot, as long as you're trying to photograph a stationary object. Shoot it in sections, and then stitch the individual segments together on the PC using a program such as Microsoft Digital Image Suite or ArcSoft Panorama Maker that lets you create a panorama from a grid of horizontal and vertical images. When you're done, you'll end up

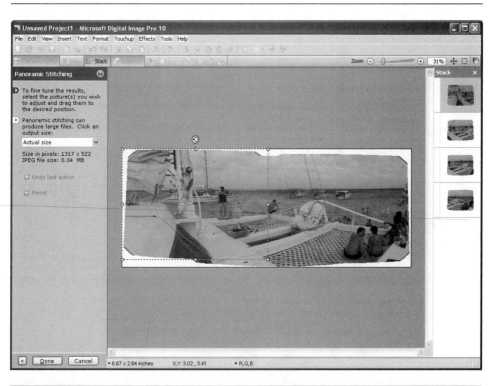

FIGURE 12-6   Automatic panorama software is a convenient way to stitch images together into impressive panoramas.

with a much higher-resolution image—one that you can even make a poster from—because it'll have a lot more pixels than a single photo would have. Figure 12-7 shows how I took six sequential photos—each one measuring about 3.3 megapixels—and ended up with a huge, super high-resolution 8-megapixel shot that's plenty big for just about any print I could possibly want to make.

Make a Virtual Reality Panorama

The panoramas we've talked about so far are very wide or tall images that go beyond the ordinary aspect ratio people expect to see when they look at a picture—that's what helps make them look so striking. You have another option entirely.

FIGURE 12-7   You can stitch several smaller images together to make a huge print.

Perhaps you've seen virtual reality (VR) movies on the Web or in online encyclopedias like Encarta. They present a scene in a small window that, when you click and drag the mouse inside, spins around so you can see a full 360 degrees, as if you were actually there. When you think about it, isn't that just a 360-degree panorama in which you only see a small piece at once? Indeed, that's the secret behind these VR movies. And that means there's nothing particularly magical about them. You can make your own VR movies and share them in e-mail or on the Web. The most common format for these interactive panoramas is Apple's QuickTime, shown here:

To make your own VR movies, you need to take a series of images that can be assembled into a complete 360-degree panorama. You also need special panorama software. The best—and most affordable—such programs that I've managed to find are Ulead's COOL 360 and ArcSoft Panorama Maker. Both of these excellent programs let you create panoramas and save them in QuickTime format, which most people can view on their computer without any additional software (or if not, and they don't already have QuickTime installed, it's available free from Apple's web site). Panorama Maker even has an option to let you save your VR movie as a web page, which makes it easier to post on the Web.

Use Adjustment Layers for Finer Control

Earlier in this chapter, we talked about how to do a wide variety of tasks—like sharpening a picture and adjusting its colors. While we did those directly to the main image, many people prefer to do the work in something called an *adjustment layer*.

What's that? Well, imagine that you want to edit a picture, so you make a duplicate copy of it (the adjustment layer) and load that into a layer on top of the original image. Then you make your changes to that photo. The original picture is underneath, but you can't see it because of the new layer. So, to finish the picture off, you reduce the opacity of the top layer, which tends to blend the two pictures together. You control the level of opacity, tweaking it until you're happy with the

How to ... Combine Images with Layers

Many sophisticated editing tasks benefit from a feature called layers, found in Paint Shop Pro and most other image editors. Here's the basic idea: your picture can be made up of many different images and selections, each occupying a different layer. Each layer has its own unique characteristics, including transparency. So you can add a ghost to an image by using the image of a person in a layer with a high level of transparency.

You can add images to a picture in layers in two ways:

■ Drag images directly to an image window from the Browse window.

■ Use the menu option Edit | Paste | As New Layer.

Once an image is considered a layer, you'll need the Layers palette dialog box to control it. If it isn't already on screen, choose View | Palettes | Layers. The Layers palette shows you all the layers in an image. To vary their transparency, double-click on a layer in the list in the Layers palette and vary its opacity. To make a lot of layers easier to manage, you might also want to rename them with more descriptive titles than Raster 1, Raster 2, and so on.

results, and then save the finished product as a new picture. This technique allows you to find the perfect balance between you original photo and the edits you applied. Here's how to do it:

1. Load a picture into Paint Shop Pro.

2. Choose Layers | Duplicate from the menu. You should now see both layers in the Layers palette.

3. Make sure that the top layer is selected and make your changes. Choose Adjust | Sharpness | Unsharp Mask, for instance, and increase the sharpness of the picture to suit your taste. In fact, you can even go a little overboard and make it too sharp.

4. Finally, drag the opacity slider in the Layers palette to the left until the less-sharp background picture takes the edge off the sharpness of the top layer.

12

5. When you're happy with the rest, save the picture.

Remember that you can use this technique to improve the brightness, contrast, sharpness, or any other aspect of your picture. Experiment!

Improve Your Sky

I bet if you browse through your photos, you'll find many of your outdoor photos lack a certain punch—the sky is washed out, cloudless, or otherwise a little boring.

There's a good reason for that. When you compose a photograph, you usually concentrate on the primary subject and pay little heed to the sky itself. Because the sky is a lot brighter than your subject, the camera overexposes it and your sky ends up looking at least a little bleached. Even if the sky is properly exposed, it sometimes just doesn't cooperate, and you'll have a cloudless, boring sky that doesn't match the mood you were trying to get. By adding some snap back into to your skies, you can dramatically improve your so-so photos.

Multiply Your Sky

The easiest way to fix a bleached sky is to multiply it. What does that mean? Well, we're going to open a photo, select the sky, and copy it the clipboard. Then we'll paste copies of the sky back into the image, using a seldom-used tool to *multiply* the colors in each layer of sky to produce deeper, darker colors. If even a little blue is peeking through your sky, this technique is ideal because it's so easy to do.

For starters, find a picture with a weak sky, perhaps like the following one. Skies rarely come more anemic than this one, so let's see what we can do with it.

Now try these steps:

1. Open the photo in Paint Shop Pro, and click on the Magic Wand tool in preparation for selecting the sky. (The *Magic Wand* is one of my favorite selection tools because it grabs parts of the photo that share similar colors.) Set the Tolerance in the Tools Options dialog box to about 20.

2. Click the Magic Wand squarely in the middle of the sky: you should see selection marks appear around a big blotch of sky. Use the SHIFT key and click all around the sky until you've selected the entire thing, without also grabbing any nonsky parts of the picture.

   Make sure you've selected the entire sky—you can zoom in and pan around the image to double-check.

3. Copy the selected sky to the clipboard by choosing Edit | Copy from the menu.

4. Next, choose Edit | Paste | As New Layer. You can tell two copies of the sky are in the picture because you can grab the top sky layer and drag it around. Position the new sky so it lines up perfectly with the original sky underneath.

12

5. Now for the magic trick that makes all this effort worthwhile: the multiply effect. Choose Layers | Properties from the menu and you'll see the Layer Properties dialog box. Set the Blend Mode to Multiply. Click OK.

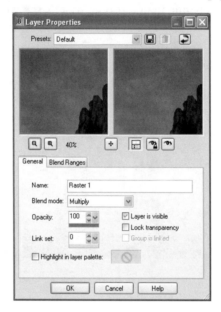

As soon as the dialog box disappears, you should see the colors in your sky immediately deepen. If you don't think that was enough of a change to suit you, don't worry. Here's where your artistic judgment comes in: because the sky is already copied into your clipboard, you can continue to paste new layers of sky into your image until you get the deep and colorful effect you're looking for. Using this technique, you can transform an anemic, pale blue sky into an angry, stormy scene in minutes.

Every time you paste in a new layer, be sure to set the Blend Mode for that new layer to Multiply, or the added layers will have no effect on the color of the sky.

Replace the Sky

The multiply technique isn't the only way to punch up a lame sky. You can also steal the sky from another photo, as I'll show you how to do now.

For starters, though, you're going to need a great photo of the sky. When I see a pretty blue sky, a swirling, cloudy day, a stormy afternoon, or a beautiful sunset, I grab my camera and start shooting. Use the Exposure Lock feature on your camera to set the exposure based on the sky or simply fill the entire frame with sky—either way, you'll capture all the color and intensity that you see through the viewfinder in the final image.

Shoot your sky shots with your camera's highest resolution, because you never know what resolution you'll eventually need. You might also want to take some pictures in Landscape mode and others in Portrait mode, so you have a selection of skies for any situation. Store your collection of sky images in a special folder, and you'll always have options available when you want to replace a bland sky.

Evict the Old Sky

Ready to try this technique? Load a picture with a weak sky in Paint Shop Pro. Then follow these steps:

1. Just like last time, use the Magic Wand with the Tolerance set at a moderate level (like 20) to select the sky in the photo.

2. After the sky is completely selected, choose Selections | Invert from the menu. You should see that the foreground is now selected and the sky isn't.

3. Copy the selected foreground to the clipboard by choosing Edit | Copy from the menu.

4. Check the image's resolution by choosing Image | Image Information from the menu. If you need to, write it down. You'll need that information in a few steps.

5. Open the image with the substitute sky in Paint Shop Pro.

6. Choose Image | Resize from the menu and fill in the proper numbers from step 4 in the Pixel Size boxes to resize this image to match the original.

7. Making sure the new image is still selected, choose Edit | Paste | As New Layer from the menu. You should see the foreground from the old picture appear in the new sky photo.

8. Drag the image around as needed until it's positioned properly in the frame. If you like the results, save the new image. You're done!

12

Chapter 13

Creating Special Effects

How to…

- Simulate a Hollywood-style blue screen effect
- Create Chroma Key effects like a news-show weather map
- Insert friends and family into pictures of celebrities
- Take science fiction shots of laser battles
- Shrink your friends and put them in jars
- Make double exposures
- Add artistic and paint-like effects to your photos
- Decolorize your photos
- Colorize black-and-white photos
- Digitally add motion blur to images

When I was a kid, I remember going to the movies and being wowed and amazed by special effects—stop motion, blue screen, animated laser combat, matte paintings—and while I'm sure a lot of people were just thinking things like "wow" and "cool," I was thinking "I wish I could do that." I was intrigued by the possibilities of trick photography, and I wanted to be able to do it myself.

Such special effects have always been possible for anyone with the time, money, equipment, and determination. I had none of the above. But when I got my first image-processing program back in 1987, I realized I could finally do what I'd always wanted to—special effects and trick photography on a budget.

Indeed, digital photography opens a lot of doors for us mere mortals. In this chapter, I'll tell you how to do some of the tricks that can make your images go beyond simple reality using, as usual, Paint Shop Pro. If your image-editing program is not Paint Shop Pro, the steps should be fairly easy to apply in the program you are using. You might not want to try all the techniques in this chapter, but I think there's a little fun in here for just about everyone.

Use a Hollywood-Style Blue Screen

What's a blue screen? Well, *blue screen* is the generic term for a technique in which action is photographed or filmed in front of a solid-colored backdrop. Later, in postproduction, special-effects technicians substitute a different scene in place

Did you know?

Blue Screens Aren't Always Blue

Hollywood has traditionally used blue screen to do special effects because it was easier before the age of computers. Movie makers could apply a red filter to a scene with a blue background, and the result would be a black matte that was easy to replace with different film footage. But, on the PC, it doesn't matter what color you use for a backdrop, as long as it's a unique color that doesn't blend in with other parts of the scene you're trying to preserve.

of the blue screen. So, a scene that looks like it happened in midair or in France or on the moon actually happened in front of a blue tarp. Separate footage is added in place of the tarp, and voilà. That's movie magic.

You can achieve the same kind of results yourself. It helps to use a real blue screen—a solid-colored backdrop that you can "paint out" afterward with a different image—but it's also possible to achieve good results with no preplanning at all.

The Chroma Key Technique

Think about the evening news. You've seen the weather forecaster stand in front of a map of the United States and point to cold fronts a million times before, but have you ever thought about how that bit of TV magic happens? Obviously, the forecaster isn't standing in front of a real map. Instead, it's a blue screen—a solid-colored rectangle. The engineer uses a technique called *Chroma Key* to replace the rectangle with video from another source. What happens is this: the engineer selects the color of the blue screen and identifies it as a "key." The second video source then overwrites anything in the scene that has the key-valued color.

Blue Screen Without a Screen

As I mentioned, in the movies they need to film in front of a special color matte to know which pixels to eliminate from the final scene. Life would be easier if you could always shoot in front of a blue screen, too. You could simply use the Magic Wand tool to select the whole background with just a few clicks. But because you don't live on a sound stage, it's a slightly more convoluted process to get a blue screen effect using your image-editing software.

13

Use the Chroma Key Technique in Your Photos

You can employ the Chroma Key technique yourself and use it for all sorts of interesting and entertaining purposes. Let's say you want to replace the view out your window with a completely different scene. It's just a matter of selecting the window (or all the little squares of glass that make up the window) and replacing them with a second image. Here's how to do it:

1. Open the picture with the window you want to modify. I'll use this one:

2. Click a selection tool from the toolbar. Depending on the image, you might want to "trace" the window with the Freehand Selection tool set

to Smart Edge, or you might have better results with the Magic Wand. In this example, I'll use the Magic Wand.

3. Click in the window and watch how the Magic Wand selects the view out the window. Hold down the SHIFT key (or, in the Tool Options palette at the top of the screen, change the Mode to Add) and continue clicking until the entire window is selected. You may need to fine-tune the Tolerance setting to make sure you only select what's outside the window each time you click.

4. Open a second image in Paint Shop Pro. This will be the image you insert into the first image to replace the view as a sort of weather map effect.

5. With the second image selected, copy the image to the clipboard by choosing Edit | Copy.

13

6. Choose Edit | Paste | Into Selection. You should see the second image pasted into the first image, as shown here:

You can use this technique in all sorts of ways. In addition to making your windows look out over an unusual vista, you can have a plain board become a famous painting or create your own news or weather effects. Experiment— it's fun and easy to do.

Suppose you want to place a subject in a completely different scene than the one in which it was photographed. In the movies, an actor would be filmed in front of a blue screen. Then a matte, or a second video source, would be substituted in place of the blue screen in postproduction. Here's how you can do it in Paint Shop Pro:

1. Open the image of the person or subject you want to transplant into another scene.

2. Create a selection area around that person or subject. Most of the time, the Freehand Selection tool set to Smart Edge works best, but you might also have good results with the Magic Wand. (In this case, the background was so uniform that I selected it with the Magic Wand and then used the Selections | Invert command to select only the airplane.)

3. When the selection is complete, choose Edit | Copy from the menu.

4. Open the second image.

5. Choose Edit | Paste | As New Layer. Your selection should appear in the second scene, but it might not be the right size:

6. To resize the image you have just pasted in, click the Raster Deform tool (it lives in the second cubby from the top of the toolbar) and then right-click a corner of the picture's selection frame. While right-clicking, drag the image to resize it to taste. Finally, reposition the image until it looks about right, and then save the finished image with a new name.

Fine-Tune the Selection

The technique I just described works fine a lot of the time, but it's just not accurate enough to create a truly convincing special effect. You can get even better results in other ways.

First, you can invest in a professional edge-detection program that largely automates the process of creating accurate selections for this kind of special-effect work. One of the best is a program from Corel (www.corel.com) called KnockOut. This program can isolate individual hairs on a person's head—it's great for this kind of image transplant.

Another, far cheaper method: if you have Paint Shop Pro, you can use the Background Eraser to delete the background from around the subject of your image, making it easy to copy and paste it into other images.

The Background Eraser works well, and is often able to leave individual hairs on someone's head intact while deleting unwanted backgrounds from around them. Select the Background Eraser from the tool palette. The only setting you generally need to make is the eraser's size; it shouldn't be too large, and you'll see why in a moment.

Click on the image, and you'll see a dialog box asking your permission to promote the target image to a full layer. (You might want to select the option to always take this action automatically.) Click OK. Now position the brush near the edge of the subject you're trying to isolate. Click, hold, and paint away the background. Be careful not to get more than half of the brush over your subject, or you'll erase a bit of the subject, too. If the brush is too large, make it smaller so you can control how much of it covers your subject at any moment. Work in bits: click, erase a little, and release the mouse. If you try to do the whole image in a single stroke and you make a mistake, the Undo button will set you back to square one and you'll have to do it all over from scratch. It's best to work in sections to avoid having to redo your work because of a glitch. On the other hand, it pays to remember that when painting with the Background Eraser the right mouse button restores the erased area.

The Background Eraser works something like the Magic Wand, erasing regions of similar color. It works best when a clearly defined edge is between the subject and background you're trying to erase. After you're done erasing the background, just select the subject and you can use it any way you like.

Shake Hands with Elvis

Now, the moment you've been waiting for—the opportunity to combine pictures of yourself or friends with famous celebrities and historical figures. It's not all that hard, especially now that you know the basic principles of working with blue screens. Let's suppose your friend, Kristen, has always wanted to meet Elvis. It's too late to set up a meeting, but you can do the next best thing. In the following steps, I'll show you how to combine a picture of her with an old shot of Elvis from the Nixon administration.

1. First, you need a suitable picture of Kristen—one in which she's more or less the same size as Elvis. Load the picture of the King into Paint Shop Pro and choose Image | Image Information to find out how tall Elvis is—or, more specifically, how tall the picture of Elvis is—in the selected image.

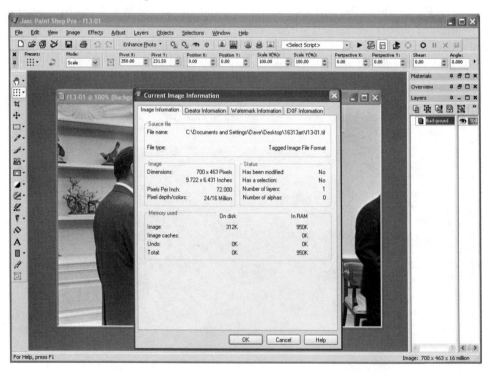

2. Armed with knowledge about Elvis, load the picture of Kristen and resize the image, using the Image | Resize menu, until she's about the right height, as shown here:

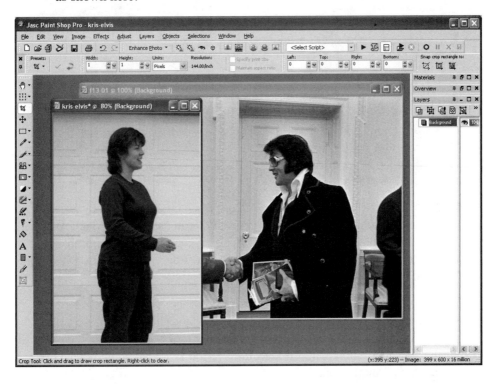

3. Now crop her so she's only seen from the waist up—like Elvis. It's okay to err on the big side, because you'll fine-tune things later. While you're here, you might want to convert Kristen to black and white (choose Image | Grayscale) to try to match her to Elvis.

4. Now for a little housecleaning. You need to erase as much of Nixon as you reasonably can, using the Clone tool techniques covered back in Chapter 12. (In this case, I used easily cloned elements of the picture, like the shelves and trim around the door, to wipe away Nixon.) You don't really need to erase all of him because you're going to position Kristen over part of this image—but the more of Nixon you can eliminate, the better, since you want Kris to look like she's really in the scene. The following illustration shows the original image (left), and what the image will look like (right) when it is getting close to good enough to paste in Kris:

5. Now for the tricky part. You need to use a selection tool to copy Kristen, but avoid including any of the background. You can use the Magic Wand or the Freehand Selection tool—whichever you're most comfortable with. Try the Freehand Selection tool set to Smart Edge, which often gives fairly good results in situations like this.

6. Once she's selected, it becomes obvious that the transition from Kristen to the background is too sharp to be believable. That means it won't look realistic in the final picture. Use the Feather tool to smooth out the edges of the selected region. Choose Selections | Modify | Feather, and then choose a value of about 4 pixels.

7. Copy Kristen to the clipboard, and then switch to the other image. Choose Paste | As New Layer. Kristen will appear onstage next to Elvis. If she's not quite the right size, select the Raster Deform tool (second from the top in the toolbar) and right-click a corner of the selection frame. Drag it to resize her.

8. Position Kristen in the new image, arranging her so their hands meet.

To make the illusion more convincing, you can try to sharpen Kristen a bit to match the original Elvis photo before you copy and paste her. Finish up by cropping away as much of the obviously faked background as you can, and save your image. The CIA might know it's a fake, but it's probably fine for your purposes.

Shoot a Sci-Fi Firefight

When I was in college, I took my geeky love of *Star Trek*, added a dose of photography, and came up with a hobby that could pretty much only be done around 3:00 A.M. Although it didn't help my grades much, it was a lot of fun to create special effects such as phaser blasts and disintegration halos. The best part? It was all done "in the lens," which means you can try it yourself if your digital or 35mm camera supports very long exposures. You can compare techniques and see if the digital way is easier. Here's how I did it in college:

1. Set the camera up on a tripod in total darkness and start a long exposure.

2. Using a flash, take a picture of the subject (like someone holding a phaser) and the target person. The flash needn't be mounted to the camera—you can just take a flash unit and hold it in your hand, flashing the subject once or twice.

3. Get behind the subject, and pointing a flashlight directly at the camera, walk to the target of the phaser blast, trying to keep the flashlight moving in a straight line so it traces what will look like a solid laser beam on the film.

4. Outline the target with the flashlight, again pointing it at the camera.

5. If you want to make the target look like he or she is disintegrating, ask the subject to leave the scene, and then flash the rear wall once.

6. Stop the exposure.

13

That's a lot of work, and the results are often hit or miss. Against all odds, you can sometimes get a half-decent one, as in this illustration:

The Disintegrating Subject

With a digital camera and a program like Paint Shop Pro, you can create this special effect a lot more scientifically. Here's an alternative way to create a similar image:

1. Take a picture of two kids posed, ready to have some special effects magic done to them. *Star Trek* clothing is optional.

2. Load the image into Paint Shop Pro and immediately store a copy of the image in the clipboard by choosing Edit | Copy.

3. As a first step toward making the target glow, carefully create a selection region around the subject. If you end up needing to make a "donut hole," as I do in this image, change the Mode setting to Remove and then outline the section that that doesn't belong (such as the small area contained between the arms and body):

4. Next, you want to make the selection bigger than the target's body. To do that, choose Selections | Modify | Expand, as shown in the following illustration, and select perhaps 10 or 20 pixels. Then feather the selection in the same way—choose Selections | Modify | Feather and set the feather to 5 or 10 pixels.

5. Now it's time to add an effect to make the subject glow. Choose Adjust |
Brightness And Contrast | Brightness/Contrast and jack the brightness up
to maximum. Click OK, and you should see a pure white region where the
subject used to be:

6. Next, add the copy as a new layer into your image. Choose Edit | Paste As New Layer. The glow should disappear because the copy of the original, unretouched image is now on top.

7. Double-click on the top layer to open the Layer Properties dialog box, and then reduce the layer's transparency until you get the effect you like—it'll probably be in the neighborhood of 20 percent to 40 percent.

You can also do variations on this. To get the target to disintegrate, take two pictures using a tripod so you have identical framing. In one image, include the subject; in the other image, just shoot the background without the subject. When you combine the images using the layer strategy I discussed in this example, it'll look like the subject is evaporating.

The Laser Blast

You've now made a pretty convincing disintegration scene, but what about the phaser blast? As I already mentioned, using a flashlight is an inexact science—it's hard to get a straight line, as you can see in Figure 13-1.

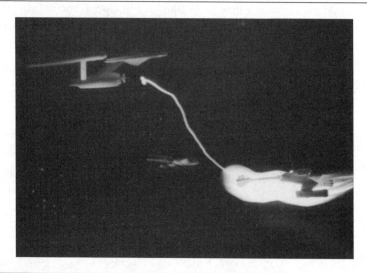

FIGURE 13-1   It's fiendishly difficult to "draw" a straight line through the air with a flashlight doing this the old-fashioned way.

With a paint program, though, you can get a perfectly straight beam. In most paint programs, holding down the SHIFT key while you draw a line locks the brush into following a perfectly straight path.

In Paint Shop Pro, click on the Paint Brush icon in the tool palette, and then select the color you want from the Materials palette. Position the paint brush where you want the beam to start, and then left-click. Hold down the SHIFT key, and click on the end point. The program draws a perfectly straight line between the two points. Here's how this particular shot came out:

Put Your Kid in a Jar

Have you ever been impressed by the fanciful digital art in magazine ads that depict the impossible or the far, far-fetched? I can't promise that you'll soon be able to photograph a cow driving your car or aliens posing with your dog while it plays the piano, but let me show you how easy it is to achieve something both cute and clever—you'll trap your kid in an old mayonnaise jar. Hopefully, when you see how easy it is to pull this stunt off, you'll want to make up a few clever gags of your own.

This exercise will show you that it's a snap to take a few pictures and combine them in layers within Paint Shop Pro, resizing them to achieve the effect you want. Do this:

1. Start by finding a nice, big jar. (When I tried this shot, I used a clear plastic peanut butter jar, but a mayo jar or any large, clear container is ideal.) Photograph someone peering inquisitively into it:

2. Next, have the person who'll be trapped inside the jar pose in front of a big backdrop. This is where a blue screen-style background (discussed earlier in the chapter) comes in handy, but you can also use a basement wall or some other background of uniform color. Don't have anything like that? Just shoot the picture outdoors, and you can deal with the background later.

13

3. Load the two images into Paint Shop Pro, but bring the trapped kid to the front. You'll work with this picture first.

4. If you managed to photograph the subject in front of a blue screen-style background, it'll be easier. Use the Magic Wand tool until the entire background is selected, leaving just the kid. Using a subtle feathering in the Tool Options dialog box can help make the picture a bit more realistic later.

5. When the background is entirely selected, choose Selections | Invert from the menu.

<table>
<tr><td>TIP</td><td>If you have an irregular background to contend with, you might want to use the Background Eraser or the Freehand Selection tool set to Smart Edge instead of the Magic Wand.</td></tr>
</table>

6. Once the subject is selected, copy it to the clipboard by choosing Edit | Copy.

7. Bring the jar photograph to the front and choose Edit | Paste | As New Layer from the menu. Your kid should now appear in the photo.

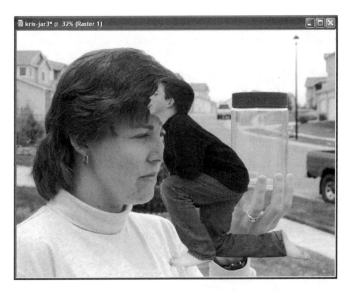

8. To shrink the new addition down to size, select the Raster Deform tool (second from the top in the tool palette) and right-click a corner of the selection frame. Drag it to resize him.

9. Click on the selection and drag it on top of the jar. If it fits, fine. If not, tweak its size with the Raster Deform tool until it fits properly in the jar.

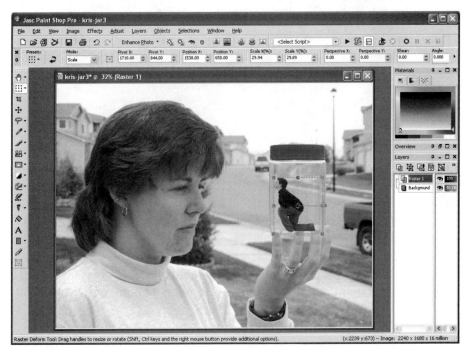

13

Once you tweak the size and position of the captured kid, your photo is done. But you can try other things to improve the photo as well:

- Photograph both pictures with similar lighting to make a more believable picture.

- Be careful about the angle from which you shoot the jar-kid in order to match the jar's perspective in the first photo.

- Select the mom's fingers, copy them to the clipboard, and paste them on top of the jar-kid as yet another layer. This way, you can increase the illusion that the subject is, indeed, inside the jar, not just pasted on top of it.

These efforts pay off—here is what the final result looks like:

Make a Double Exposure

Now let's return to Earth for an easy trick that mimics double-exposure photography. In the world of 35mm photography, double exposures are fun but hard to do well. You can go for far-out stuff that combines two completely different kinds of subjects or a simple artistic effort like the double-exposed flower in Figure 13-2.

The good news is that double-exposure shots in digital photography take seconds to do and don't require any of the elaborate planning or in-your-head

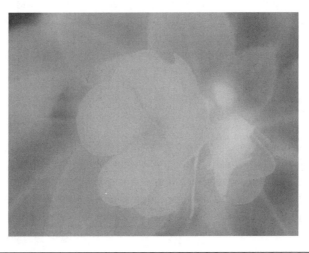

FIGURE 13-2   A double exposure like this one can add an ethereal quality to your photograph.

exposure calculations you'd need to do with film. And you can combine any number of photos into your multiple exposure. Here's how:

1. In Paint Shop Pro, load two photos you plan to combine.

2. Make sure they're both the same pixel size by choosing Image | Image Information from the menu. If one is larger, resize it so both are the same size.

3. Select one photo and choose Edit | Copy to put it in the clipboard.

4. Select the other photo and choose Edit | Paste | As New Layer. You should see the first photo appear over—and completely obscure—the selected photo.

5. If the Layers palette toolbar isn't already on the screen, open it by choosing View | Palettes | Layers.

6. In the Layers palette, double-click the top layer, and then drag the transparency slider for Layer 1 back from 100 percent until you can start to see the underlying image. Setting the slider at 50 percent will give you equal amounts of both pictures, though you might want one of the images to be significantly more prominent. If so, drag the slider back and forth until you get just the right multiple-exposure effect.

When you're happy with your multiple exposure, save the image. To get the double exposure-style image of the flower in Figure 13-2, I took one photo in sharp focus and a second exposure with the flower completely out of focus, and then combined them. I kept the out-of-focus image mixed back around 35 percent.

Paint Like Van Gogh

An easy way to transform your images into unique works of digital art is with the filters that are built into image-editing software such as Paint Shop Pro and Adobe Photoshop. A *filter* is graphics talk for a tool that lets you edit or manipulate your image. A filter is so named because when you run it, software changes your image according to a specific mathematical process, filtering the original data in a certain way to deliver a modified image. A common and relatively boring example of a filter is *sharpening*, which adds contrast to the pixels in an image, increasing the apparent sharpness.

Filters can do a lot more than just sharpen (or blur) your images, though. Hundreds of filters are out there, and many programs (like Paint Shop Pro) come with a few dozen. The best way to find out what a filter does is to experiment. I say that because it's one thing to read an explanation of the filter, but it's quite another thing to process a picture with each filter to see the effect. In general, you probably won't use many of these filters very often. But it pays to try them out, because you

Plug-Ins Expands Your Image-Editing Options

Many image editors, including Paint Shop Pro, can use something called a *plug-in*, or a *plug-in filter*, which are filters originally designed for Adobe Photoshop. Photoshop filters have become something of a standard in image-editing software, and many programs can use these filters. You can download filters from the Web, purchase them in stores, or sometimes they come with other image editors. Back in Chapter 7, for instance, I talked about a program called LensDoc, which lets you straighten images that got distorted because of wide-angle and fish-eye lenses. Well, LensDoc is a plug-in for Photoshop. It's a filter that processes your image within an image editor.

Filter	Description
Blur	Blur filters average nearby pixels to give the impression of blur, poor focus, or motion.
Sharpen	Sharpen filters increase apparent sharpness in an image by increasing the contrast between pixels, either throughout an image or only along edges.
Edge	Edge filters typically enhance and trace edges—regions defined by high-contrast borders between pixels.
Noise	Noise filters can add or remove "noise" in an image. Noise manifests itself in digital images as specks of high-contrast color, like snow in a TV transmission.
Geometric effects	These tools let you distort and skew parts of an image. They're good for displaying an image in a different perspective. You can change the orientation of an image in three dimensions or perhaps distort images within circles, cylinders, and other shapes.
Artistic effects	This is the general name for a slew of filters that do everything from add bas relief, watercolor, charcoal, mosaic, and more to your images. This is where you should go when you want to make your image look like it was hand painted or give it a unique, nonphoto-realistic look.

TABLE 13-1   Common Filter Types

never know when a certain effect will be just what you're looking for. Table 13-1 provides a quick summary of the most common filter types you might run across.

There's no limit to the kinds of effects you can achieve with filters, but beware: many of them are somewhat clichéd. Use your judgment when applying them. Check out Figure 13-3. Here you can see the original strawberries, as well as what they look like with Brush Stroke, Stained Glass, and Colored Pencil filters applied. In Paint Shop Pro, you can find all of these effects—and many others—in the Effects menu.

Lots of companies sell add-on plug-in filters for Photoshop and other graphics programs. More plug-in packages are available for Photoshop, Photoshop Elements, and Paint Shop Pro than I have room in this book to list. Just to name one, Xenofex 2, from Alien Skin Software (www.alienskin.com) is one of my favorites. It includes 14 filters—you can add lightening or a gorgeous blue sky to your images, or transform an image into a TV-style graphic, complete with old-fashioned, picture tube-esque curved edges and video scan lines. You can add burnt edges to a picture,

13

Original   Brush Stroke

Stained Glass   Colored Pencil

FIGURE 13-3   A variety of artistic effects are applied to the same original image.

shatter it like broken glass, or turn it into a virtual jigsaw puzzle. And that's only about half the effects. Figure 13-4 shows a night photo that's been transformed with the addition of an oversized moon (added via Paint Shop Pro's Layers feature, plus lightening and a TV effect from Xenofex 2).

Decolorize Your Pictures

This effect is a lot of fun. Surely you've seen television commercials in which everything is black and white except for one item—a person, perhaps, or the featured product—which is in full color. It's an effective trick because your eyes are drawn to the color image in a sea of gray.

FIGURE 13-4   A creepy sci-fi look is created after just a few minutes in an image editor with filters.

On television, this effect is typically done with two cameras. On the PC, though, you can do it after the fact with a single image—you didn't even have to have this effect in mind when you originally took the shot. Best of all, it's not hard to do. It's particularly easy if your image editor supports layers. The basic idea is this:

- Stack two copies of the image in separate layers.
- Convert one to grayscale.
- Select most of the image in the color version.
- Delete the selection, leaving a small color subject on top of the grayscale image.

13

Specifically, here's how to do it in Paint Shop Pro:

1. Open the image you want to use and make a copy of it by choosing Edit |
   Copy. Don't paste it anywhere yet; just let it stay in the clipboard.

2. Select the image and convert it to a grayscale picture by choosing Image |
   Grayscale. Then turn the image into a 24-bit file by choosing Image |
   Increase Color Depth | 16 Million Colors.

3. Rename this image's layer to **grayscale** so it's easier to keep track of. To do
   that, double-click the layer in the Layers palette and change the name in the
   Layer Properties dialog box.

4. Now add the color image on top of this one. Select the image and choose
   Edit | Paste | As New Layer. You can prove it worked by sliding the
   transparency control of the top layer until you can see the grayscale image
   peeking through. Now the second layer sits on "top" of the grayscale layer,
   as you can see in the Layers palette:

5. With the new color layer selected, use the Selection tool to trace out the subject you want to keep in color. Trace as carefully as possible. (In this example, I'm selecting just the flower petals, which will be a vibrant violet against a sea of gray.)

6. When you're done, choose Selections | Invert to select everything *except* the subject you want to keep in color.

7. Choose Edit | Cut to cut most of the color image away.

8. Choose Selections | Select None to finish.

You should now have a grayscale image with a single element in color. Save the image with a new name.

Colorize an Image

Now try the opposite technique: instead of taking color away from your picture, here you'll add color or change the colors in your photos. Colorizing digital images—or even old black-and-white photos you've scanned into your PC—is easy, though it takes a little artistic skill to do well. Some folks use the colorizing technique to see what their car or basement walls would look like painted another color, while others want to enhance old photos they found tucked away in a family

13

photo album. Whatever your motivation, the mechanics of colorizing your photos is easy. Try this:

1. Start by loading a picture into Paint Shop Pro and selecting just the part of the image you want to colorize. If you're trying a new paint scheme on your car, use the Magic Wand tool to select the car's body without also capturing the windshield, chrome, or surrounding background. If you want to paint the basement, select the walls. As usual, you should fine-tune the Magic Wand's Tolerance setting and use the SHIFT key to select the entire region.

2. Now click the Flood Fill tool, and in the Tool Options dialog box, change the Blend mode from Normal to Color:

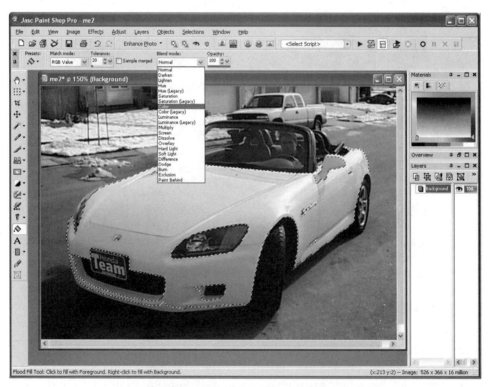

3. Left-click in the color palette to select the color you'd like to paint.

4. Click anywhere in your selected region, and you should see the color change without losing any of the underlying texture in the selected region. In other words, you've changed the color of your subject.

Another Kind of Colorizing

You can create an interesting work of art using the Colorize tool. Colorize converts your image into a picture with uniform hue while maintaining the original brightness levels, and that means you get a monochrome image that isn't grayscale. Instead, it's bluescale, redscale, or whatever scale you happen to choose. Want to get an image that looks like it was photographed through night-vision goggles? Try to colorize it with a hue of 75 and a saturation of 80. But keep experimenting—some images can look dramatic when rendered in just a primary color.

Add Digital Motion Blur

Life is full of little paradoxes. They bother to display nutritional information on the wall at McDonalds, for instance. And, in the world of photography, people often try to capture the essence of motion in pictures, which are by their very nature totally static, two dimensional, and frozen in time.

That's what makes motion-themed photos so compelling, though: the notion that you can somehow capture motion and freeze it for all eternity on an unchanging computer screen or sheet of photo paper. Back in Chapter 6, I talked about motion blur techniques when you actually took the picture; now let's add it digitally after the fact. My guinea pig is a C-130 cargo plane that I photographed at an airshow.

In the following photo, the C-130 is frozen with a pretty fast shutter speed:

13

As you can see, I've stopped the action so thoroughly that even the propeller blades hang frozen in the air. As a result, the picture lacks soul.

To make the image look like it's moving, do this:

1. Start by adding another layer to the picture, which you can use to help fine-tune the motion blur effect later. Choose Layers | Duplicate. You should now have two layers in the Layers palette called Background and Copy Of Background.

2. Make sure that the top layer—Copy Of Background—is selected by clicking on it in the Layers palette.

3. Choose Adjust | Blur | Motion Blur. In the Motion Blur dialog box, you can set two important options: the Angle of the blur and the Strength of the effect. Set the strength around 50 percent, and then adjust the angle of the blur until it's roughly in line with the direction of the subject's motion. As you can see, I've added blur to this image, but unfortunately, it just looks, well, blurry. It's as if someone bumped into me right as I took the picture.

4. Use the Eraser to fine-tune the blur. Click the Eraser tool, which lives in the seventh cubby from the bottom of the toolbar. The Eraser does just what it sounds like—it erases pixels from the picture. But since you have the original image in the layer underneath, what the Eraser will do is let you combine blurry and nonblurry sections of the picture by revealing pixels from underneath.

5. Set the Opacity to 100 and adjust the size of the Eraser, if necessary, so you don't wipe away too much of the picture with each stroke.

6. Use the Eraser to sharpen the leading edges of the plane—the nose, the wings, and the tail section—and sharpen the inner sections of the body

as well, leaving just the trailing edges blurred. The final image looks something like this:

Blur the Background

That's one way to add motion blur to an image. It's akin to keeping the camera stationary while you snap a picture of a moving subject. Another technique you might want to try is akin to panning (see Chapter 6). For that, you want to blur the background and leave the subject intact.
To do that, follow these steps:

1. Select the subject using whatever technique you prefer. But, because you want to apply motion blur to the background, you need to invert your selection—that will select the entire background, leaving the vehicle itself unselected. Choose Selections | Invert.

2. Next, choose Adjust | Blur | Motion Blur. Again, set the Angle and Strength, and then click OK.

You'll should see a pretty plausible example of motion blur, as in this illustration:

13

Chapter 14

Creating Projects

How to...

- Add text to digital images
- Fill text with other images
- Create text drop shadows
- Turn images into wallpaper for the Windows desktop
- Turn images into screen savers
- Make photo collages
- Add small images to letterhead in Word
- Create greeting cards on the PC
- Make photo filmstrips
- Turn your photo into jigsaw puzzles
- Make your own newsletter

Over the course of this book, I've shown you how to do all sorts of things to your images—everything from the mundane, like sharpening, cropping, and brightening your images, to adding sophisticated special effects like Chroma Key and abstract effects.

Sometimes, though, all you want to do is add a caption or turn a picture into a birthday card. In this final chapter on image editing, let's talk about the various ways you can add text to your images to turn them into true multimedia works of art. I'll even show you some simple tricks for creating stuff like Windows wallpaper, greeting cards, and letterhead with your images.

Add Text to Pictures

If you're used to using a word processor like Microsoft Word, you might be surprised to find that some image editors don't let you type directly onto the canvas as if you were writing a letter to your Mom.

Instead, many image editors (such as Paint Shop Pro, for instance) require you to type your text into a dialog box, and it only appears in the image after you accept the text entry. In fact, the Text tool in Paint Shop Pro plays by a few unusual rules:

- Unlike some image editors, such as Adobe Photoshop Elements, you can't type directly onto the image. Instead, you need to type your text in a dialog box and then transfer it to the image when you finish. You can see the Text Entry dialog box used by Paint Shop Pro in Figure 14-1.

- The color of the text will usually be painted in the currently selected background color, so make sure it's set to the right color before you click the Text tool.

- Text is an editable object when you first position it. That means you can position it, stretch it, transform it, and so on—but, depending on which mode you're in when you insert the text, it might only be editable initially. If you change tools and do something else, that text typically becomes a permanent part of the image.

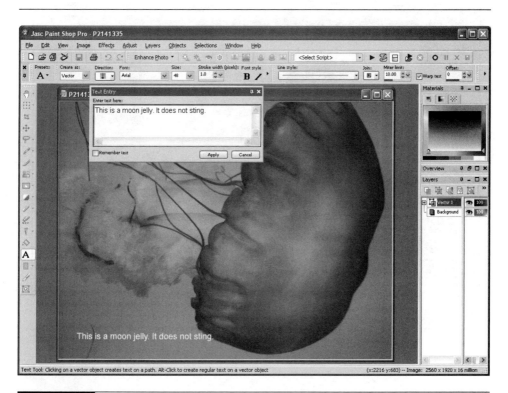

FIGURE 14-1   The Text toolbar and the Text Entry dialog box let you specify the style, color, and size of the text you add to a digital image.

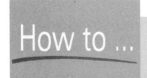

Add Text to a Picture in Paint Shop Pro

Occasionally, you may need to add text to a photograph. It's easy to do, and you can get suprisingly fancy effects with very little effort. Here are the basics:

1. Right-click in the color palette on the desired color to change the background color to whatever you want the text to be.

2. Click the Text button in the tool palette. The mouse pointer will change to the letter *A*. In the text toolbar, set the Create As drop-down menu to Floating or Vector. Set the font and size as well, but you can adjust those in a moment.

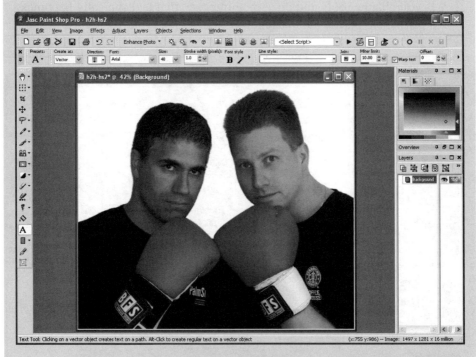

3. Click in the image where you want the text to be positioned. The point that you click will be the lower-left corner of the text box.

NOTE *The timing of these steps vary in different programs. In Adobe Photoshop, for instance, there's no text box at all. In older versions of Paint Shop Pro, you don't see the font selections until you click the image.*

4. When the Text Entry dialog box appears, type your text into the space provided. You can adjust the font and size by selecting the text in the box, and then changing its characteristics using the toolbar.

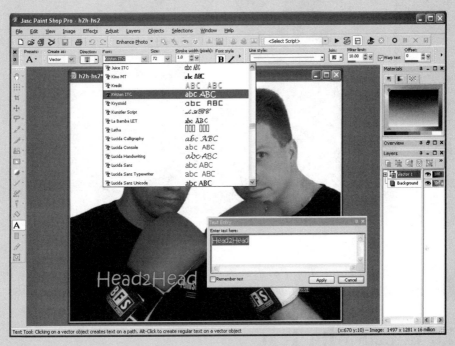

5. Click Apply. The text should appear in the image at the place you positioned it in step 3.

6. For the moment, the text is treated as an object you can edit. You can reposition the text by dragging the box in the center of the text box. If you selected Vector text, you can also resize the text by dragging the small boxes in the sides of the text box. To keep the text in its

original proportions as you resize it, right-click and drag it by one of the corners.

 *Notice that Paint Shop Pro displays the text you enter in the dialog box as you type, but it doesn't become a part of the image until you click Apply.*

Special Effects with Text

You can do a lot with text in an image—so much more than pasting letters down in some primary color. Attractive text, in fact, is what makes or breaks documents such as posters and greeting cards. A lot of text tricks are so easy to do that you can experiment and create your own. I have a few you might want to start with, though.

Create Picture-Filled Text

One of my favorite tricks is to make an image show through the text, as if it were a digital stencil. Look at Figure 14-2, for instance. As you can see, I've made the word "Flying" from a photo of a bird in flight, and the word "Tiger" from, well, a tiger. This is an interesting exercise in creating an eye-catching picture, so let me show you how to do this yourself.

FIGURE 14-2   You can convey the spirit of a word using patterns from pictures as stencils.

Here's how:

1. Open the image you want to show through the text.

2. Click the Text icon in the tool palette.

3. Set the Create As drop-down menu in the text toolbar to Selection. This will create the text as a selection instead of as solid-colored text. Set the font and size in which you want the text to appear. You'll need to make the text big and fat for this effect to work. For starters, I suggest you choose a font like Bauhaus.

4. Click in the spot where you want to grab the photo as text, and then enter your desired text. It's okay to be approximate, since you'll be able to move the text around in a moment.

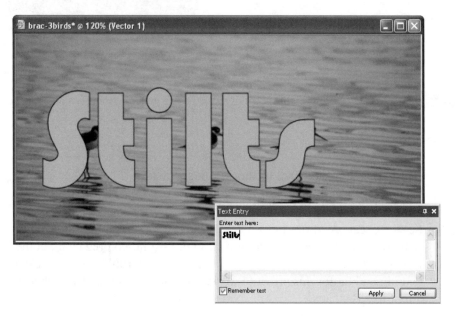

In Paint Shop Pro, the spot you click becomes the lower-left corner of the text.

5. Click OK. The text appears as a selection in the image. You can now reposition the text by right-clicking and dragging. The pointer will change to four arrows when you can drag it.

6. Copy the text to the clipboard by choosing Edit | Copy.

7. Open the image to which you want to add the text.

8. Choose Edit | Paste | As New Selection from the menu. The text should appear in the image.

9. Position the text to your liking and choose Selections | Select None.

The finished text should look something like this:

Add a Drop Shadow

Drop shadows, as shown in Figure 14-3, are a cool embellishment that can add a lot to the visual appeal of your text. They can even make it more readable,

FIGURE 14-3   Drop shadows are a great way to lead the eye to text in the image.

particularly on pictures with very busy color patterns. Some programs come with a drop shadow tool built in, making it a snap to add drop shadows to your text. But, if your program doesn't have a drop shadow feature, you can achieve similar results simply by making two copies of the text in different colors and arranging them by hand, so they look like text and shadow.

To achieve this affect, try this:

1. In the Materials palette, set the background color to black. This will be the color of your shadow text.

2. Click the Text button in the tool palette and enter the text, font, and size. Select the Vector option in the Create As drop-down menu.

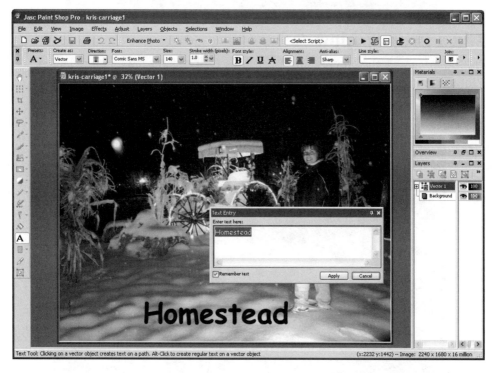

3. Now, click in the image to specify where you want the text to appear. The Text Entry dialog box should appear. Enter your text, click Apply, and then position the text precisely where you want it in the finished image.

4. Now go back to the color palette and change the background color to white.

5. Click the Text button in the tool palette again. In the Text Entry dialog box, don't change anything. You'll want the font, size, and text to be exactly the same as the shadow text you've already entered.

6. Click in the image. You needn't be precise about where the text will go right now because you'll move the text with the mouse in a few steps. Type your text, and then click OK to paste the text into the image.

7. Position the mouse pointer over the center of the text, and then drag the text until it's positioned over the shadow text, offset just enough so it looks like a drop shadow.

8. Choose Selections | Select None.

TIP

You can also apply a drop shadow effect to text more directly. To do that, add text to an image and then select Effects | 3D Effects | Drop Shadow from the menu. If necessary, click OK to create a new layer and then fine-tune the effect from the Drop Shadow dialog box. The look of the text will vary depending on whether you choose Vector or Selection text.

14

Create a Drop Shadow from the Image

This last text trick is so simple you're going to say it's hardly a trick at all, but I'm including it to show you how easy it is to come up with cool effects with little effort. The effect: text filled with a picture, like we've already done, but this time the underlying picture is the same as the text. How can you see the text at all, you wonder, if it's filled with the same image as the background? The text is bordered—on two sides, at least—by a drop shadow. Check out Figure 14-4.

Here's how to do it:

1. Change the background color to white using the Materials palette.

2. Click the Text button. Make sure the Stroke and Fill styles are set to solid color, and then choose Selection in the Create As drop-down menu. Set the font to taste.

3. Click in the image to specify where the text will be pasted.

4. Enter the text, and then click Apply to paste the text into the image.

5. You should see a selection shaped like the text. Grab the text and drag it a short distance. In place of the text, you should see lettering that will serve as your drop shadow. Don't move the text too far or the image text will get lost in the surrounding image.

FIGURE 14-4   This effect is subtle, but one of my favorites.

Cool Projects for Your Digital Images

Now that you know how to edit, manipulate, and embellish your images, you probably want to apply those skills by using images in projects that go beyond e-mailing images to your friends. One of the benefits of digital images, of course, is the ease with which you can incorporate them into projects such as posters, greeting cards, newsletters, and business cards. Let's take a look at how you can get started doing this yourself.

Use Digital Images as Wallpaper

Let's start with something that's not only easy, but also can make your PC a bit more fun. Your Windows desktop can display any kind of image as long as it's been saved in a JPG, GIF, or BMP format. If your desktop still has that same old background that it had when you took it out of the box, you can use an image from your digital camera to brighten things up.

To display one of your images on your desktop, do this:

1. Make sure your image is in JPG, BMP, or GIF format. As you know by now, most digital cameras save images in JPG format, so you're probably ready to go. (Windows can't display a TIF or RAW image on the desktop, however.)

2. Right-click the desktop and choose Properties from the Context menu. The Display Properties dialog box appears.

3. On the Desktop tab, click the Browse button to choose the image.

4. If you want the image centered in your display, choose Center in the Display drop-down menu. If you'd prefer the image to repeat itself all across the display, choose Tile instead.

5. Click OK to close the dialog box.

14

NOTE   *You might want to resize the image in a program like Paint Shop Pro to match the screen resolution you run on your PC. That way, the image will take up the entire screen. The original resolution of the image should be close to your desktop size (or bigger). If you start with an image that's much smaller than the desktop, the result will often be quite ugly.*

If your image is too small for the display, it'll either be tiled to fill the screen or centered in the display with a lot of blank desktop around it. For photographs, I think centering looks good—tiling photographs just looks busy and annoys me. Of course, stretching a photo to fill the desktop can be unattractive as well (see Figure 14-5). Of course, it's your computer—you can experiment and arrange your display any way you like.

a.

b.

c.

FIGURE 14-5   The same image shown a) centered, b) tiled, and c) stretched

If the various members of your family all have their own separate logins for the computer, everyone can select their own wallpapers, and the appropriate one will start when each person logs onto the PC.

Turn Your Pictures into Screen Savers

The same is true of the Windows screen saver—everyone in the family can select their own, and the chosen screen saver will start displaying after a certain period of inactivity. These days, most monitors don't need screen savers to protect them from old-time dreaded "burn in," but screen savers are still fun to watch, which is why so many people use them.

Windows XP has a screen saver that works by showing off your digital photos. To use it, do this:

1. Right-click on the desktop and choose Properties.

2. On the Display Properties dialog box, click the Screen Saver tab.

3. From the Screen Saver list, choose My Pictures Slideshow. Now, you can click OK and Windows will use some smart default settings to show the pictures in you're My Pictures folder whenever you stop using the computer for some short period of time. But you can customize the settings by continuing on to the next step.

14

4. Click the Settings button to see the Options page. Here, you can specify how frequently the pictures change, how much of the screen they should take up, and if Windows should use transitions between the pictures. Most importantly, you can tell Windows exactly where to find your photos, which is handy if you keep them somewhere other than the My Pictures folder, or if you only want to show certain images.

5. When you're happy with the screen saver, click OK twice.

Make a Photo Collage

As the saying goes, everyone loves a parade. And a photo collage is a veritable parade of photos—which probably explains why they are so darned popular. A collage (which is just a collection of photos arranged on a single page) is easy to do and is a great way to showcase and share a collection of pictures from a special occasion. Here's an easy way to make one:

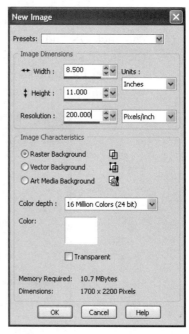

1. Since a collage is just a collection of photos, you'll need a blank page on which to arrange them. You can make your collage small (for e-mail, perhaps) or large (for printing), but let's create this one big enough to print nicely on an ink-jet printer. Choose File | New, and when you see the New Image dialog box (see the following illustration), specify a size of 8.5×11 inches. Since Paint Shop Pro needs to know how many pixels to put in this blank page, also set the resolution to 200 pixels/inch. That will create an image that's 1700×2200 pixels. Click OK. You should now have a blank white canvas, ready to be populated with pictures.

2. Now you're ready to start adding stuff. Find a picture that you want to add to your collage and open it in Paint Shop Pro.

If you're using Paint Shop Pro, you might want to use the program's browse mode for this. Click and drag the picture from the Browse window into the canvas.

3. Once the picture is open, tweak it however you like. You might want to run One Step Photo Fix from the Enhance Photo button in the toolbar, for instance, or correct the color and exposure manually. While you're working on it, crop the picture to taste using the Crop tool. At this point, you workspace might look something like this:

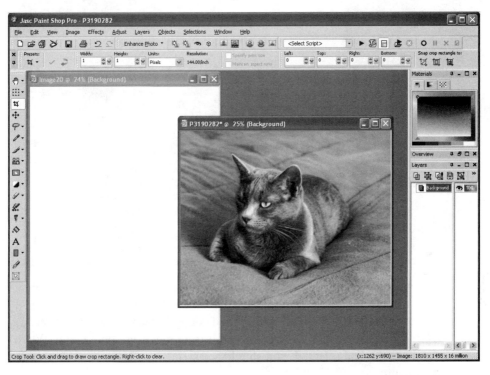

4. Now it's time to insert your first picture into the collage page. Click the picture to make sure it is selected and then choose Edit | Copy to copy the picture to the clipboard. Then switch to the blank canvas and choose Edit | Paste | Paste As New Layer. The picture should appear in the blank canvas, but it's entirely possible that it'll completely fill or be too big for the page. That's fine; you'll fix that in a moment.

5. Select the Move tool in the toolbar. Click in the picture you just pasted and drag it until you can see the lower-right corner of the picture, like this:

6. You want to see the lower-right corner so you can use the resizing handle that will appear there in a moment. To get the resizing handle, select the Raster Deform tool. It shares the second cubby in the toolbar with three other tools, so you may need to choose it from the drop-down menu. When you have the tool selected, you should see sizing handles appear all around the picture.

7. Move the mouse over the bottom-right corner of the picture. Don't click and drag; if you do that, you'll actually deform the picture by changing its aspect ratio. Instead, right-click the sizing handle and then drag it while holding the right mouse button down. Then left-click anywhere inside the picture and drag it to position the photo inside the collage page.

8. Now that you've positioned the first picture in your collage, adding more is a piece of cake. You can use this technique to add any number of images, give them unique sizes and positions, and make your collage as visually interesting as you like. Pictures can overlap or have white borders—it's all up to you. Here's what my collage looks like after using this technique:

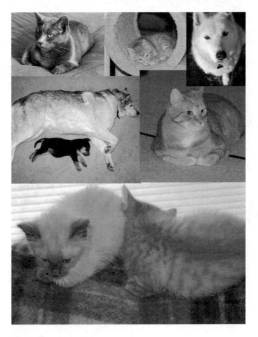

Add an Image to Letterhead

If you use Microsoft Word and send a lot of letters, you might want to try this next project—creating your own personal letterhead with an embedded digital image. Here's what to do:

14

1. Open Microsoft Word. If you don't already have a new blank document open, click the New Document icon in the toolbar.

2. Design the letterhead any way you like. You should set your formatting to single space and try to keep your text smaller than about 11 points.

3. To insert an image from your digital camera, choose Insert | Picture | From File and locate the image you want to include. The image will appear in your document.

4. To make the image easier to move around and position on the page, you need to put a frame around the picture. Right-click the image and choose Format Picture.

5. Click on the Layout tab and choose Tight.

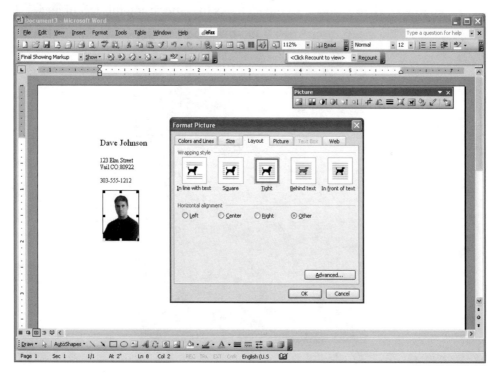

6. Click OK.

7. Position the image in the letterhead region of your document, such as to the left of your name. Notice how the text moves to accommodate the image.

8. Finish the letterhead by drawing a thin horizontal line under the text and image (see Figure 14-6). To do that, activate the drawing tools by clicking the Drawing icon in the toolbar. Then click the Line tool and drag out a horizontal line, holding down the SHIFT key at the same time. The line will snap to the horizontal automatically.

Create Your Own Greeting Cards

You can make greeting cards using your computer in two ways: the easy way and the not-as-easy-but-still-not-very-hard way. The easy way is by using one of the

FIGURE 14-6   Images can make your letterhead quite elegant (unless it's a picture of me...).

many greeting card software packages on the market (see Figure 14-7). Not only can you import your digital camera images into these programs, but they also come with a considerable collection of clip art and premade card templates.

If you don't have one of those programs, you can still make your own greeting cards in a page layout program or Microsoft Word. Because Word is the lowest common denominator—almost everyone has it—let's create a card in that. Before we get started, though, it's worth pointing out that you can make a greeting card on the PC in two common methods: the single-fold and the dual-fold.

Single-fold cards are simply made from 8.5×11-inch paper or cardstock and folded once down the middle, so the card measures 5.5×8.5 inches. This is a slightly oversized card, but it's a good size and the one I usually use. The alternative is a dual-fold card that's folded once lengthwise and again widthwise,

14

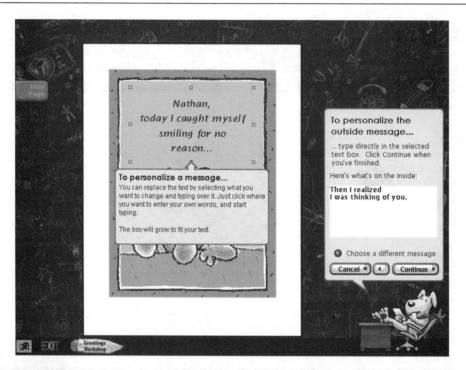

FIGURE 14-7   Greeting card programs let you import your own digital images into their greeting card templates.

for a card that measures 5.5×4.25 inches. The disadvantage to this kind of card is that it's a bit small and it has a potentially amateurish double-fold along one edge (see Figure 14-8).

You can't make dual-fold cards in Word because that kind of card requires one of the panels to be printed upside down. So Word is best at single-fold cards, and I describe how to do that in this example:

1. Open Word and create a new document.

2. Change the document into a landscape orientation. Choose File | Page Setup. The Page Setup dialog box appears.

3. Click the Paper Size tab and select Landscape from the orientation section. Click OK.

Single-fold

-side	one-
Back	Front

-side	two-
	Inside
	Right

Dual-fold

	Front
Inside Right	Back

FIGURE 14-8   You can make either single-fold or dual-fold cards on your PC with almost any program.

4. Now you need to give the document two columns. Each column will be a panel on the finished card. Choose Format | Columns.

5. In the Columns dialog box, select Two and click OK.

6. Now you can enter your text. The left column on the first page is the rear of the card. If you want to, you can add something to the bottom of the rear panel like commercial greeting cards have. Press ENTER enough times to get to the bottom of the page.

7. Now it's time to create the front of the card. That's the right column on the first page, so press ENTER to get there. You'll probably want to insert an image there using Insert | Picture | From File. You can place text above or below the image, or you can integrate the text in the image in a program like Paint Shop Pro first. Be sure to experiment with large and stylish fonts for this card.

14

TIP   *Microsoft's WordArt is a cool way to dress up a greeting card in Word. Choose Insert | Picture | WordArt to insert WordArt into your project. WordArt lets you turn plain text into a fancy 3-D piece of art.*

8. The inside of the card is on the second page. The left inside panel is the left column, and the right inside panel is the right column. Enter text and images as necessary to lay out the card you want to create.

9. When you're done, you need to print your card manually so it doesn't print the second page of the document on a second sheet of paper. To do that, you have two choices:

   ■ Only load a single sheet of paper in the printer. When the first page is printed, turn the paper over and load it back in for the second pass.

   ■ Change the printer settings. In Word, choose File | Print. Choose Properties to open the Printer Properties dialog box and change the printer's paper source to Manual.

If you're printing on an ink-jet printer, make sure you wait for the first side to dry before turning the paper over and printing the second side. See Chapter 15 for more information on printing.

Make a Photo Filmstrip

When I showed this particular project to my 12-year-old daughter, I said that I didn't really know what to call it. My intention, as I explained to her, was to arrange photos in a line to look like an old-fashioned filmstrip, with the center picture popping with color and all the other images somewhat bleached or devoid of color. I envisioned making this sort of thing as a gift, with a recent picture in the center and older snapshots on either side. Here's what I showed her as my working example:

She suggested calling it a "lifestrip," and I suppose that's a pretty good title. Here's how to make your own:

1. First, pick a series of pictures to include in your own filmstrip. Five to seven pictures is a good number. Pick your pictures and load them all into Paint Shop Pro.

2. Now you need to make sure each and every one of the pictures is exactly the same height. That'll be important later, when you paste them into the filmstrip. If you were planning to make a very small lifestrip—just 300 pixels high, for instance—you'd probably want to make all of the pictures 300 pixels square. Select one of your pictures and then click the Crop tool. In the Tool Options palette, select Square from the list of presets. Now adjust the size and position of the frame in the picture to taste, and click the checkmark to accept your crop. Finally, choose Image | Resize from the menu and set the width and height to 300 pixels. Click OK. You've now cropped your picture and sized it to fit perfectly in the lifestrip panel. Go ahead and repeat the process on all the other pictures, and leave them open in Paint Shop Pro.

3. When you're done resizing your photos, it's time to make the filmstrip. Choose File | New from the menu. In the New Image dialog box, create an image that's wider than the combined width of all the images and exactly the same height as each picture. Click OK.

14

4. Select a picture and choose Edit | Copy from the menu. Switch to the filmstrip and choose Edit | Paste | Paste As New Layer. Click the Move Tool and drag the picture to the far left of the filmstrip.

5. Now it's more lather, rinse, and repeat—copy each picture, paste it into the strip, and then position each picture beside the next. You should now have a strip that looks like this:

6. Finally, you can use saturation to draw attention to the center picture. Click the Move tool and click on the center picture. Then choose Adjust | Hue and Saturation | Hue/Saturation/Lightness from the menu. Drag the Saturation slider up to about 30, and then click OK. You should see the center picture "pop" a bit, since its colors have been enhanced.

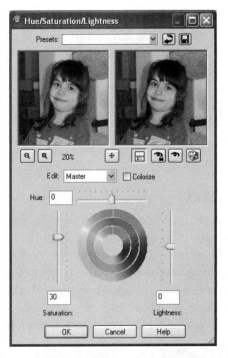

7. Now start on the far left of the lifestrip. Click on the furthest picture and choose the Hue/Saturation/Lightness control again. Lower the saturation to about −60 and click OK. Lower the saturation of all the other pictures (except the center one, of course) in a similar way.

When you're done, you can save and print your project. As an alternative, you don't have to paste the pictures into a strip: you can instead make seven individual prints and mount them on your wall in individual frames.

14

Make a Photo Jigsaw Puzzle

When is a digital photo a game that the whole family can play? When it's also a jigsaw puzzle. If you're looking for a new and unique activity for the family, consider turning pictures the family takes into jigsaw puzzles that you can then solve together or give to the kids to solve on their own. You can make pictures into real, live puzzles by gluing a print of your photo onto a piece of cardboard (the thicker the better) and then cutting it carefully into curved pieces.

If you're not that handy with glue and scissors, you can solve your puzzles just on the computer screen. There are a number of computer games that let you turn your own digital photos into jigsaw puzzles. Consider BrainsBreaker, for instance;

it is one of a number of programs you can find on the Internet that lets you solve an onscreen jigsaw puzzle made from any picture on your computer.

BrainsBreaker lets you import a photo, crop it down to just the part you want to turn into a puzzle, and select the number of and shape of your puzzle pieces. Then the desktop turns into the digital equivalent of your dining room table, complete with puzzle pieces lining the screen edges, a clear work area, and even a slew of "boxes" for storing pieces you don't need to work with right away.

You can download a free trial of BrainsBreaker at www.brainsbreaker.com. If you like it, the complete program costs $20.

Create a Newsletter

Equipped with Microsoft Publisher or a similar page layout program, you can create professional and attractive newsletters for the office, family, or your club or organization. Publisher comes with most versions of Microsoft Office, and I highly recommend it for generating your own newsletters (as well as business cards and other projects). Publisher is a wizard-based program. All you have to do is follow the directions to set up the overall look and feel of your document, and then fill in the text and replace the placeholder images with your own pictures.

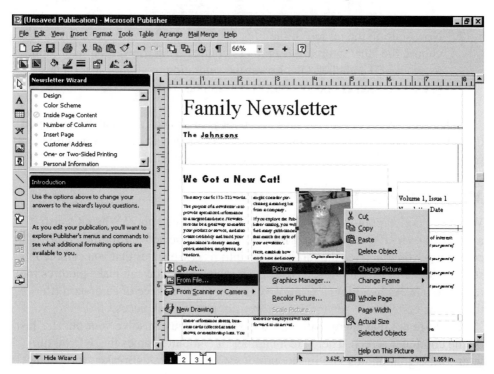

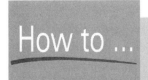

Create Gifts from Pictures

Many web sites and local photo stores can take your digital images and use them to create all sorts of interesting gifts, like coffee mugs, T-shirts, refrigerator magnets, jigsaw puzzles, and even food (your picture can be added in edible food dyes to cookies, cakes, and candies). Sites like ClubPhoto.com, ofoto.com, and PhotoWorks.com all offer these basic services. If you're shopping for a picture-apron or you want to eat some vacation shots, check out these web sites.

Make a Magazine Cover

At gift time, I believe photos are some of the most personal and most appreciated gifts you can give. But just handing someone an 8×10-inch photo lacks that certain *je ne sais quoi*, as the French like to say. So I like to do things with my pictures that are a bit unusual. The next time a birthday rolls around, here's a clever gift you can make all by yourself, without any help from a bakery: a framed mock magazine cover featuring your guest of honor.

This is easy to do. All you need is an appropriate, high-resolution photo and an image-editing program to make some surgical changes. Then send it to the printer and it's ready for framing. Because this will eventually be printed on an ink-jet printer at 8×10-inch size, you should start with a 2- or 3-megapixel image. For this example, I'm going to make the debut issue of *Kristen* magazine. Here are the steps to follow:

1. Your first order of business is to give your picture a magazine-like outline. Load it into your image editor and add a blank border area around your image. You can make it any color you like, but for my picture I think a nice fire-red border will be very magazine-ish. In Paint Shop Pro, there's an easy way to do this. Choose Image | Add Borders, and then choose a color from the color box in the Add Borders dialog box. Next, enter a border dimension. If you're using a 3-megapixel image, you might need about 100 pixels of border to get the right effect, but experiment until you see something you like. Be sure to set the border to Symmetric, so all four sides are the same. Click OK to create the border. You should see a red border added around the outside of the image.

14

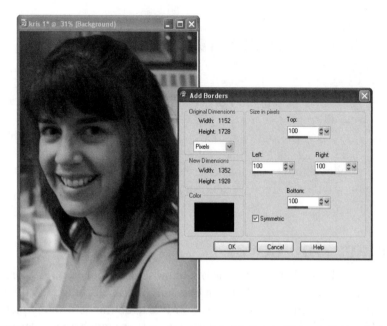

2. What's a magazine without a catchy title? Mine will be called *Kristen* magazine; after all, it's the place people go when they want to read all about Kris. Click the Text button and adjust the font style, size, and color. Set the Create As drop-down menu to Vector. Click in the upper half of the picture, more or less where the title should end up. You'll then get the Text Entry dialog box. Type a title, and then select it with your cursor, drag the text around the screen, and even change its size. If you want to get fancy, you can even rotate it by clicking-and-dragging the small box to the right of the center of the text.

3. From here, it's all up to you. Add some "cover lines" to your magazine to make it look more like a real publication. Add an issue date, some revealing new feature, and more. If you're ambitious, you can photograph a bar code from a real magazine with your digital camera and paste it into the cover. My first draft looks something like this:

Part IV

Using Your Images

Chapter 15

Printing Your Pictures

How to…

- Choose the printer that's right for you

- Distinguish among laser, ink-jet, and dye sublimation printers

- Shop for a printer

- Match resolution to print size

- Choose the right kind of paper for your print job

- Print an enlargement with Paint Shop Pro

- Configure your printer for paper and quality

- Determine what side of the paper to print on

- Care for prints after they come out of the printer

- Let someone else print for you

A lot of the time, it all comes down to this: no matter how versatile the digital medium is, a digital camera isn't very useful unless you can make prints. Great prints. Prints that look every bit as good as what you can get from a 35mm camera and the local photo shop.

If that sounds like something you would say, you're in luck. Recent advances in print technology have made it possible to make your own prints that look just as good as what you can get from a 35mm camera. In some ways, the results can be better. With a digital image, you can tweak it so it looks exactly the way you want it to, and you can print it any way you like, from wallet size all the way up to near-poster 13×19 inches.

In this chapter, I'll talk about everything you need to know to get great prints from your digital images. When you're done, you'll be able to frame your creations, and no one will be able to tell that the pictures came out of a computer printer.

Use the Right Printer

Not all that many years ago, there was a time when computer printers had a reputation for, shall we say, substandard output. Of course, everyone thought the printers looked pretty good at the time, but there was no way anyone would mistake what came out of a computer printer for a real photograph. Printers couldn't depict enough colors.

The resolution was too low. Obvious bands of different intensity colors ran through images like venetian blinds on a window. And those were just the most vexing of the output problems.

Then, a few years ago, it all started to change. Around the same time that scanners became affordable and digital cameras began to hit the scene, printer manufacturers had new incentives to make their products work better. By the late 1990s, most mainstream printers could create passable prints from computer images, and the top-of-the-line printers made prints that were essentially photo-realistic.

In the last few years, not a lot has changed dramatically. For most practical applications, it's not possible to make prints look any better to the casual viewer, so printer manufacturers have turned their attention to other aspects of digital printing, like making the prints last longer before they fade. I'll discuss this area in more detail in the section "What to Look For."

Choose a Printer

Before we get started printing, let's talk about the printers themselves and how to choose the right one. Buying a printer isn't an easy decision because not only are many different brands of printers competing for your attention—and lots of different models from each manufacturer—but you also have to figure out what kind of printer you want. If you're serious about printing digital images, I suspect you'll want an ink-jet printer. But, to be sure, let me tell you about the variety of printers you can choose from.

Laser Printers

Laser printers are like specialized photocopiers. Using the digital image in the computer's memory as a template, they electrically charge a piece of paper. The printer then allows *toner*—a fine ink-like powder—to come into contact with the paper. (See Figure 15-1 for a look at a typical toner cartridge.) The toner sticks to the paper in places where it has an electrostatic charge, and finally, the toner is permanently melted into the paper by a hot fusing wire.

15

Laser printers have a lot of advantages. They can print quickly (many personal laser printers can generate as many as eight or ten pages per minute), and the toner lasts a long time, yielding a low cost per page. My HP LaserJet 1200 prints about 3,000 to 5,000 sheets of paper for each $80 toner cartridge. Those advantages add up to a good all-around office printer that handles most common print jobs pretty well. Personal laser printers can be had for between $100 and $500, with many excellent models priced under $300.

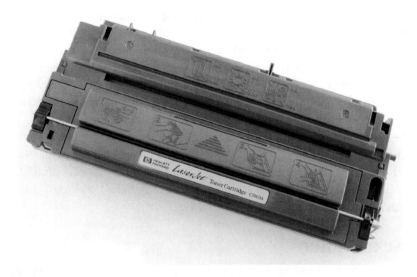

FIGURE 15-1 A laser printer's toner cartridge is generally good for several thousand prints.

Unfortunately, laser printers tend to be better at printing text than graphics. That's mainly because most laser printers are black-and-white devices, able to generate just shades of gray. Color laser printers are available, but because they're priced at $500 and up, they're more expensive than many people want to invest. Even if you could purchase a color laser printer, I wouldn't recommend it for printing digital images for framing. Color laser printers tend to produce prints that don't look much like traditional photo prints and, thus, they don't look good framed. They also limit you to a print size of 8×10 inches. Color laser printers might be okay for printing business graphics (like PowerPoint slides) and making fast draft prints of photos, but they're not up to the task of making framed photos. The same is true of black and white lasers—they simply don't make photo-quality prints, even if you're only printing in black and white.

Laser printers can certainly be used to print images, and they can do it well, as long as your needs don't include color. You can print a large quantity of family newsletters with a laser printer faster than with an ink-jet, for instance.

Ink-Jet Printers

If you want to print images, I think ink-jet printers are the best all-around printing solution for most people. They produce excellent color output, but can also print text at a reasonable speed—as long as you don't need to print a lot of it.

FIGURE 15-2 The print head slides back and forth across the page, spraying dots of ink as it goes.

Ink-jet printers are, in some ways, a simpler technology than laser printers. Simply put, they work by spraying microscopic droplets of ink onto paper. You can see an ink-jet's internals—complete with ink cartridges—in Figure 15-2. Of course, it gets a lot more complicated than that. Printer manufacturers exert a lot of effort making sure that the dots are small; that they combine with other dots to mimic thousands of distinct colors; that they dry fast enough so they don't spread, run, or smear; and that the paper is optimized to handle the ink's chemical characteristics. It's a highly technical business.

Nonetheless, you generally don't have to worry about most of that stuff. What matters is that they create stunning output and they're pretty affordable, typically running between $50 and $500 (though professional-caliber ink-jets can cost more than a thousand dollars).

Don't worry about image quality from a good ink-jet printer. Ink-jet technology has improved to the extent that it can be difficult to distinguish between a 35mm print and a quality ink-jet print made on photo-grade paper. My walls are covered with digital images that I've printed, matted, and framed (see Figure 15-3). No one can tell the difference.

15

FIGURE 15-3   These pictures were printed on the Epson Stylus Photo 1270.

Dye Sublimation Printers

The smallest segment of the printer market is occupied by dye sublimation printers (also called *dye-subs* for short). Look inside a dye-sublimation printer, and you'll see a long roll of transparent film that appears to be sheets of red-, blue-, yellow-, and gray-colored cellophane. The film is composed of solid dyes corresponding to the four basic colors used in printing: cyan, magenta, yellow, and black (CMYK). The print head heats as it passes over the film, causing the dyes to vaporize and permeate the glossy surface of the paper before they return to solid form. Because the dye gets absorbed and goes just below the surface of the paper, the process is called *dye-sublimation*. Because the color infuses the paper, it's also less vulnerable to fading and distortion over time. Dye-sub printers also create "continuous tone" images—they have no dots whatsoever, something you tend to get with ink-jet printers. Bottom line: the results from dye-sub printers are nothing short of stunning—they typically look just as good as 35mm prints and even magazine photos.

You May Need Two Printers

I have two printers. I use an HP LaserJet 1200 for routine text printing—I do a lot of that—and an Epson Stylus Photo 1270 for all my image printing.

Do you need two printers? It might seem a bit decadent at first, but it's really not, depending on how much printing you do. Both ink-jets and lasers are reasonably affordable these days, but owning just an ink-jet means that your ordinary text printing will be quite slow. Worse, ink is expensive. If you do a lot of routine printing, you can easily find yourself spending more on replacement ink cartridges each year than a cheap laser printer would have cost. Finally, if you have several computers in the house and find your kids fighting over access to the printer, having a second one is not such a bad idea!

The downside is this: dye-sub printers aren't much good for printing text, so your dye-sub printer will have to be a second printer, which you only use when you're expressly printing photos. For me, a bigger disadvantage is that most dye-sub printers only create 5×7-inch and 8×10-inch prints—nothing larger. Also, the selection of printer models is much more limited and much more expensive. You can find some printers in the $300–500 range, but full-page, 8×10-inch prints require bigger printers that tend to start at $1,000. These printers are more commonly used in the professional arena, where publishers can inexpensively make test prints that show what output from the final printing press eventually looks like.

Make no mistake: output from dye sublimation printers looks great. But, given all the disadvantages, I think you're better off choosing an ink-jet.

What to Look For

Okay, so now you know you want to buy an ink-jet printer. At least, that's the assumption I'm making. If you don't agree with me, you're shopping on your own. Actually, I'll talk about laser printers as well. I hope you're happy.

Where do you start? Walk into a store and all printers tend to look more or less the same. And, in my humble opinion, salespeople are not particularly helpful

15

unless you already have a pretty good idea of what you want. So use this checklist to help choose your printer:

- **Resolution**   Resolution is measured in dots per inch (dpi), which simply means how many dots or pixels of information a printer can pack into every inch of paper when printing. The higher the resolution, the better the quality. Virtually all laser printers print at 600 or 1200 dpi. In the ink-jet world, resolution varies quite a bit, though better printers will typically be advertised as either 2880 dpi or 1440 dpi. These numbers are deceiving, though—for all intents and purposes, they still print around 300 dpi. Most ink-jet printers, regardless of the thousands-of-dots-per-inch rating on the box, have a much lower effective resolution. I explain why in the section "The Right Resolution."

- **Number of colors**   This is irrelevant for a laser printer, of course, but when ink-jet shopping, look for a printer that uses a pure black cartridge instead of mixing all the other colors to mimic black. (The result is a muddy gray-brown instead of black, and these printers use up their ink exceptionally fast.) Better ink-jet printers use five or more individual colors to create more realistic photo prints, but four colors (black plus three colors) is the absolute minimum you should accept. Some of the best printers use seven or even eight colors for the most realistic prints. Note that the number of ink colors a printer has is different than how many individual ink cartridges it has—some printers supply each ink in its own cartridge, while most printers pack several colors into a cartridge. You can save money on replacement inks by buying a printer that has separate cartridges for each color. That way, when one color runs low, you don't have to replace all the inks at once. But from a quality perspective, it shouldn't matter whether a seven-ink printer supplies the ink in seven cartridges or just two.

- **Speed**   You should pay attention to the printer's speed, measured in pages per minute (ppm) and resolution. Slow laser printers run at 8 ppm; the fastest are around 24 ppm. Remember, ink-jets print much more slowly; color is their selling point, not speed.

- **Print quality**   No matter what the specs say, a printer is only as good as the prints. Try out printers in the store before you buy. Most computer stores have demo models set up that spit out prints when you press a test button. And, as I mention in the section "Working with Paper," remember, the paper is just as important to print quality as the ink and the printer itself—so after you bring the printer home, you'll only get great prints if you use high quality photo paper.

- **Ease of use**   Once you get the basic specs down, you might want to consider some less-tangible factors such as ease of use. Most printers come with status monitor software that lets you get important information about your printer—like how much ink is left—right from the Windows desktop. If you have a notebook PC or a handheld computer, you might want to print directly to your printer via the wireless infrared port. Few printers have infrared support, however, so you'll have to shop around. An emerging feature is Bluetooth printing. *Bluetooth* is a wireless networking standard that cell phones, PDAs, laptops, and other gadgets can use to exchange data. Epson is one of the first printer companies to directly support Bluetooth printing, and it sells a Bluetooth adapter for a handful of its ink-jet printers. Other companies, like AnyCom and MPI, sell Bluetooth adapters for common printers.

- **Direct printing**   Many printers let you connect your digital camera directly to the printer—or insert the camera's memory card into the printer. This lets you circumvent the PC for fast and painless printing.

- **Size and capacity**   Although most major manufacturers like Epson, Canon, and HP all make good printers that generate excellent results, they differ dramatically in terms of what kind of paper they can print on. Most printers print up to 8.5×11 inches. You'll have to buy a wide-format printer if you want to create 11×17- or 13×19-inch prints.

- **Dye versus pigment**   If you're shopping for an ink-jet printer, you should know that most models use dye-based inks, while higher-end designs sometimes rely on pigment-based inks. If you're concerned about generating prints that are highly resistant to fading, investigate pigment-based printers. On average, you'll find that run-of-the-mill (dye-based) ink-jets can make fade-resistant prints last for 10 to 20 years. Pigment-based printers generate prints that last for 100 years. On the other hand, cheaper, dye-based inks are brighter and more vivid than more expensive (but longer-life) pigment-based inks.

15

Print Your Images

So you're all ready to print. You've downloaded your pictures from your camera to your PC. You have a printer connected to the computer. All you need to do is print. Let's talk about the things you need to ensure great prints.

The Right Resolution

The resolution of your image is one of the two most important factors that determine how good your pictures look when printed. Printers do vary, but in general you can use this rule of thumb:

Type of Printer	Resolution (in dpi)
Laser	600 or 1200
Ink-jet	200–300

Experimentation is key, though. Choose a high-quality image and sample it at several different sizes. Print each one and compare them to see where the quality threshold lies with your printer. In other words, determine what minimum resolution you need to eliminate obvious pixels and jaggedness from your prints.

Let's assume that 300 dpi is about right for your printer. Suppose you want to print an image on an ink-jet printer. To determine how big your image should be before you print it, just multiply the output size (in inches) by 300. The following chart illustrates the minimum dimensions of your image for a variety of common print sizes with an ink-jet printer:

Print Size (Inches)	File Size (Pixels)	Camera Resolution Needed
4×6	800×1200	1 megapixel
8×10	1600×2000	3 megapixel
11×17	2200×3400	6 megapixel
13×19	2600×3800	10 megapixel

Wow. Surprised? It takes a lot of pixels to make high-quality prints. So what does that chart mean—that you should have a 10-megapixel camera to make a 13×19-inch print with a wide-format ink-jet printer?

Well, yeah, that's exactly what it's saying. But there's good news: you can cheat. Many printers will still give you great results, even if you feed them an image that's underpixeled. In other words, suppose you have a 1600×1200-pixel image. You might still get quite decent results by printing it at 11×17 inches or perhaps even 13×19. Try it out and see.

Increase Print Size with Resampling Software

Need to print an image at a certain size—like 8×10 inches, for instance—but don't have nearly enough pixels to make the picture come out sharp? Or perhaps you have a 6-megapixel picture that you want to crop a bit, yet still turn into a poster.

You might want to try resampling the picture with a program like Genuine Fractals or pxl SmartScale.

Both of these programs can digitally enlarge your image while preserving quality using a complicated mathematical procedure that does a pretty good job of reducing noise and digital artifacts.

Make no mistake: these programs aren't magical and can't add information to a picture that wasn't there to begin with. But they do an amazing job nonetheless. In my experience, you can often increase the size of a photo by several factors with little to no visible loss in print quality. That's pretty amazing.

Genuine Fractals (available at www.lizardtech.com) is available in several versions, with a consumer version selling for about $50—though it won't input an image any bigger than 1500×2100 pixels, and it won't let you enlarge the image to a file size any bigger than 64MB. That makes this version affordable, but means you can only use it to work with images that are 3 megapixels or less. You can also get a $150 version that has no file size limits. pxl SmartScale on the other hand, is available from www.extensis.com for under $200.

Using either program is a piece of cake. Essentially, you simply choose to save your picture in the new, resampled format from any plug-in compatible program, such as Adobe Photoshop or Paint Shop Pro. When you open your saved file in SmartScale, for instance, you can choose how much to enlarge (or resample) it via a set of controls that look like this:

15

Did you know?

The Real Resolution of an Ink-Jet

Confused? I said earlier that ink-jet printers come in resolutions up to 2880 dpi, yet now I claim they print around 300 dpi. Which is it? How can one number be so different from the other?

I agree: it is confusing. The simplest answer is that printer companies aren't being entirely honest with you. The resolution they advertise on the box isn't a measure of how many pixels per inch (ppi) the printer can accurately lay down on paper. If it were, 2880 dpi ink-jets would be capable of printing photos professional magazine quality, and that's clearly not the case. So something else must be going on.

Indeed. Here's the deal: the advertised resolution of an ink-jet printer is a measure of the accuracy of mechanical systems like the step motor that drives the print head around on the page and the precision of the nozzles themselves. Certainly, you want the printer to be as accurate as possible, but remember, it takes several steps for the print head to make even a single dot on the paper—and it's the dots, in the end, that limit the printer's maximum resolution. So, an ink-jet with a resolution of 2880 dpi isn't necessarily a whole lot better than an ink-jet with a resolution of 1440 dpi. Visually, prints made with one printer might look a bit better than the other, but certainly not twice as good. It's like buying a 3 GHz computer. It's faster than a 1.5 GHz PC, but it's not twice as fast.

Put another way, a printer with a lousy step motor can visibly degrade the quality of a print. But buying a printer that has a 10,000 dpi resolution via the way that companies like Epson measure that sort of thing today, will only result in more perfectly formed pixels. The pixels themselves will be limited by other factors.

The printer's top resolution is, indeed, important, but other factors play an important role as well: using the sharpening filter on your image and choosing the right paper can have just as much of an effect on the final print quality.

So what resolution should you use when you print? The honest-to-goodness dpi of most ink-jet printers is still in the range of 150–300 dpi. If you start with a sharp image and plan to use high-quality ink-jet paper, you might see a small difference in image quality if you feed the printer a 300 dpi image. But the difference will be small, and you can generally get decent results with as little as 200 dpi. If you send images of lower resolution to the printer, you'll be able to tell the difference.

Too Much or Too Little Resolution

As I already mentioned, a 4×6-inch ink-jet print typically requires an 800×1200-pixel image to start with to avoid pixels and jagged edges in the final image. That's almost twice the resolution that a VGA-resolution, 640×480-pixel digital camera can muster. What happens if you print an image that doesn't have enough pixels for the size you want to achieve? You get something like what is shown in Figure 15-4.

If the output size isn't as important to you as having a sharp, quality print, then just print the image smaller. Cramming those pixels together on paper in less space will make the print sharper.

In reality, you might still get adequate results printing even a 640×480-pixel image at 4×6, even though that only works out to 100 dpi. If you look carefully at the finished print, you'll find that you can see jagged edges where there weren't enough pixels to fill in. For best results, pick a size that lets you print around 200 dpi, or whatever resolution best matches your particular printer.

That's what happens when you print too few pixels for the size you're shooting for. What about too many pixels? Can an image that's too high-res ever be a problem? The answer is generally not. Too many pixels isn't really a problem, though it does make your image file bigger than it has to be, and it can potentially bog everything down.

15

FIGURE 15-4   When bad things happen to good pictures: this sort of thing happens when you try to print a low-resolution image too large.

The bottom line is this: if you pack more pixels than you need into an image—above 200 dpi, for instance—odds are good that you won't improve image quality very much. Instead, you'll just make the file bigger, which takes more storage space on your hard disk and can slow down the printing process.

TIP   *Test your own printer by generating prints in high-quality mode at 150, 200, and 300 dpi. Use these to figure out what the resolution threshold of your printer is, and strive to use that setting as often as possible.*

Of course, all this advice is specifically for someone who wants to know how much resolution an image needs to print well at a certain output size. If you just want to print an image and don't care how big it turns out, just print it. Most image editors have an option to let you print the image at full-page size or at the image's normal size. If you choose normal size, the image will print smaller than full page and probably look just fine. It's only when you force the image to print at a certain size that the image's original resolution becomes important.

On the other hand, you should set the print size yourself whenever possible. If you allow the printer driver to resize the image on its own, it'll usually just scale the image and introduce a lot of pixelization in the process.

Understand DPI

Some image editors and print programs use dpi instead of, or in addition to, pixels. And I've found that a lot of people are flambuzzled when it comes to understanding the relationship among resolution, dpi, print size, and pixels. What, really, is a dialog box telling you when it says an image is 4 by 6 inches, 72 dpi?

The important thing to understand is that measurements like "4 by 6 inches" and "72 dpi" are meaningless while the image is still on a PC. A computer deals only in pixels. An image can be 640×480, 1280×1024, or 2240×1680 pixels, for instance. And the "size" of the image on a computer screen depends on two things: the screen size of the Windows desktop and the zoom factor of the application displaying the image. If you show a 640×480 pixel image on a Windows desktop that's only 640×480 itself, the image takes up the whole screen. If you show it on a PC that's using a 1280×1024-pixel screen, then the image will be tiny, because the screen can show more pixels when set to that display mode.

So repeat after me—and this is really important—"there's no such thing as a 72 dpi digital photo." Even if a program appears to be telling you that a picture is 72 or 144 or 300 dpi, it's simply not true. A dpi value only has meaning when you take a picture that has a certain number of pixels and you then print it on paper at a certain size.

So far so good? It's worth pointing out that zoom can also be a factor when viewing images onscreen. Some image programs automatically fit images to the screen, shrinking them as necessary. Other (usually older) programs try to display the image at full size, which can result in images that you have to pan around to see properly because they're larger, pixel for pixel, than the computer screen itself. The bottom line: when still in the virtual world of a computer, the only image size that has any real meaning is the number of pixels used to create it.

Only when you're getting ready to print a picture does a size like "4 by 6 inches" have any meaning. If you assume there's a one-for-one relationship between a pixel and a printed dot, then the size the image prints at is determined by dividing the number of pixels in the image by the dpi rating you hope to print with.

Consider the same 2240×1680 pixel image. It can make a

- **7.5×5.5-inch print** when set to 300 dpi (good for a color laser printer)

- **15×11 inch print** when set to 150 dpi (which might look okay coming from an ink-jet)

- **31×23 inch print** when set to 72 dpi (on a computer screen), if displayed at full size

Remember, dpi and print size is just a way to measure how large you can print a digital image—the numbers that really tell you the true size of the image are the number of pixels.

Paper for Laser Printers

If you have a laser printer, you might be wondering what kind of paper is appropriate for that printer as well. I suggest you use ordinary 20-pound laser or copier paper. Decent laser paper shouldn't cost more than about $7 per 500 sheets (a ream). I'd be reluctant to buy really inexpensive paper ($3/ream or less) because loose paper fibers in budget-priced paper can, over time, clog your printer, affecting its performance and, eventually, even damaging it.

Use Good Paper

Here's a common scenario: you see great, photo-realistic prints in a computer store and think, "that's the printer for me. It's only $150 and it makes outstanding pictures!" So you buy the printer and bring it home. But when you get the printer set up and send your first few images to it, you're devastated. The output is horrible. The prints look flat and lifeless. The paper curls. What went wrong?

It's the paper. What you failed to consider is the choice of paper is so important to the quality of your prints that it's essentially *more important than the printer itself*! A handful of printers on the market can generate photo-realistic prints. But, unless you use quality paper, they will all disappoint you.

Which Paper Is Best

Unfortunately, choosing paper isn't easy, even if you know you want to get the best. There are a lot of choices, and it isn't generally clear which kind is best based on the name or description on the package. This is especially true for ink-jet printers. I honestly don't know why paper manufacturers make this so hard; it seems counterproductive to sales.

As a general rule, you'll find store shelves stocked with paper divided into four quality levels: ink-jet paper, high-quality ink-jet paper, photo-quality paper, and glossy photo paper.

So where do you start? Let's begin with daily use that doesn't involve printing photos—I suggest you use either plain paper or ink-jet paper. Even when printing on plain paper, use quality stock because cheap paper can plug the nozzles and decrease the effective resolution of the printer. For general-purpose printing, you can use the same stock I recommend for laser printers. Of course, I'm assuming the majority of what you print is test prints, text, and other routine output. If every print you make is destined for the Louvre, then you might want to skip directly to the section where I talk about photo paper.

When you're ready to step up to some higher-quality printing, you have a number of choices on store shelves (see Figure 15-5). Here's a general overview of the various grades available.

- **Plain paper** As I've already mentioned, this is good for general text and ordinary graphics printing. The paper is inexpensive, but the ink tends to absorb quickly into the paper and blur the image. The paper also curls and distorts.

FIGURE 15-5   With so many choices on store shelves, it pays to experiment with a few to find the paper that delivers the best output with your printer.

- **Ink-jet paper (and high-quality ink-jet paper)**   This is a step up and embeds clay or some other ink fixture into the paper to stop the inks from spreading before they dry. For most printing, you won't notice a big difference, but this paper makes for better draft-quality photographic prints.

- **Photo paper**   A variation of coated paper, photo paper is generally bright-white coated paper that's designed explicitly for photographs. If you're looking for paper in an intermediate price range that can give decent results, try this stuff.

- **Glossy (and matte) photo paper**   The best paper around, this stuff is expensive, generally costing about a dollar a sheet. Certainly you won't use it all the time, but if you plan to frame a picture or give your digital "prints" away to family or friends, definitely use the special photo paper. Note that you can only print on one side of photo paper; the back side looks like the back of a photograph and generally has a logo printed there. I don't recommend printing on the back of glossy paper, even on a laser printer.

15

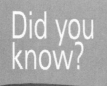

Did you know?

Other Specialty Papers

In addition to ordinary plain, coated, and photo paper, printer manufacturers and paper vendors sell a variety of other specialty papers. You might want to investigate these papers because they can be a lot of fun and enable you to do all sorts of things with your printer that you never imagined possible:

- **Greeting card paper**   Greeting card paper and matching envelopes let you make your own greeting cards with your printer and some greeting card software.

- **Transparency paper**   This clear film media is perfect for printing color overhead slides for business meetings. You can use this to print PowerPoint slides or any other kind of image or document.

- **T-shirt transfer paper**   This special paper is an iron-on transfer that you can run through your printer, and then apply to clothing. When you print on T-shirt paper, be sure to use special T-shirt transfer software or just reverse your image before you print. (Create a mirror image of what you want it to look like.)

■ **Fabric sheets**   This unique kind of printing media is fabric that gives your prints texture. You can print on it just for its own sake or use the print to make cross-stitch designs and other craft projects.

Which Brand?

What brand of paper should you use? Should you use Epson paper in an Epson printer and Canon paper in a Canon printer, or should you buy paper from a company like Ilford—known in 35mm photography circles for their excellent paper—instead? This is a good question. Obviously, each printer company wants you to use its own brand of paper with its printer.

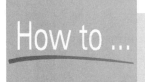

How to ... **Make a Print**

Now that you have all the parts in place, it's time to print. I'll show you how to make a print of a specific size in Paint Shop Pro; other programs use a similar method. Of course, if printing the picture at a very specific size (such as 5×7 or 8×10) isn't important to you, just click the Print button and get it over with. But, if you want to print your image so it fits properly in a traditional picture frame, here's how. Specifically, let's say you're going to make a print at 8×10 inches. Do this:

1. Load the paper in your printer. Make sure you put it in with the appropriate side set for printing, and only load a single sheet at a time.

2. Load the picture you want to print in Paint Shop Pro. The first thing you want to do is crop it to print at the right proportion. Click the Crop tool and drag it through the image, creating a rough crop of your image. At this point, it's not important to be accurate; just make a crop box.

3. In the Tool Options toolbar at the top of the screen, set the Units to Inches, and then enter the dimensions of your print—in my case, width of 10 and height of 8. Select the check box for Maintain Aspect Ratio.

(You could also click the Presets menu and find the entry for 8×10 in horizontal.)

4. Now position the crop box precisely on the screen and resize it by dragging one of the corners. Because the aspect ratio is locked, it'll keep the proper proportions for our 8×10-inch print. When you're happy with the final result, select the check box to make the crop, and you'll get an image that's proportioned exactly right for an 8×10-inch print:

5. Now we're going to select the paper size and orientation. Choose File | Print from the main menu. You should see the Print dialog box.

6. Click the Portrait or Landscape button in the Orientation section of the dialog box to get the image oriented properly.

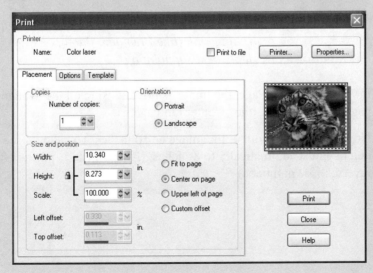

7. Click the Printer button to open your printer's preferences and find the paper size selector. Choose Letter or 8.5×11, if it isn't already selected. While you're there, select the appropriate type of paper, such as ink-jet paper or photo glossy. Click OK to close the printer dialog box.

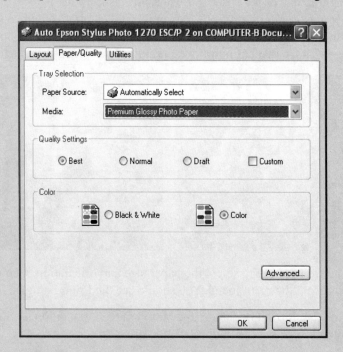

CAUTION *If you don't tell the print driver about the kind of paper you're printing with (like Premium, Photo, or Plain paper), the results will invariably be disappointing.*

8. If you click Fit To Page, the image is printed using all the available page space. Instead, click Center On Page.

9. Now specify the width of the image as 10 inches. You should see the height adjust automatically to 8 inches. (If your print is portrait style, reverse those numbers.)

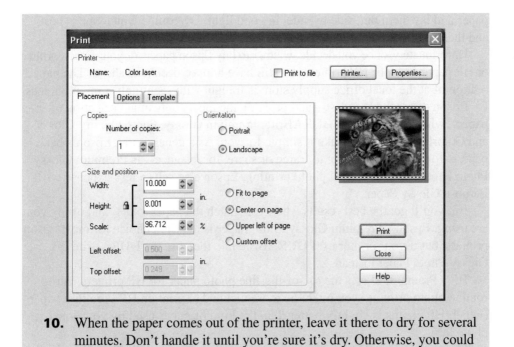

10. When the paper comes out of the printer, leave it there to dry for several minutes. Don't handle it until you're sure it's dry. Otherwise, you could smudge it.

In truth, vendors like Canon, Epson, and HP go to great lengths to fine-tune their paper to match their inks so colors won't bleed and they'll be as vivid as possible. My own Epson Stylus Photo 1270 does best with Epson's Premium Glossy Photo Paper, and I tend to use that paper almost exclusively. When I first got the printer, I tried a dozen different kinds of papers, including paper from companies like Ilford and Tetenal, which came highly recommended by computer and photography store salespeople. After being disappointed with all those other brands, I tried Epson's own Premium Glossy paper, and was blown away—the results were dramatically better. I've had similar experiences with other printers, though I have to admit they weren't as dramatic as with the Epson printer, which was clearly engineered with specialty paper in mind.

So what should you do? If you have a few dollars to spare, buy a bunch of different paper packages and try them. Print the same image on different kinds of

15

paper and lay them out, side by side, in good light. Determine which one is best, and then stick with that brand of paper.

Unfortunately, once you decide whether to buy Epson paper for your Epson printer or HP paper for your HP printer, you still have a lot of decisions ahead. The paper section of at the local office supply store is fraught with seemingly similar choices.

Epson offers the broadest—and possibly the most confusing—selection of papers, with names such as DURABrite, Premium Glossy, Photo Quality Glossy, and ColorLife. But I can make it simple for you. As a general rule, Epson's best paper—for pictures you plan to frame or share, for instance—is Premium Glossy Photo Paper. For less formal photo printing, Epson also sells a less-expensive All Purpose Glossy Paper.

But you'll get the best results when you match the paper to the kind of ink you are using. Epson's Premium Glossy Photo Paper is the right choice for most Epson printers, but if your printer uses DURABrite ink, then use the DURABrite Ink Glossy Photo Paper instead.

HP's Premium Plus is the top-of-the-line photo paper for HP printers, but for routine photo printing, you might be more inclined to print on HP Premium paper (which HP claims is slightly better than the kind of paper used by your local photo lab).

Canon has made its paper even easier to choose. Just look for the colored stripe that runs down the center of all its paper packages; papers with a gold stripe are premium blends intended for the highest-quality prints, while bronze identifies the paper as an everyday variety.

Which Side Is the Right Side?

Often, it matters which side of the page you print on. Plain-old laser paper is the same on both sides, so if you print on a laser printer or you use plain paper in an ink-jet, it doesn't matter. But if you print on specialty paper in an ink-jet printer, make sure you load the paper the right way. Keep these tips in mind:

- Usually, the brighter or shinier side of the paper is the printing side. Occasionally, it's rough, like sandpaper.

- If you're printing on photo paper, the back will probably have a company logo on it.

- Many paper types label the paper with small marks to indicate the proper print side.

Be sure you look carefully at the print directions the first time you try a new paper. Ink won't adhere well—or at all—to the wrong side of specialty papers, and you could end up with a real mess in and around your printer if the ink runs everywhere.

Can you print on both sides of the paper? I get that question a lot. And the answer is this: it depends. Don't ever try to print on the back of glossy premium paper, but you can usually print on both sides of ink-jet and high-quality ink-jet paper without any trouble. If I'm printing a newsletter or a greeting card, I might print the pictures on one side and use a laser printer to add text to the back. You can also find paper that's intended for double-sided printing. Check the paper aisle of your computer or office store to see what's available.

Care for Your Prints

All picture colors tend to fade over time, but ink-jet photos tend to fade somewhat faster. In fact, ink-jet inks are sensitive to ultraviolet light, and your images will fade faster if exposed to direct sunlight for extended periods. If you plan to frame pictures and leave them exposed to sunlight, consider using UV-shielded glass, available at some framing shops.

> TIP *Keep original image files on your hard disk or archived on CD-ROM, so you can reprint them when the fading becomes noticeable.*

Some newer printers are marketed specifically as models that create prints with more *lightfastness* than older printers. You can probably guess that lightfastness is a print's capability to resist fading when exposed to light. In particular, a number of Epson models offer a lightfastness of ten or more years—check out this chart of Epson photo papers, for instance:

Epson Photo Paper	6 years
Epson Premium Glossy Photo Paper	10 years
Epson Matter Paper Heavyweight Paper	25 years
Epson ColorLife Photo Paper	27 years

15

In addition, you can find some ink-jet printers designed to offer extremely long resistance to fading, such as pigment-based ink-jet printers, like the Epson Stylus Photo 2200. Intended for serious photo enthusiasts and professionals, pigment-based ink-jet printers are a bit more expensive than dye-based ink-jets, but they can deliver a print life of over 100 years. By comparison, 35mm prints tend to be lightfast for only about 50 years, so newer printers can create prints that last longer than traditional prints.

No matter what kind of printer, ink, or paper you use, you should protect your prints from fading from the moment you print them. Here are a few precautions you can take:

- **Cover your prints.** Cover the print with glass or plastic as soon as it's completely dry (wait 12–24 hours after the print is complete). Contaminants in the air can fade a print quickly, but if you put it under glass or in a photo album, the print is no longer in direct contact with air and, thus, is protected. Some ink and paper combinations can cause a print to fade dramatically in a matter of days if left exposed to the open air.

- **Avoid sunlight.** Keep the print out of direct sunlight, even when under glass. Hang the print where the sun doesn't shine directly on the wall.

- **Don't touch the ink.** Avoid handling the print in such a way that you touch the ink with your fingers.

If you've spent much time in the world of 35mm photography, you might also be familiar with acrylic UV-blocking sprays that you can apply to prints. These sprays "fix" the print and give it a longer life before fading, especially when the print will be framed and hung where it could be exposed to direct sunlight. Can you—or should you—use these sprays on digital images?

Well, that depends. I'd avoid using a photo-fix product designed especially for traditional film-based prints. I've tried it, and it seems to work, but I've neither been able to test a wide variety of ink and paper combinations nor have my tests observed the prints for a long period of time. Indeed, I asked several printer companies what their opinions are of these sprays and, for the most part, they were all a bit wary. Epson, for instance, said this: "We recommend avoiding UV sprays since the effect on lightfastness of one color ink could be different than another ink, and may actually lead to the visual acceleration of fading or color shifting." On the other hand, a few companies make a special spray just for ink-jet printers, and I think these "ink-jet fix" sprays are a lot safer for your digital prints.

Calibrate Your Monitor

A lot of people run into a problem with their printers that can be summarized thusly: "I just printed a photo on good-quality paper, and it doesn't match what's on the monitor."

This common problem stems from the fact that the two output devices—the printer and monitor—are calibrated differently. If you want what's on the screen when you edit a photo to exactly resemble what comes out of the printer, then you need to correct one or the other so they're in agreement. It's easier to adjust the output of the monitor (printers don't come with any sort of calibration tools), so that's what most people commonly do.

If you don't mind spending money, a few solutions are available that are designed to help you calibrate your monitor. OptiCAL, from Pantone (www.pantone.com), is a popular program—but, priced around $200, it's probably too pricey for you unless you happen to be a true graphics professional. A lot of folks like ColorBlind Prove IT (www.color.com), which works with a sensor (called a spider) that clips onto the front of your monitor to help calibrate it. Priced around $300 with the sensor, ColorBlind is also a bit costly—but it's a good deal if you want the most accurate results for the least effort. Finally, Colorific (www.colorific.com) offers an affordable color-matching and monitor calibration system. It's priced at a reasonable $50. The truth is, though, that it's possible to calibrate your monitor manually, without buying any software at all. It does take a good eye and some judgment, though.

Set Your Display Properties

If you're ready to optimize your monitor, the best place to start is with the Windows Display Properties. You can do a few things here to render images onscreen more accurately and to improve the overall look of your display at the same time.

Right-click on a blank portion of the desktop and choose Properties from the drop-down menu. You should then see the Display Properties dialog box. Click the Settings tab to see the details about your computer's display settings. First, check the screen resolution. If should be at least 800×600 pixels, and higher is generally better. If the resolution is too low, you won't see as much onscreen, and digital images won't look as sharp. Experiment by increasing the resolution and clicking the Apply button. Keep the resolution comfortable; if things get too small, revert to a lower resolution. I think 1024×768 is a good value for a 17-inch display, and try 1280×1024 if you have a 19-inch monitor.

Also, set the color quality. If it's set too low, then images will look dramatically different onscreen than they do when printed. The best setting is 24-bit. For working with digital images, 32 bits doesn't really improve the look of images on the screen, and it can be a drag on your system's performance. After you choose 24-bit color and the resolution you like, click the OK button for the changes to take effect.

Print a Test Photo

The most important tweak you can make is to match the monitor's settings to a real print from your ink-jet printer. So load a picture you like—choose a daylight photo

15

that includes a person with natural skin tones—into your image editor and print it at highest quality onto a sheet of good, glossy photo paper. Let the picture dry out of direct sunlight for a few hours to let the colors set permanently.

Now you're ready to get to work. Make sure your monitor is set up the way you usually use it, with the same level of ambient light as you typically have when editing photos. Eliminate any harsh glare by closing window shades or angling the monitor.

Next, set the monitor's contrast and brightness levels to their halfway point. Most monitors have buttons or dials on the front of the case; you might need to experiment or check your monitor's user guide. Now open the image file on the monitor and set the picture you printed right next to the monitor, so you can look from one image to the other. From here, it's just a matter of adjusting the brightness, contrast, and color levels until the printed and onscreen images agree with each other.

Unfortunately, there's no magic bullet for monitor calibration. It takes a good eye to tweak the red, green, blue, brightness, and contrast levels to match a test image, like the one you just made. But tons of useful web sites are out there that can lend a hand with fine-tuning your monitor. If you want to read more, check out one of these web sites that offer monitor calibration tutorials:

- **Bryce Alive Network**   www.bryce-alive.net/calibrate

- **ePaperPress**   http://epaperpress.com/monitorcal

Let Someone Else Do the Printing for You

Let's be honest: most of this chapter is about making prints on your own. And there was a time when the only way to get prints from your digital camera was to set up an ink-jet printer, pick the right paper and toner, make your own prints and wait while they dried, and resupply the paper and toner when you were finished. This process can be time-consuming, though, and these days I'd be remiss not to mention another alternative: upload your photos to an online photo service, or take your memory card to a local photo printer.

You can experience good and bad results from any photo printer in town or on the Web, so it pays to spend a few dollars and have some sites make some test prints for you. Some of the most common online printing services include:

- **Shutterfly**   www.shutterfly.com

- **Kodak EasyShare Gallery**   www.kodakgallery.com

The Difference Between Home and Professional Printing

So, you can make your own prints from home or order prints from professional photofinishers. Which is better? Which should you do? For the most part, it all comes down to the actual printing method.

Professional photofinishers use a process called continuous tone printing, while ink-jet printers at home use halftone printing. *Continuous tone printing* gets its name from the fact that the pigments used to make the picture work like the grains on film—they can exhibit gradual color change without any abrupt transitions because the printer can generate any desired color for each dot. It's the best and most realistic way to print a picture.

Ink-jet printers can't create continuous tones; instead, they lay down dots of distinct color. And, as you may remember from school, when you place two colors right next to each other and step back, the human eye perceives a third color, rather than the primary colors. That's the essence of *halftone printing* at home: lots of little color dots creating a rainbow effect.

While halftone printing can look great—just check out the sample prints in the printer section of an electronics store to see for yourself—professional prints will usually look better because continuous tone printing can generate sharper images from the same number of pixels.

Technology aside, online printing has a few other advantages. You don't have to mess with ink, paper, and configuring your printer. If you want to do red eye correction and cropping, you can usually do that right from the web page before you order the prints. And you can order multiple prints and have them mailed directly to any number of different recipients, so you can send pictures to everyone in your family with very little effort.

15

- **Snapfish**   www.snapfish.com
- **PhotoBox**   www.photobox.com

In general, all these sites work the same way. You upload a batch of photos, store them in an online photo album, and then select the pictures you want to print. After clicking through a short ordering process, the prints are made much like traditional 35mm prints and then mailed to your home. They are very affordable—usually just a few cents per print—and you can make enlargements and photo gifts using the same service.

Order Prints Online

Suppose you want to try out this brave new world of online photo printing. You can visit Shutterfly and order a few pictures by following these steps:

1. If the pictures you want to print aren't already stored on Shutterfly, begin by adding them. Click the Add Pictures tab at the top of the page. Choose whether to add the pictures to an existing album already on Shutterfly or to create a new one. Then click Next.

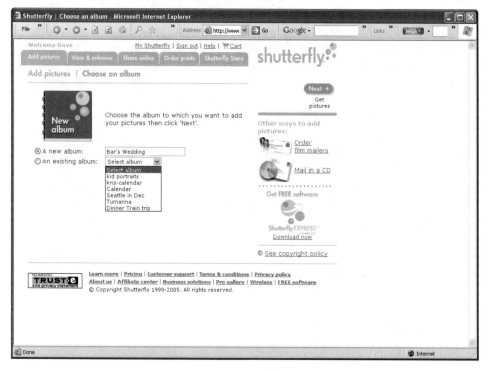

2. It's time to add the pictures to Shutterfly from your computer. You can either drag file icons from Windows directly onto the drag-and-drop area of the web page or click Choose Pictures and pick them from the dialog box. After you select some pictures, they'll upload automatically. Bigger image files will take longer to complete. When they're done, click View Pictures.

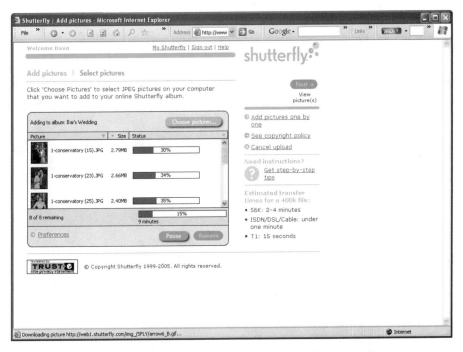

3. Click a picture in your album, and you'll see it appear in the View & Enhance tab.

Note that the Prints Best Up To information (see the next illustration) under the picture suggests a maximum print size based on the resolution of the image.

4. If you want to make any changes to the picture before it prints, now is the time. You can use the tools right on the Shutterfly web site to remove red eye, crop, and otherwise modify your picture.

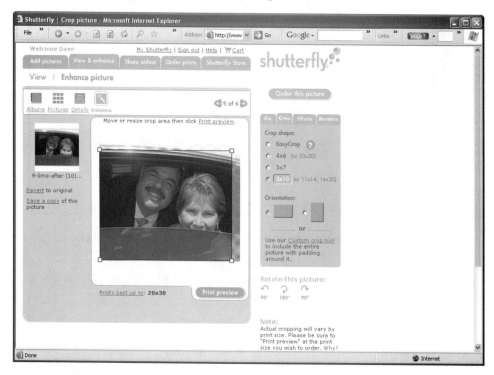

5. Click the Order Prints tab. On the next page, you can select how many and what size to print. The default quantity and size in each order is one 4×6 print. Also located at the top of this page is an option to select which type of paper finish you would like: matte or glossy. By default, the filename of each picture will be printed on the back of each print. You can, instead, choose to type in your own custom text up to 80 characters. When the order is set up the way you want it, click Next.

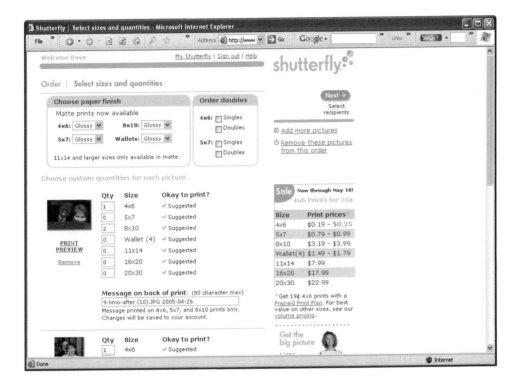

If you are planning to make three copies of a single picture and you want to send one of each to three different people, specify only one print on this page. When you select the recipients on the next page, each will get one print. If you select two prints on this page, each recipient will get two copies.

6. Select the recipients for your prints. It's easy to send prints to as many people as you want. On the Select Recipients page, simply check the boxes next to the names of the people you want to send prints to. You can customize each recipient's order on the next page. To add someone new to the list, click the Add New Address button.

7. Once you finish selecting recipients and have reviewed your order, click the Next button to select payment options. Review your billing info (and edit it, if necessary), enter a gift certificate code if you have one, and then choose a payment method (credit card or check) and click Place My Order Now.

A confirmation and thank you appears, letting you know your order has been placed. An order number and further instructions are provided (for instance, instructions on how to cancel your order within the first hour of placing it, or instructions on sending a check for payment). Your prints will arrive in a few days.

15

Chapter 16

Sharing Your Pictures

How to...

- Send and receive images via e-mail
- Choose the right file format for e-mailing pictures
- Compress images for e-mail and disk
- Choose a web design program
- Prepare images for display on the Web
- Store images on the Web without programming
- Show off pictures on a Palm handheld (PDA)
- Display images in a digital picture frame
- Create a video slide show with your camera and a VCR
- Create a video slide show using PowerPoint on your PC

Taking pictures is one thing; sharing them with friends, family, and coworkers is something else entirely. Of course, this is one area where your digital camera has a leg up on 35mm cameras. To share traditional prints with someone, you need to physically give them a copy. That means visiting the photo finisher and having duplicates made. Or, you could scan the images and distribute them electronically.

Digital camera images are electronic to begin with, though, and that makes everything a whole lot easier. Want to share your images? E-mail them. Or, you can post them to the Web or show them off with a digital picture frame or a PDA. In this last chapter of *How to Do Everything with Your Digital Camera*, I'll show you how to easily make your images available to other people.

Send Images via E-mail

E-mail is perhaps the most common way to share digital images with people who live far apart. Not only is e-mail good for casually lending images to friends and family, it's also the medium of choice for professionals. When I create images for print in newspapers, magazines, and books, I typically send the files via e-mail unless they're so large that e-mail is impractical.

So how do you do it? Sending pictures within e-mail is simply a matter of including one or more images as attachments in your mail message. *Attachments* are binary files—as opposed to plain text—that your mail program can deliver to another person's mail system.

Most of the time, attachments work just fine. Occasionally, though, you'll run into problems sending images as attachments. That's because the original Internet wasn't designed to accommodate the sending of binary files such as pictures via e-mail, and encoding schemes were "tacked on" after the fact. Here are some snags you might run into:

■ **Beware of sending files that are too big.** Many e-mail systems can't deal with a single e-mail file that's bigger than about 2MB—a few older or "free" e-mail systems even have a 1MB limit. Personally, for most e-mail transmissions, I'd consider 1MB as your upper limit on file size, though broadband users (that is, users with cable modem or DSL access) can sometimes receive files as large as 5MB without trouble. The bottom line is that it isn't always easy to know how large attachments can be with any given e-mail system, and if you send a very large file to someone, it can get "stuck" in their mail server, clogging up messages that are trying to come in afterward. It's a good idea to check the file size of your attachments (see Figure 16-1) before sending them. To be sure that they'll be small enough (in megabytes), I recommend resizing images that you plan to e-mail down to around 800×600 pixels.

NOTE   *When you attach a digital image to an e-mail message, the attachment usually ends up about 10 percent larger than the original image because of the encoding necessary to send it across the Internet.*

■ **Older versions of America Online can only receive a single attachment.** Even though most mail systems can accept multiple attached files in each e-mail message, if you know someone still using an old edition of AOL, their PC won't quite know what to make of that kind of message. Only one of the attachments will get to the recipient, and the others will simply disappear. On the other hand, the newest versions of AOL handle multiple files in a single message just fine—they assemble all the images into a single, convenient ZIP file.

16

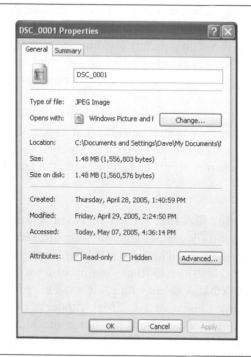

FIGURE 16-1 This 1.5MB file is, for many folks, simply too large to e-mail effectively. Resize it or change it into another file format so it's under a megabyte.

Shrink Images for E-mail

Having a lot of resolution is a good thing for printing, but 2- and 3-megapixel digital images are cumbersome to send through e-mail. You should resize pictures in your favorite image editor before attaching them to electronic messages (see Chapter 11). In general, e-mail-bound images should be cropped and/or resized down to 800×600 pixels and saved in JPG format. If you remember to do that, you'll never get any complaints from friends or family that your images are too big and are clogging their e-mail systems.

If you don't mind spending a few dollars, you can get a specialized program for cropping and resizing images as well. A Smaller Image, from TriVista (www .trivista.com) is a great little program for prepping your photos for e-mail.

This simple $15 program is designed from the ground up to crop and resize photos. After you drag an image into the application window, you can move a cropping frame around the screen until you've composed the picture just the way you want. The cool part is this: you can configure the cropping frame's proportion based on how large you

 **View Images Someone Sent to You**

In most e-mail programs (like Netscape Messenger, Microsoft Exchange, Outlook, and Outlook Express), your attachment appears as an icon that you manipulate like any other file icon. Here are your most common choices:

- With the message window open, right-click and choose the View option to see the image on the desktop without opening a large image-editing program.

- Double-click the image icon to launch a preview window or an image-editing program and display the image.

- Drag-and-drop the image icon from the message window to the desktop or another Windows folder for permanent storage.

want the resulting photo, so there's absolutely no guesswork. Set the end photo size to 800×600, for instance, and the cropping frame is proportioned exactly right for the job. You can also scale the cropping frame to include more or less of the original image in the new, resized photo. It's all very clever and makes you wonder why no one ever thought of that before.

A Smaller Image also includes sharpness, brightness, and contrast controls, an optional graphic border for your images, and a simple text tool for adding captions. If you frequently resize photos for e-mail, the Web, or printing, A Smaller Image is a handy tool.

Attach Pictures in E-mail

Although the process varies from one program to another, attaching one or more images to an e-mail message isn't hard. The basic procedure is this: drag-and-drop an image file directly into your open e-mail message, or use a menu option to insert a file into the message. In addition, almost all mail software uses the paperclip icon as a standard symbol to represent an attachment to your message,

16

 **Send E-mail with Outlook**

If you're a Microsoft Outlook user, here's how to attach a pair of images to an outgoing message:

1. Click the New button in the Outlook toolbar to create a new mail message. A blank, untitled message should appear.

2. Address the e-mail by typing the appropriate e-mail address in the To box.

3. Add a subject by typing in the Subject box.

4. Enter some message text. It's generally a good idea to write a personal, specific note rather than sending a blank message with attachments—that way, the recipient knows it's not some sort of virus.

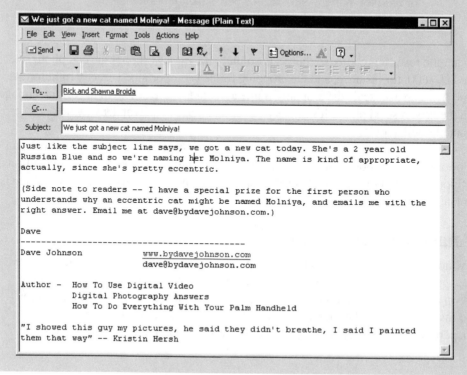

5. If you have a folder with pictures open on the desktop, you can drag an image file from that folder over the message window and drop it, as shown in the following illustration. You should see an attachment appear in the message.

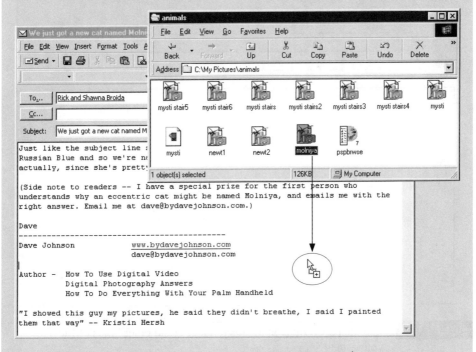

6. To add another image to the message, choose Insert | File from the message window's menu, or click the Attachment button (shaped like a paperclip). You should see the Insert File dialog box.

7. Navigate to the appropriate folder and select the image file you want to attach. If you want to attach multiple files from the same folder, you can hold down the CTRL key while you click each image file.

8. Click the Insert button to close the Insert File dialog box, and then insert the images in the message.

9. When your message is complete, click the Send button to send it to its recipient.

16

Click this button to attach a file.

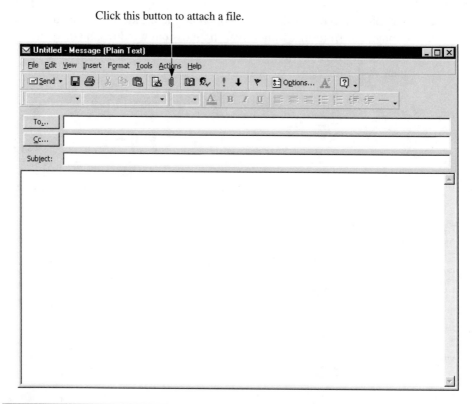

FIGURE 16-2   Use the paperclip icon to attach images (and other kinds of files) to your e-mail.

so look for that button and use it to specify files for inclusion in your e-mail (see Figure 16-2).

If you're sending an image to someone using any modern PC (including a Mac or Windows), almost any file format is fair game, but JPG is probably best because the files tend to be so small. Because JPG is an efficient file format for sending photographic images, you're best off sending images in JPG format exclusively.

Distribute Images on Disks

Because JPG images are so small, you can often copy a lot of images to a floppy disk and pass them around that way. After all, almost everyone has a floppy disk drive, right?

Even better, pretty much everyone can read PC floppy disks—even Mac users. The Macintosh floppy drive can read PC floppies. That means you can copy a few JPG images to a floppy and give it to a Mac user, and he or she will be able to read the images just fine.

One caveat, though—PCs can't read Macintosh floppies. So Mac users need to be sure the disk is formatted for a PC before doing the handoff. The same is true of Zip disks. A Zip disk made on a Mac can't be read on a PC. Instead, you'll see an error message saying the disk isn't formatted.

The New Floppy Disk: CD-R

Floppy disks have some important limitations, though. They don't hold much data, they're slow, and despite the fact that they've been around forever—or perhaps because of that—they're starting to lose popularity. Some new computers come without any floppy drives at all, in fact. The heir to the floppy throne? The CD. These days, many new PCs come with CD-RW drives, which can write data to blank CD-R and CD-RW discs. Don't have a CD-RW drive? That's OK—you can add a CD-RW drive to a PC very inexpensively. I suggest using a CD to share images because a CD-R disk is readable by any CD-ROM drive, making it handy for sharing. (I don't recommend creating CD-RW disks, because they often can only be read by the computer that created them.) For details on copying images to CD, see Chapter 10.

Writeable DVD drives, like DVD-R, DVD+R, and RVR-RAM are getting popular as well. You can use any of these devices to store your photos. As an added advantage, DVDs hold so much data (over 4GB) that you can easily store a vast number of full-size images without the need to resize anything.

Strategies for Sharing Lots of Images

If you need to send someone a lot of images and you want to minimize the total file size, you have a few ways to get the data to the recipient. Often, you'll need to combine these techniques. Here are some things you can try:

■ Use a compression program like WinZip (www.winzip.com) to shrink the images to a smaller size. (If you are using Windows XP, a WinZip-like compression program is built in. Just select your pictures, right-click, and choose Send To | Compressed (zipped) Folder.) If your image files are already compressed (such as if you use the JPG or compressed TIF formats), then zipping won't do much to your total file size. But if you're trying to send uncompressed images (such as TIF), this compression program can be a lifesaver.

■ Break the image collection into several e-mail messages, with each message weighing in at less than a megabyte or so.

■ Use the compression feature in the JPG format (usually an option when you save the JPG image) to reduce file size. With many images, you can compress the image significantly before you start to see any obvious degradation due to compression. This is great if you're just passing images around among friends, though I'd be more careful about images you're planning to print.

■ Instead of e-mail, mail a CD-R. Because a CD holds 650MB of data, you have an awful lot of room to work with. It's certainly more efficient than using the Internet.

Create Your Own Web Pages

The Web is a great place to store and share your digital images. Your pictures are probably already in a convenient web format—like JPG—and most of your friends and family probably already own a computer with Internet access. If you have a web design program such as FrontPage, FrontPage Express, or Netscape Composer, you can drag-and-drop your way to a nice little web page with a minimal amount of effort. Figure 16-3 shows FrontPage being used to edit a typical web page. For simple web pages, the learning curve is similar to what you might expect from a program like Microsoft Publisher.

Using a web design program, you can enter text, drag-and-drop graphics and pictures, and then edit and format the web site's appearance with simple toolbar and menu controls. Many good web design programs are on the market. Some are free and some are retail products. Here are some of the most popular programs:

■ **Microsoft FrontPage**   www.microsoft.com/frontpage

■ **Sausage Software HotDog**   www.sausagetools.com

■ **Avantrix Koala HTML**   www.avantrix.com

■ **Netscape Composer**   www.netscape.com

■ **Macromedia Dreamweaver**   www.macromedia.com

It's worth noting that you can also create web pages with some Microsoft products that aren't even designed specifically for the Internet. Publisher, for instance, has a feature that lets you publish documents to the Web. It's not a great

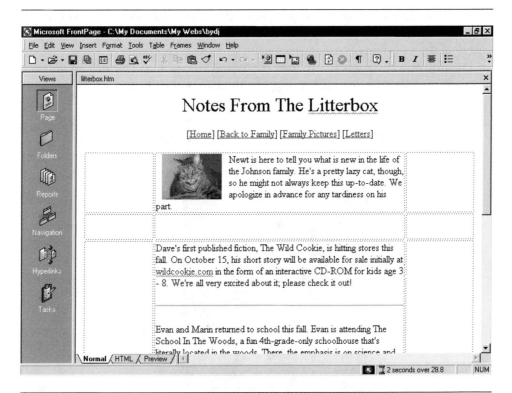

FIGURE 16-3 If you can handle programs like Publisher, PowerPoint, or Word, you can probably slap together a simple web site in a program like FrontPage.

web design program, but it'll let you get pictures up on the Web with a minimum of fuss and with software you already own.

Choose an Image Size and File Format for the Web

Many digital cameras take pictures in resolutions as low as 640×480 pixels, but this can be too big for a web page. Not only does an image that big take a while to download, it consumes a lot of space on the screen. Instead, I recommend that you shrink your images down to about 600 pixels across. (See Chapter 11 for details on how to do that.)

Two file formats are commonly used on the Web: GIF and JPG. CompuServe originally developed the GIF format, which stands for Graphic Interchange Format (making the term "GIF format" somewhat redundant). GIF is a compact file format commonly used in web pages. The major disadvantage of GIF, however, is that it limits

16

images to just 256 colors (or less, depending on the settings you use when saving the file). That can affect the quality of the image onscreen, though that's generally not too important if your priority is making the pictures very small for the web.

Usually, web designers like to use GIF format 89a, which is the newest version of the GIF format. GIF format 89a supports three important features:

- ■ **Transparency** *Transparency* lets you specify a color in the image that will be treated as transparent. That way, you can make the image's background or border transparent. If you have an irregularly shaped image, like a diamond or an oval, this feature can look cool, as you can see here:

No matter what kind of background you use, a picture with a transparent background will blend in.

- ■ **Interlacing** An *interlaced image* downloads to a web browser first as a chunky, low-resolution image, and then it increases in quality as more information is retrieved. Otherwise, the image would normally load a few lines at a time, so you'd see the top of the image display before the bottom. Interlacing isn't faster than the alternative, but it gives the viewer something to look at, and so it can seem faster. This is a good option to use when you know that people with slow Internet connections will be viewing your images.

- ■ **Animation** An *animated GIF* is just a sequence of individual images played one after the other. Not really fast enough to give a sense of cinematic motion with large images, animated GIFs are usually used to slowly display one image after another, like a slide show.

The JPG format was created by the Joint Photographic Experts Group to be a scalable file format that could be compressed to yield low file size or be left

Which File Format Is Best?

You can use the file format—GIF or JPG—that best suits your needs. It's perfectly all right to mix JPG and GIF images in a web site, even on the same page. This chart should help you decide which is the appropriate file format.

Use JPG:	Use GIF:
To display full-color photographs compressed to a small file size	To have a transparent background
	To interlace the display of an image
	To display an image with a few colors

uncompressed for higher quality. Unlike GIF, JPG images can display a full 16 million–color palette. Depending on how much you compress a JPG image, however, the image quality can vary from nearly identical to the original all the way down to unrecognizable.

You can specify the level of compression to use when saving a JPG file. Most programs default to a fairly low compression level, preserving image quality. In reality, though, you can often compress the image much more aggressively than the default and still get adequate quality for a web page.

Share Images on the Web Without Designing a Web Site

Certainly, you can design a web site that shows off your pictures to friends and family, and as I just mentioned, quite a few tools are around to help you do just that. If you aren't thrilled by the idea of learning how to manipulate a web design program, though, there's an easier solution—one that requires no programming, no eye for page design, and no real Internet skills. The solution? A photo-sharing web site.

These sites take the arcane drudgery out of designing web sites from scratch and posting photos to the Internet by enabling you to upload images to a commercial site via a simple interface. The site itself arranges your images into an attractive layout, complete with thumbnail views (which you can click to see a full-sized version of the image), captions, and even printing services that can print your favorite images

16

and mail the hard copy directly to you. These sites are a convenient way to publish your images online for friends, family, and strangers to browse, and you needn't learn anything about web site creation.

A year or two ago, as many as two dozen of these sorts of sites existed, and they all tried to deliver free photo-sharing services. I recognized at the time that this was a business plan disaster waiting to happen, and guess what? I was right! Most of them are gone now. Of course, a few are left, and those that remain are excellent:

- **Club Photo**   www.clubphoto.com

- **Kodak EasyShare Gallery**   www.kodakgallery.com

- **Shutterfly**   www.shutterfly.com

- **Flickr**   www.flickr.com

- **smugmug**   www.smugmug.com

- **dotPhoto**   www.dotphoto.com

Club Photo, for instance, lets you arrange your photos into albums and display them for visitors (see Figure 16-4). The site lets you drag-and-drop images from your desktop directly to the web browser—a convenient way to upload images.

Another option is Kodak EasyShare Gallery. This site has a clever image-editing tool built right into the web page. You can crop, rotate, and even remove red eye from your pictures right from an upload assistant program, which you can download and use to store images on the web site. And there's Shutterfly, a nicely organized site that works with both digital and film pictures.

The bottom line is you can't expect sites like these to stay in business on advertising or good thoughts. If you find one you like, I highly encourage you to pay the subscription fee and keep it in business. That's what I've done with Club Photo because I'd like my digital images to still be online 6 months, a year, and even 2 years from now.

> TIP
>
> *Even if you maintain your own personal web site, you can save yourself the time and trouble of arranging digital images on a photo page by linking from your own web site directly to your album on a photo-sharing site. That's what I do; to see it in action, go to www.bydavejohnson.com and click on the Photography link to see how I connect to the Club Photo site.*

FIGURE 16-4   Club Photo automatically arranges your uploaded digital images in an elegant manner.

Show Off Images on a PDA

A popular way to show off traditional 35mm pictures is by carrying them in your wallet. Wallet photos and digital imaging don't mix that well—or at least they didn't, until recently. Now you can transfer images from your hard disk and store them on your Palm OS handheld (like the Zire 71, Tungsten T, or Sony Clié) or Pocket PC device. A typical PDA (personal digital assistant) can store dozens of images on a memory card and let you display them a picture at a time or in slide show mode.

16

Flickr Makes Tagging Popular

It seems like there's a human compulsion—driven perhaps at the genetic level—to share pictures we've taken. That's why sites like Shutterfly and Club Photo are so popular. Whether the pictures are of your pet, European vacation, grandkids, or car, there's nothing quite as satisfying as showing them to someone else.

Flickr is becoming one of the most popular photo-sharing web sites, and for good reason. It works a bit differently than most sharing sites: in my opinion, it feels more like a true community of photo fans than most other services I've seen. The most compelling feature is the way it lets you tag pictures with keywords. Not just your own pictures—you can tag other people's photos as well, and then quickly browse all the photos at Flickr with specific tags. It may not sound like a cool feature, but trust me, it changes the way you interact with photos. Here's an example—try visiting this URL at the Flickr web site: www.flickr.com/photos/w00kie/sets/180637. The page you'll see looks like this:

Billed as a collection of "Transparent Screens," it looks like all of the computer displays shown in these photos truly have transparent screens that show whatever is behind the computer. You can see right through them to whatever is behind the PC!

The truth is that they're all carefully staged photos using custom-photographed desktop wallpaper images. There's no high art here, but it's a lot of fun to click through the various images.

You can add people with photos you like to your contacts list, leave comments for other photographers, and converse in Flickr's forums. And believe it or not, all that is just scratching the surface—there are other features, too: some simple photo-editing tools, the ability to organize your photos into albums, and a slew of other group sharing features. Flickr is free, but you can also subscribe (for about $40/year) to get more features, such as unlimited photo storage and no advertisements.

Applications abound for storing and displaying images on a Palm device. Here are a couple of the best choices:

- **AcidImage**   www.red-mercury.com
- **SplashPhoto**   www.splashdata.com

Figure 16-5 provides a glimpse of what some of these applications look like. Your PDA might come with image-viewing software. Sony often includes its Clié Viewer, for instance, and Palm bundles SplashPhoto with many of its devices.

If you have a wireless modem connected to your PDA, or your handheld is a Smartphone like the Handspring Treo or Samsung i330, you can wirelessly e-mail pictures to other PDA users and ordinary desktop e-mail accounts as well. One way to do that is via a program called Pixer, from Electric Pocket (www.electricpocket.com).

Pixer is a program that mimics the European MMS (Multimedia Messaging Service) experience. MMS enables mobile phone users to send digital images, hand-drawn sketches, and written notes between mobile handsets. It's quite literally a multimedia alternative to SMS text messaging, which is popular in the United States. You might have trouble finding recipients for your MMS on a mobile handset in the United States right now, but Pixer lets you send and receive digital images on a Palm via e-mail—both between PDAs and between a PDA and the desktop.

16

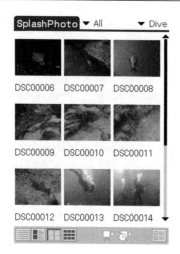

FIGURE 16-5 A variety of photo applications let you display images and even videos on any PDA.

Show Off Images in a Digital Picture Frame

Another way to display digital images is in a digital picture frame. Digital picture frames are inexpensive LCD displays mounted in a picture frame shell. Equipped with a memory card, the picture frame can show digital images in a slide show format. Digital picture frames are readily available. Models include the following:

- **Digi-Frame** www.digi-frame.com
- **Ceiva** www.ceiva.com

Sony's CyberFrame uses Sony's Memory Stick to display both still images and MPEG movies in a small LCD screen, which you can place on a tabletop like an ordinary picture frame. If you already have a Sony digital camera that uses Memory Stick memory storage, the CyberFrame is a good choice because you can simply remove the memory card from the camera and insert it directly in the picture frame to begin displaying images.

The Digi-Frame is product similar to the CyberFrame, though it uses both CompactFlash and SmartMedia memory cards, so you can insert the memory card from most digital cameras to view your images.

The Ceiva, which you can see in Figure 16-6, is unique in two ways: in addition to a small cache of internal (nonremovable) memory, it also connects to the Internet via an ordinary telephone jack. Using a built-in modem, it regularly connects to the Internet and downloads images you've stored on the Ceiva web site. With the capability to rotate among 20 images stored in the Ceiva's memory each day, you can have a constant supply of images on display with minimal effort. Likewise, Ceiva makes it possible to share images from your digital camera with other Ceiva picture frame owners. So you can establish a community of friends and family who exchange images among their picture frames via the Ceiva web site.

16

FIGURE 16-6   Digital picture frames put an always-changing slide show of your digital images right on a tabletop.

Show Pictures on TV

No one likes to admit it, but many of us spend the best hours of our lives in the family room within a stone's throw of the television. So while the Web and framed enlargements are two good ways to show off your pictures, nothing beats watching them on the familiar old television. Heck, I can even think of a non-couch-potato reason to show your pictures on a TV: it's the biggest screen in the house, so everyone can see your photos without craning their necks.

Thankfully, showing your digital images on television is easy. Most digital cameras have video-out ports built right in that can directly display the contents of your camera's memory card on a TV screen. Don't lose the video cable that comes with your camera, though; one end is a standard RCA jack for connecting to the video-in port of a TV or VCR, but the other end is a specialized connector for your camera. It's expensive to replace and is only available from the camera manufacturer.

Your camera is designed to take any picture on your camera—even big 3-megapixel ones—and fit them on the TV screen. That's fine, but it can be slow because the camera has to read a lot of useless data from the memory card, pack it down to a smaller image size, and finally, pump it to the TV. If you want to make a faster slide show, use your PC to convert the images to 640×480-pixel images, and then copy them back to a memory card. Insert the card into your camera, and you're ready to rock and roll.

You're not limited to showing your digital pictures on the TV. Most cameras will output any image on the card to the television. This means you can convert PowerPoint slides, graphics, and other images to JPEG images, store them on a memory card, and display them on a TV. That makes your camera a portable, general-purpose projector system.

Create a Slide Show on Videotape

Another way to show your images on TV is by making a videotape slide show that people can pop into their VCRs. This is a convenient solution for folks who might not own a computer. For years, photography stores have offered video slide show services for a fee: they'd copy your old prints, slides, and negatives to videotape with a musical soundtrack. Now you can do it yourself.

If you're shopping for a new DVD player, it might be worth looking for one that can play audio and video files from CD and DVD you've recorded on your PC. This way, you can play your slide show on your DVD player and record the output on a VCR.

Record Video Directly from the Camera

You can make your own video slide show in two ways. If your camera has a video-out jack, you can do it quickly and easily without even using your PC. Here's what you can do.

1. Start by arranging the images you want to show off on your camera's memory card. Delete any images you don't want to show, for instance. You can also copy other images from your PC to the camera's memory card, and then insert the card in the camera. Also, make sure they're all oriented properly—sideways images taken by holding the camera on its side should be removed.

2. If your camera has the capability to display transitions between each image during playback, turn that mode on now.

3. Attach the video-out port of the camera to your VCR. If you want musical accompaniment, connect your CD player to the VCR as well, and queue up some music. Set the VCR on pause.

4. When your tape is ready to record, start recording, and then start the CD player and the camera's playback mode simultaneously. You should end up with a slide show of images with music recorded on tape.

Use PowerPoint to Make a Video Slide Show

Using the camera to create a slide show is easy, but it's fraught with compromises. Usually, there's no way to precisely time the transition from one image to another in your slide show, for instance, so you can't easily synchronize the images to music. Also, images tend to roll slowly onto the screen as they're read from memory. This might look cheesy, particularly if you're used to seeing pictures "snap" rapidly onto the screen.

Instead, you might want to try the second, though obviously more elaborate, solution if you have the necessary gear. For this approach to work, you'll need a PC, a program like PowerPoint (which you might already have, especially if you use Microsoft Office), and a video-out port on your PC that you can connect to a VCR or camcorder.

To create a slide show using PowerPoint, do this:

1. Start by making sure all the images you plan to use are 640×480 pixels. If they're bigger, resize and save them using a different name. It's often easiest to create a special folder for all your slide show images, and then delete that temporary folder when you're done creating the slide show.

16

2. Launch PowerPoint and choose Blank Presentation from the New Presentation dialog box.

3. You need to choose a slide style—it doesn't matter which one, so pick the blank slide from the bottom.

4. Choose Insert | Picture | From File. Find the image you want to add to the slide.

5. When the image appears on your slide, resize it, if necessary, so it takes up the entire slide, from top to bottom and side to side:

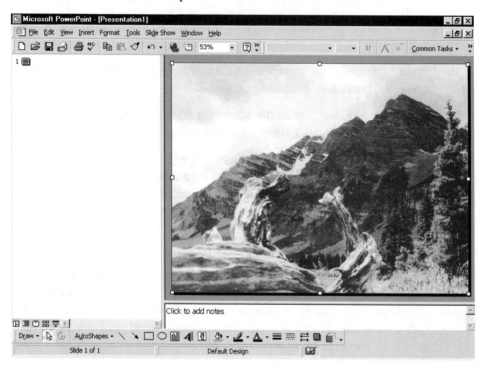

6. Now add another slide by clicking the New Slide option from the Common Tasks drop-down menu, and then add another blank slide.

7. Add another image to this new blank slide.

8. Continue this process until you've created a complete slide show.

9. To add a common transition to every slide in your presentation, choose Slide Show | Slide Transition, and then select a transition from the

Transition drop-down menu. The Dissolve transition is a good choice. To apply this transition to every slide in your slide show, choose Apply To All.

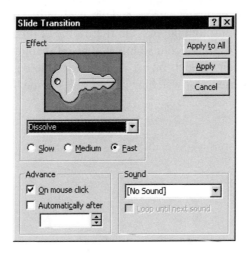

You can apply transitions to a particular slide or apply them to all the slides at once. In my opinion, slide shows that use a different effect for every transition have a decidedly unprofessional look. I suggest you stick with a subdued, single-transition approach throughout the entire presentation.

   10. Save your presentation by choosing File | Save As.

   When your slide show is complete, you can plug your PC into a VCR or camcorder, and then record the show to tape, using your own mouse clicks as timing for when to change the slides. You can also add a CD audio source to the VCR to add a soundtrack as you record the show.

If Your Camera Has No Video Output

Not all digital cameras have video-out ports, and if you have one of those video-deprived models, showing your pictures on the big screen can be difficult. If this sounds like you, consider getting a stand-alone device that displays digital images on a TV without needing a camera with a video-out connector. The SanDisk

Digital Photo Viewer (www.sandisk.com) is a box that connects to your TV, but it has an array of slots for inserting CompactFlash, SmartMedia, Memory Stick, SD, and MMC cards. The device is designed for no-nonsense simplicity. Just insert a memory card from your digital camera and use the bundled remote control to view, zoom, rotate, and step through photos. Or, there's the eFilm Picturevision, from Delkin (www.delkin.com), which also lets you insert memory cards from digital cameras and display their contents on a TV. Any one of these gadgets can bring back the old-fashioned experience of watching 35mm slides in the living room.

Index